OTHER BOOKS BY PHILIP YOUNG

Ernest Hemingway (1952)

Ernest Hemingway: A Reconsideration (1966)

The Hemingway Manuscripts: An Inventory (1969)

Three Bags Full: Essays in American Fiction (1972)

REVOLUTIONARY LADIES

Philip Young

REVOLUTIONARY LADIES

Alfred · A · Knopf
New York
1977

THIS IS A BORZOI BOOK
PUBLISHED BY ALFRED A. KNOPF, INC.

Published in the United States
by Alfred A. Knopf, Inc., New York,
and simultaneously in Canada
by Random House of Canada Limited, Toronto.
Distributed by Random House, Inc., New York.
Library of Congress Cataloging in Publication Data
Young, Philip [date]
Revolutionary ladies.
Bibliography: p.
Includes index.
1. Women—United States—History. 2. Women—
United States—Sexual behavior. 3. Camp followers.
4. United States—History—Revolution, 1775–1783.
I. Title.
HQ1418.Y68   301.41'2'0973   77–1111
ISBN 0–394–49992–1
Manufactured in the United States of America
First Edition

To the Author's Ladies,

KATHERINE & ROSALIE

A great deal has been placed to the General's fondness for,
and attachment to, Mrs. L———g. . . . You think,
I dare say, I am descending to tea-table chat and little scandal.
What I tell you . . . you will, at some time,
hear such evidence of as will surprise you.
O Tempora! O Mores!

—ANON., 1778

Contents

Acknowledgments

This book was conceived in historical innocence, and its author is grateful for considerable support in delivering it—financial from the Pennsylvania State University's Institute for the Arts and Humanistic Studies, liberal from its College of Liberal Arts, bibliographical from the various departments of its Pattee Library, moral from Robert Lescher, and total from Katherine Young. A special debt, textual, is owed the bright eyes and sensitive ear of Wilma R. Ebbitt, who gracefully assumed the burden of the writer's prose, clarifying, smoothing, and augmenting it from cover to cover. His other extraordinary obligation, factual, is to Richard E. Winslow III, who not only checked out endless details on his own initiative but also supplied quite a few of them.

REVOLUTIONARY LADIES

Chapter One

CASTING
THE MOLD:
PRELUDE

JOHN ADAMS had another question for Thomas Jefferson. "What," he demanded to know, "gave Pompadour and Du Barry the Power of making Cardinals and Popes?" He was already sure of the answer—"Their beauty." Take, he wrote, the "daughter of a green Grocer." She

walks the streets in London dayly with a baskett of Cabbage, Sprouts, Dandlions and Spinage on her head. She is observed by the Painters to have a beautiful Face, an elegant figure. . . . Sir William Hamilton . . . sends her to Schools . . . and marries her. This Lady not only causes the Tryumphs of the Nile of Copinhagen and Trafalgar, but seperates Naples from France and finally banishes the King and Queen from Sicilly.

Such is the Power of beauty. "Millions of examples might be quoted. . . ." But to find women like these, he begs, "For mercy's sake do not compell me to look to our chaste States and Territories."

It was November, 1813. The topic of correspondence was Jefferson's Natural Aristocracy. There was agreement on one important point, "vizt. That 'there is a natural Aristocracy among men; the grounds of which are Virtue and Talents.'" But for

3

Adams that was about half of it. Female aristocrats, he pointed out, are "nearly as formidable" as male. And "What chance have Talents and Virtue in competition with Wealth and Birth? and Beauty?" Any one of them, witness his ladies, can overbear either or both of the other two—even if the likes of Emma Hamilton were not to be found in America. Jefferson, who had dreamed of an agrarian society's moral superiority, did not respond to the question.

Enthusiasm for the green Grocer's daughter suggests that Adams was hoodwinked by Southey's "sublime" *Life of Nelson,* just published, and profoundly influenced by the work of a hack hired by the lady herself to promote her fancies. Her father, who died when she was newborn, was a blacksmith. She had gotten her schooling through the man Hamilton obtained her from. When the Battle of the Nile was won, she was scarcely acquainted with Horatio Nelson. After becoming his mistress, she had no more to do with defeating the Danes or with Trafalgar than that he went to battle "hot—or cold," as is written, "from her embrace." Though she was sufficiently intimate with Maria Carolina of Naples to cause a good deal of lubricous talk, she had no part in separating the place from France. When the Queen was banished from Sicily it was the work of Ferdinand the King. Certainly Mmes. Pompadour and du Barry, as successive mistresses of Louis XV, had influence at court, but neither came close to naming a religious or political leader.

Carried away in one direction, Adams was diverted from another. Just as his country's States and Territories were emerging from its Provinces, exactly such women as he could not discover in the general chastity had started to blossom in the homeland. And where the foreign aristocrats he urged on Jefferson were but partly to his point, his compatriot ladies were wholly. Pompadour's origins were utterly bourgeois; Lady Hamilton's were humbler; du Barry's mother was a penniless seamstress and her father, very likely, an obscure monk. But in the New World their sisters in spirit could add to Beauty, Talents, and easy Virtue both Birth and Wealth. As for Power, one of them was credited with having all by herself lost England its colonies.

The first of them had emerged, to be sure, nearly four decades back. Understandable that Adams had lost them in his memories of the struggle with Great Britain. But entirely curious that historians spading Revolutionary America from every conceivable direction, increasingly assisted by specialists trained to turn up females of the time and place, should after two hundred years have failed to find not just native women of the kind an ex-President of the Republic was thinking of but a distinctive, if small, group of them.

Revolutionary Ladies, vizt., a gathering of provincial American girls, all beautiful, well born, well-to-do, Loyalist, and Anglican, who grew to uneasy fame in a greater world by far. All of them caught up in the double jeopardy of sexual scandal and war, driven in a losing cause to adventures in exile, buried in the land of their ancestors, and virtually forgotten. The aim is to introduce to our consciousness of the nation's past a cluster of women it had been unaware of. In an age that offered females little latitude, their individual lives had such dimensions and complexity as to achieve a size that has seemed impossible. Collectively they establish a presence that Americans have not believed their tradition ever embraced. Even an ardent Patriot might have chosen them over those he presented to Thomas Jefferson.

᠔ I

THE COUNTRY could scarcely have produced notable offenses against sexual propriety any sooner than it did. Early American scandal is very small potatoes. Among the reasons why there's a germ of truth in the rumor that the colonies were "a paradise on Earth for women." In London, as Moll Flanders complained, there was a shortage of men, who "play the game all into their own hands." In the provinces, particularly the southern ones, there had been from the start a shortage of women. No need for wealth or beauty. As George Alsop in seventeenth-century Maryland observed,

Women that go over into this Province as servants, have the best luck here as in any place of the world besides; for they are no sooner on shoar, but they are courted into a Copulative Matrimony, which some of them (for aught I know) had they not come to such a Market with their Virginity, might have kept it by them untill it had been mouldy.

If a woman lost her mate she was unlikely to go uncopulated long. The speed record for remarriage was held in London, where a lady whose husband had died one evening at eight o'clock married the next noon the draper who'd come that morning to sell her widow's weeds. But colonial Virginia was not out of contention. When the wife of the first American Washington died, John courted Anne Gerrard, who had already enjoyed two husbands and was accused of keeping a bawdy house. Her sister Frances was charged with being a whore, as well as the mistress of the Governor; together they were said to have entertained a gentleman on a bed in the dark. In 1675 the ancestor of the father of his country married Anne. After her death, Frances, bereft of her third husband, took John Washington as her fourth, which in Virginia was perfectly legal. Of course it didn't actually hurt to have money; the *Virginia Gazette* was pleased to report that "Mrs. Sarah Ellyson, aged eighty five, a spritely old Tit, with three Thousand Pounds Fortune," had married.

Alsop's imported women were potential problems, since but for one embarrassment or other many of them would never have left England. William Byrd encountered in Virginia a serving girl who was the daughter of a baronet; she had been sent to this country because "her complexion being red hair'd inclined her much to lewdness." On board his ship headed here another gentleman noted the presence of a "lady of high family and great wealth"—sent over by her parents "as she had been guilty of some indiscretion." All Charleston knew how in England Sir Egerton Leigh had fathered a child on the "hellion" who was his ward, his wife's sister, and the niece of a man who would soon be President of the Continental Congress. It was widely believed that young ladies and gentlemen who were sent to Great Britain for their education brought back more than was good for them.

A larger problem might have been the one which had Johnson grumbling to Boswell that Americans were a race of convicts. He could have been thinking of Moll Flanders. "Twelve Year a Whore . . . Twelve Year a Thief," she had been deported to Virginia like her convicted mother before her—who observed that Newgate "half peoples this colony." The remark was prophetic. Between 1700 and 1770, something like ten thousand female felons were shipped, chiefly to the southern provinces, from Great Britain; Franklin proposed that in return we export rattlesnakes. And there is little doubt that prostitution was among the commonest of offenses. In this country the newcomers were at first indentured servants; some escaped and were advertised for. "N.B.," a *Gazette* would remark, "She is fond of Drink and likes Sailors Company much"; another "has run away several times and knows a great many noted men." A London magazine carried the story of a servant in South Carolina who for a time successfully set herself up as a Princess, the sister of Queen Charlotte. But the curious thing about these hordes of fallen women is the apparent rarity with which, once here, they got into further trouble. Of London it was said that Covent Garden and Drury Lane alone would furnish "lewd women enough to fill a colony"; it is possible that prior to the Revolution there were more whores in those two locations than in all colonial America. The inference is unavoidable that the majority of jades from the jails of England, "Brides from Bridewell," served out their indentures here or escaped from them and, either as married or common-law wives, reproduced. William Byrd, who slaked his passion almost nightly in London, on two occasions searched the length and breadth of Williamsburg for a woman to hire and both times failed.

It is not quite true, as has been remarked, that "it was well into the eighteenth century before Boston was troubled by professional whores." By the end of the seventeenth it had become a seaport with a waterfront, and "the sweet sin of Lechery" was heard on the land. A woman had been convicted of keeping a tavern where "Lewd Lascivious . . . persons of both Sexes" had "opportunity to commit carnall wickedness," and the General Court found it necessary to enact a law prohibiting "a stews, whore house, or brothel house." The "Whores of Boston"—if not, as elsewhere claimed, notorious—existed. What is remarkable is that there were so few of them. Between 1670 and 1680 exactly twelve cases of prostitution were brought to justice. But it was not a shortage of women in colonial Massachusetts, which was settled familially, that helped account for the relative absence of vice. Nor was this absence to be attributed to the religious zeal of the Puritans. The important fact appears to have been that women were not, by and large, driven to whoring for money. It has clearly been shown that, once a colony was established, the settlers "could confidently hope to enjoy a considerably higher standard of living than they had in the Old World."

Theocratic Massachusetts could, to be sure, produce tiny scandals. As early as 1642 Governor Bradford was bewailing "ye breaking out of . . . incontinencie between persons unmarried." One unhusbanded woman kept her parish busy putting her on probation each time she gave birth. Another, dragged into church to be excommunicated for her third such offense, disputed the theology and walked out on the proceedings. A third, victim of rumors of unchastity, asked her church to investigate and clear her; investigating, it decided the reports were true. Her name was Mehetable Goof. A minor folk hero of western Massachusetts was Samuell Terry, caught outside the meeting house "even in sermon time" with his face to the wall "chafing his yard." (Six lashes.) Some time later, when Samuell's bride of five months spawned, the "Corte concluded it manifest that they did abuse one another before marriage." (The choice: "Whipt on their naked bodyes with 10 lashes appiece or fyned 4 £" [fyned].)

Sober researchers have concluded that among the Puritans, "premarital sexual relations were the rule"; carnal knowledge "in time of contract" or betrothal was clearly distinguished from fornication. Anyway, what the Seventh Commandment forbade was adultery. When the Calvinist leaders cried out against sin what they had in mind, more often than not, was cards, dancing, cosmetics, and periwigs. In early New England, moreover, dramatic offenses against sexual propriety were made difficult by the equalizing tendency of Puritan beliefs. The social and economic realities of frontier life afforded little room for privilege. The Commonwealth did not by definition permit or in fact support an upper class; if there was one it was made up of clerics. (When a nameless woman came to the eminent clergyman Cotton Mather and beseeched him "to make her mine," he was so consumed with the Foul Fire in the Male that he confessed to thoughts of self-destruction, but he refused her.) There were just not enough people elevated enough to fall far enough to cause a fuss. "Greatest scandal," Shakespeare noted, "waits on greatest state."

But if solvency promoted morality, prosperity undermined it. Complaints of "wages large" and "gold and garments gay" began issuing from Massachusetts pulpits as early as 1650: once-penniless servants were found now to be worth "scores, and some, hundreds of pounds." When it was explained to Increase Mather, father of Cotton, that tithes were falling because of poverty, he had a quick question: Were there not whole "Towns in New-England in which the Inhabitants spend more at the tavern, than they do to uphold the Publick Worship of God?" He was the Mather who first detected, precisely three hundred years ago, a dire new development that had a remarkable future: the direct importation of corruption from Mother England. He had the whole heart of the matter. "A proud fashion no sooner comes into the country but the haughty Daughters of Zion in this place are taking it up," he announced, until "the whole land is at last infected." Exactly a decade later, when Sir Edmond Andros arrived as Governor of "the Dominion of New-England," a touch of aristocracy began to color the region. The first Anglican church was built in Boston; it was alleged that the Governor "admitted the Squaws dayly to him; or else he went out and lodged with them." The colonists abided Sir Edmond for three years, then arrested and deposed him in a little preview of things to come.

By the dawn of the eighteenth century Increase Mather's trickle of fashion had swelled to an estuarial tide. Colonial society had become more prosperous and more urban. A gentry was clearly emerging—a worldly, affluent little group which in a few cases was establishing an indigenous aristocracy. English clothes, styles, airs, manners were to be found in all major cities, such as they were, of the New World. As if to embody the trend there had arrived from England the concept of the Fashionable Woman. No one has improved on Oliver Goldsmith's understanding of the term: "a woman cannot be a woman of fashion till she has lost her reputation." Even in New York, where a stubborn Dutch conservatism is said to have slowed developments, a young belle of the town could by 1760 exult that "we follow the London fashions." Things were not, she confessed, so gay as in Boston, but the girls were getting bolder. So in Philadelphia young ladies were beginning to earn fame "for their want of modesty." Living there just after the Revolution, a Frenchman claimed that socially prominent young women were, for a fee, available.*

By that time Abigail Adams was complaining that Philadelphia was becoming "as vile and debauched as London—nay more so." Such grief in the wife of the President of the Republic suggests that rejection of England had meant a desire for moral as well as political independence. And that helps explain why, during the war, no woman of both social stature and public scandal was a Patriot. As a British import, Fashion was a significant part of what indignant Americans wished to be rid of. The idea of "what men call gallantry," as Byron would put it, "and Gods adultery" was odious.

But the notion that America's capital rivaled England's for vice was a provincial delusion. George III looked on his scene and pronounced it "the wickedest age that ever was." Thoroughly prepared for by the Restoration court of Charles II—"one vast brothel" with the monarch in charge—eighteenth-century London is reckoned to have housed twice as many whores as Paris. Marylebone, a single parish, is thought to have had more prostitutes than Philadelphia had citizens. Girls under ten walked the

---

*Moreau de St. Méry is thought reliable, but sometimes sounds like a Frenchman rebuffed. Other young ladies, he charges, not only "give themselves up to the enjoyment of themselves" but "seek unnatural pleasure with persons of their own sex." He may also have been an imperfect observer: these girls are, he concedes, beautiful at fifteen, but by eighteen, "their breasts, never large, already have vanished."

streets or were sold into brothels; virgins, some of them professionally such, fetched a great premium. Competition was keen, and included middle-class women by moonlight, during which time the action was often in the streets; the fastidious Boswell chose the privacy of Westminster Bridge. The brothels were a recent import from France and a great success; upper-class and expensive, a few were available for ladies seeking gentlemen, or other ladies (a taste, it was believed, originating in Turkey). In Paris dildoes sold privately; in London one woman kept an open shop. *Crim.-Con.* or lurid cases of Criminal Conversation, details taken mainly from divorce proceedings ("disgusting" to a modern anthropologist), was highly popular reading. But it was chiefly the world of Fashion that set the tone for "Whoring, nowadays mistaken for Gallantry and Politeness."

A new breed of British, with their upper-class folkways, brought to the colonies a moral as well as a physical shock. The steamy climate of the American Revolution got steamier as the English army moved from Boston to Halifax to Philadelphia to New York. In the city of fraternal affection colonial gentlemen anguished over "wanton wives and wicked daughters," taken by British officers "almost without a trial—damn them." A Hessian observed that for vice the town need not yield to Sodom and Gomorrah. But there was a shortage of companionable women, some of whom were coming down with Redcoat Scarlet Fever. It is rumored that whores were brought in from New York; it is known that around the old Southwark Theatre, home of Howe's Thespians, enterprising soldiers sold their wives to their officers, a few of whom advertised for mistresses in the newspaper.* The boast was that for every rebel killed a bastard would be fathered, and by the time the English left Philadelphia it was charged that "most of the young ladies who were in the city with the enemy and wear the present fashionable dresses have purchased them at

---

*There was apparently some sharing of favors. When General Charles Lee, long an English prisoner, was returned to Washington's headquarters at Valley Forge, he showed up late for breakfast next morning, having spent the night just behind Martha's sitting room with a "miserable dirty hussy" he'd brought from Philadelphia—"a British sergeant's wife."

the expense of their virtue"—also that a remarkable number were "carrying before them . . . an extraordinary natural weight."

Visiting New York, a Philadelphian observed that except for the Van Horne girls the young ladies were less fashionable than those she knew at home. Yet they were more forward: " 'Tis here I fancy always leap year." Indeed the belles have "made the men so saucy that I sincerely believe the lowest Ensign thinks 'tis but ask and have. . . ." As for public women, New York was full of them. If all the stories told were true, one resident out of four— woman, man, slave, child—was a whore. Crowded around King's College were the resorts of Katie Crow, Quaker Fan, Man-of-War Nance, and others. The area surrounding St. Paul's Church, awash with "bitchfoxly jades, jills, haggs, strums," was known as Holy Ground. When the brothels burned down with much of the rest of the city in 1776, business continued in the charred cellars, covered with old tents and sails and now called Canvas Town. It was rough trade; even though the place was off-limits after nine, Colonel Baldwin (to whom we owe the apple) wrote his wife that excavations in the region had unearthed a good many male bodies "ciled by the hoars." A Patriot embargo on British goods, fol-lowed by a huge influx of Loyalists when the British took the city, produced a shortage of nearly everything legal and forced people into practices that were not. It has been computed that women who but for penury and the war would have been middle-class wives were servicing one Redcoat every fifteen minutes.

Where women were not readily available the problem was rape. The seven-month occupation of New Jersey was especially hard on females—"stripped of their clothing and exposed to the inclemency of the winter and to personal insult and abuse of almost every description." Sixteen girls in a group were raped at one little town; six men nearby violated a child of thirteen; "seven or eight different officers" had their pleasure of another young woman of the province. By April of 1777 a committee of the Continental Congress was formally protesting the "lust and bru-tality" of the enemy forces. Six months before that, in the hon-ored tradition of military hypocrisy, General William Howe was deploring the "present licentious behaviour of the troops" as a "disgrace to the country they belong to," and sentencing to death for rape a soldier named Lusty. Others in command took a lighter view. As one of them reported from Staten Island,

The fair nymphs . . . are in wonderful tribulation. . . . A girl cannot step into the bushes to pluck a rose without running the imminent risk of being ravished, and they are so little accustomed to these vigorous methods that . . . we have most entertaining courts-martial every day.

Nymphs in the southern colonies, he remarked, were more philosophical. He recalled "a woman who having been forced by seven of our men" came to complain—" 'not of their usage,' she said; 'No, thank God,' she despised that, but of their having taken an old prayer book for which she had a particular affection." (Southern females, some of them "violent rebels," were not always passive. A British captain reported that outside Charleston "several ladies" were assaulted by English dragoons, and Mrs. ——, "a most delicate and beautiful woman . . . most barbarously treated"; they eventually escaped, Lady —— receiving "one or two wounds with a sword.")

But no American women, wanton, whoring, or raped, were as conspicuous as the camp followers of the British army. A very few of these women were sufficiently remarkable that they are better remembered than the husbands they followed. One of them, the foremost heroine of contemporary England, spent the early part of the war on a farm in the American south. After the Battle of Culloden, the young Flora Macdonald had helped Bonny Prince Charlie escape to the Isle of Skye disguised as her maid, was imprisoned in the Tower of London, and released under pressure of popular acclaim. She then married Allan Macdonald, bore him six children, accumulated debts in Scotland, and with her family joined a colony of Highlanders in North Carolina. With the advent of the war she became famous again—for traveling through the woods on a white horse, inspiring her compatriots to the royal cause, and reviewing troops whom she addressed in Gaelic. In a minor echo of Culloden, and under command of Donald Macdonald, a thousand kilt-and-plaided, pipe-and-drummed Scotsmen at Moore's Creek Bridge were wiped out in a matter of minutes. Flora's husband was captured, her estate confiscated, her daughters stripped of their gowns by rebel swords. They all returned to Scotland. When she died, there was a colossal funeral, and she was buried in a sheet that both the Young Pretender and Dr. Samuel Johnson, another admirer, had slept in.

Baron von Riedesel, commander of Brunswick troups in America, was an effective General when he got the chance. But because his Baroness published the record of her six-year tour of duty with or in pursuit of him, Frederica is more often recalled than Friedrich—as a highly proper hence frequently shocked lady who was in truth, as alleged, the very "symbol of devoted conjugal love." The enemy wife who caught the public fancy was Lady Harriet Acland, painted by Sir Joshua Reynolds as a bride. Major Acland was brave, according to the Baroness, though "drunk almost every day"; his lady was neither, but "the lovliest of women," warm and "romantic," who moved about the country caring for her husband when he was sick or wounded, until he was shot through the legs at Saratoga and left to the rebels. Burgoyne so admired Harriet that he gave her a note to the American commander; with it, her maid, the Major's valet, and a chaplain, she set off down the Hudson at sunset in an open boat to join the captive. After a storm, a Patriot sentinel on shore was "filled with superstitious fear" when he hailed something afloat in the dark which answered in "the clear, silvery tones of a woman's voice." She eventually reached her husband, who, according to legend, was later killed in a duel back in England, whereupon she became "a maniac" and married the chaplain. Actually, she died after thirty-seven years of widowhood. By then she had long been famous in this country as the subject of a painting, not by Reynolds, of her "highly graceful and delicate form" precariously balanced in a little vessel, as she waved her handkerchief and trilled into the night.

There were in fact exactly three such elegant camp followers. What "truly astonished" an American lady at Cambridge was first sight of the real thing.

I never had the least of Idea that the Creation produced such a sordid set of creatures in human Figure. . . . Great numbers of children . . . bear feet, cloathed in dirty rags, such effluvia filled the air while they were passing, had they not been smoking all the time, I should have been apprehensive of being contaminated by them.

Not that the American army had no trouble with females. Washington more than once issued orders to "prevent an inundation of bad women." But usually he inveighed against their riding in the wagons with the men instead of with the baggage where they belonged. More American women probably tagged along with the British, who already had more than they needed. As an allotment of wives—many of whom doubtless were wives—they had brought from England something like five thousand. Each outfit had its quota. But these figures were exceeded "beyond any Idea of Imagination"—augmented by such recruits as indentured servants who'd served their time or escaped, and were "passed about a bit." Burgoyne's army was allotted about three hundred women; at the time of his defeat they numbered more like two thousand. Prostitutes swarmed after the British wherever they went, taking "fierce pleasure in annoying and insulting the prudent and decent women . . . adjacent to their line of march." A more serious problem was that in addition to themselves they sold untold quantities of rum—this despite the fact that the British commissary spent three times as much on it as on all its meat, flour, and bread combined. Somehow the women trafficked heavily in the same commodity, further disturbing what peace there was by persisting in selling it to Indians. Their next best source of income was stripping corpses after battle.

No one knows what happened to these creatures in human Figure; five thousand biographies, any one of which might be worth reading if we had it, never got written. They did not, by and large, return to England with its defeated armies; apparently the country digested them as it had the convicts who came earlier.

There is, however, a story of what became of a closely related group of women. When British troops posed a threat to wives of American Loyalists in New York, the war office in London is said to have commissioned a Captain Jackson to bring in 3,500 females as the "intimate property" of the British army. Chiefly from the brothels of the largest cities, Jackson is said to have gathered them, for a fee paid him of £2 per body, and stuffed them into twenty hulks bound for the New World. (The load of one ship lost at sea was replaced with a cargo picked up in the West Indies.) The presence of these women, housed in stockades at Lispenards Meadows, explains the frequent references in Rivington's New York newspapers to soldiers visiting Jackson's Whites and his Blacks. When the British eventually evacuated the town, some three thousand whores made their way north, somehow crossed the Hudson River, reached the Ramapo Mountains, and settled in. Breeding with Tuscarora Indians, runaway slaves, and Hessian deserters whose names a few of them still bear, their descendants are today called "Jackson Whites"—a storied group of inbred and reputedly degenerate outcasts yet to be seen, now and then, not an hour from New York City.

These people look as if there might be Indian blood in them, though there is no evidence that the Tuscaroras ever reached the Ramapos. Censuses of the area show no influx at the end of the war, nor any German or Hessian names. Equally unknown to the British Records Office are Captain Jackson and his contract; New York papers of the time make no mention of Jackson Whites, a name which conceivably derives from "Jacks [runaway slaves?] and Whites," and never saw print until the late nineteenth century. The legend that they derive from some English whores was first published in this century. The Hessian names—Van Dunk, De Groat—are Dutch, and it was by examining early marriage and baptismal records of the Dutch Reformed Church that a clever graduate student discovered their origins in some pioneering Negro farmers of the Hackensack River Valley—freed slaves given land outside New Amsterdam, in the mid-seventeenth century, by their Dutch owners.*

---

* Their descendants refuse to believe what David S. Cohen has demonstrated; they insist that their ancestors were Hessians and Tuscaroras, as they have been taught.

It is easier to invent stories about women who never existed than to discover much about a couple of hapless ones who did. About, for instance, the whore—a "subtile shrewd jade"—who at length was "proof against every threat and persuasion" that George Washington could think of in order to discover the author of a coded letter found in her stocking. It was intelligence for the British; the relentless General finally broke her down, and she named him: Dr. Benjamin Church, distinguished Boston Patriot and chief physician to Washington's army. A Harvard man who had dismissed wife and children for this "Infamous Slut," now pregnant (and "he owns himself the father"), Church was deported on a ship that was lost at sea. The letter she carried on her leg, whose cipher was instantly cracked by a method Poe would triumphantly unfold a half century later, survives. And so does one she herself wrote about it ("pray com as swon as posebell"). But no one knows what happened to the woman, or even her name.

Nor the real name of the beautiful, delicate girl of good family, not yet fifteen and married to

an American officer, who was dastard enough to abandon her at Fort Washington in York Island, where she was taken in the powder magazine by a private soldier of the Hessians. . . . This unfeeling wretch . . . blind to her beauty and tears, only as they inflamed his lust . . . compelled her to be subservient to all his brutal desires.

She was eventually sold, for a shilling, to a British officer who sent her into town, set her up in acceptable fashion, and then was killed in a skirmish. Next she fell victim

to the avarice and iniquity of one of those . . . of her own sex, that always contrive to make a property of unfortunate beauty.

It was in this situation that she had come on board the *Daphne* on a visit . . . and carried to sea. . . .

Headed for British-held New York on that man-of-war, an astonished diarist encountered the lady—"young, handsome, and graceful." She was named "Sukey *Washington,* after the fort where she was taken, and by that she is pretty well known in New York." Perhaps so, but nothing has been discovered of her since.

IT IS DEPRESSING that a book published in 1975 should celebrate exactly the same Revolutionary heroines as were exalted a century ago—cherished Patriots whom Americans have clung to and hoarded like a few old coins. Heads and tales wear thin after excessive recounting. Especially when they are chiefly those of ladies acceptable to the nineteenth century which inexpensively minted them—not the eighteenth, which was less circumspect, or our own, which is "bored," says Simone de Beauvoir, "by 'good' women." These tin goddesses are not, moreover, really remembered as women at all, but as appendages to their husbands— wives, homemakers, hostesses, Martha Washingtons—or as make-believe men, dispensing water on the battlefield, manning field-pieces, Molly Pitchers. This, as everyone explains, because females had little opportunity to earn immortality. "A climate conducive to women's achievement did not yet exist. A woman's place was in the home. . . ."

For the most part, no doubt true, though the place of upper-class women was also in society, and there were a great many lower-class women who did not really have homes. Thus readers are still regaled with Deborah Sampson, who apparently did, disguised as a man, serve in the army for a considerable period. (It was her second enlistment, the first having terminated when she got drunk in a saloon and blew her cover.) The intimate logistics of her masquerade have been ignored, but she is believed to have survived a wound which if treated would have exposed her, and to have been found out only when, defenselessly ill with "malignant fever," a doctor reached for her heart. He is said to have kept his secret, but his niece fell in love with the soldier, who after a couple of close calls in a carriage wrote the impassioned girl a letter signed Your Own Sex, was discharged, pensioned by Washington, married, and raised a family.

Best known Molly Pitcher was Mary Ludwig Hays, who did sure enough carry water in battle at Monmouth, and service a gun when her husband was wounded. Likewise another wife replaced her husband as an assistant gunner and suffered a "shredded breast." One woman is remembered for whipping off her dress and running for the powder that saved a fort; it is conceivable that another did shoot or hang six Tories at her cabin. And the business of Mrs. Murray of Murray Hill, Manhattan Island—wondrous siren who for hours beguiled the British generals while a large part of Washington's army escaped easy capture—is still transacted in prose, verse, and theater. The D.A.R. installed a plaque, and generations of patriots in the know have chuckled over this ultimate revelation of the power of Revolutionary Woman.

Nearly forgotten is Patience Wright, whose husband neglected her for scarlet women, whereupon she demanded to know why she ceased to satisfy, and he did shun

These faithful arms and eager run—
to some obscure unclean retreat
With fiends incarnate glad to meet.

The reason is unknown, but on his death Patience took the children to England, gave up poetry for modeling in wax, and became famous. Even the King and Queen, whom as an ardent republican she claimed to address as George and Charlotte, visited her London studio. According to a report of the time she "found herself the avenues to get information of almost every design"—which she shipped to Benjamin Franklin in Paris. Armed with this intelligence (thus goes a recent account), "his mission gained new successes each month," until the alliance with France which eventually won the war was signed. Franklin was so pleased with her model of his head that he donated an old suit of his clothes to enhance it; some of her handiwork is still on display in Westminster Abbey.

After the war Patience Wright alerted Thomas Jefferson to her proposed return to this country, then died in England. His reaction is unknown, but may have been relief. Franklin certainly tried hard, though unsuccessfully, to stop her from coming to Paris. Her reputation as a spy was her own creation; the one letter to him that the British intercepted was of little or no import to either side. An American in Paris described her expression as "appalling . . . a maniac's," and her language an acute embarrassment. Abigail Adams referred to her as "the Queen of Sluts." As for the "incredibly beautiful Mrs. Murray," it is quite possible that the British command, having taken their objective, enjoyed a glass of Madeira at Murray Hill, though it had nothing to do with their failure to take up the rebels. And Circe was a middle-aged Quaker lady with twelve children.

Only the real Molly Pitcher improves with time, and that because of a recent republication of the obscure narrative of an obscure soldier who happened to be at Monmouth, and saw how, as she reached for a cartridge,

a cannon ball from the enemy passed directly between her legs without doing any other damage than carrying away all the lower part of her petticoat. . . . She observed that it was lucky it did not pass a little higher, for in that case it might have carried away something else

and went about her business. The heroic Tory-killer was in life "ugly, illiterate, and vulgar." The wounded gunner took to drink, became known as Dirty Kate, remarried unpromisingly, and occasioned Washington's aide to ask how it was that with so ancient and decrepit a husband she was so pregnant. Deborah Sampson wrote and published her own story, took to the lecture circuit, and climaxed her performance by appearing in uniform and executing the manual of arms.

HISTORY HAS REMEMBERED these women out of hunger for more attractive ones, and in recognition of the fact there simply must have been women of the period worth preserving. But there is nothing more to be learned of Patriot wives and hostesses. And the females we have honored for military courage are not very formidable when put beside such ladies of the French Revolution as risked their necks right up to the guillotine that chopped them, or to lady terrorists plotting against the Czar of Russia a century later, or the fifteen hundred women wounded, captured, or killed in the Russian Revolution at Petrograd alone—not to mention women of the Spanish Civil War or the War of Liberation in Israel. It is natural that Americans should remember best such people as were on the winning side. A few lesser known ladies of the time suggest that victims may be viable as victors. Four of them, to be exact, whose scandal was grist for the American novel at its start.

When just a girl in Chichester, England, Charlotte Stanley, daughter of the eleventh Earl of Derby, eloped—so goes the story —with a young lieutenant named John Montresor. Ordered to this country during the war, he promised marriage, and she sailed with him. They landed, the months passed, and she was pregnant —"her open shame known to all New-York." She was dowerless as well, and Montresor deserted her to marry a woman with an income. Charlotte bore a daughter—apparently in 1775—and died in the event. She was buried in Trinity Churchyard, her grave still visible from the sidewalk on Broadway.

Charlotte had a cousin whose daughter was also desperate and legendary. A close relative of Pierpont Edwards, son of Jonathan Edwards, and of Aaron Burr, Jonathan's grandson, Elizabeth Whitman was the "lively, beautiful, and vain" daughter of a Hartford clergyman, and at the time of the Revolution rejected offers of marriage from two other ministers, both Yale men and one so much a hypochondriac that she feared "abstinence and self-renunciation." What course she chose instead is unknown, but at thirty-six she moved into a tavern at Peabody, Massachusetts, one June day, explaining that her husband would be joining her. There was no husband; in July she gave birth to a dead infant, and in two weeks died herself of puerperal fever. Both her "riotous cousins" Edwards and Burr were fingered as the father, as was still another relative she had entertained "at unseemly hours." The newspaper was harsh: "she coquetted past her prime . . . and fell into criminal indulgences." Her epitaph was kinder if confusing: "Let candor throw a veil over her frailties. . . ." A piece of wallpaper from her room at the tavern and a silver spoon are carefully preserved.

Livelier scandal afflicted Sarah Wentworth (Apthorp) Morton, striking beauty of three portraits by Gilbert Stuart, and her sister Frances, namesake of their aunt Frances Wentworth, whom Copley had captured. Sarah was called the "American Sappho," the country's best known woman poet. She married Perez Morton: Harvard, Boston lawyer, orator, pillar of King's Chapel and irresistible, as his wife had reason to know, to many ladies. They had three children in four years, and when Frances—also considered a beauty, younger, and "pliable"—came to town, she was welcomed into the Morton mansion on State Street. "All accounts agree" that she "readily yielded" to her brother-in-law. And continually. At last she became pregnant, gave birth to a daughter who was removed to the country to be raised, and took up her bed where she left it. The affair became notorious; as defined by the Boston Incest Bill, it constituted incest. Frances wrote her "once lov.'d Morton . . . the first and last man I ever knew," not to let "my sweet Infant suffer . . . you are the father of it," took poison, and died.* Sarah, newly pregnant, wrote verses "To a recently united husband." After all, subject to his "ardent sway, / How many hearts were left to weep . . . ?"

There was far more weeping over Jane McCrea—best known of these tragic women—the "beautiful girl of sixteen" scalped and killed near Saratoga by some of Burgoyne's Indian scouts while waiting to marry her lieutenant. Recalling a near-miss of her own, Margaret Moncrieffe long ago told the tale as it wildly circulated at the time:

She, alas! found *no* mercy; her charms served only to stimulate the furious passions of her brutal ravishers: arrayed in her bridal robes, awaiting the arrival of him, the lover, who was to crown her joys . . . she

---

*The "guilty Innocent," as Frances repeatedly calls herself, also wrote six incoherent and not entirely legible pages for what appears to be her journal, and another letter. In the former she begs her sister's forgiveness, and remarks: "I have felt from the first that this matter would go against me but I have resolved never to live after it has." To a letter in the same vein dated August 27, 1788, she added a florid "Finis" and, according to the *Massachusetts Gazette,* she died the next day. All three documents were found in a book in a second-hand bookstore in New York 110 years after they were written.

was three times violated by Canadian savages in *British* pay, and afterwards, (oh horrible to relate!) in *cold blood, scalped, and murdered!*

Michel René Hilliard-d'Auberteuil, an early student of the case, took much the same view. The Indians

stripped her of her garments; and having performed on her all that their fury and brutality could suggest, they scalped her and displayed her long tresses . . . under the very eyes of her lover.

She was found both scalped and naked, but there is no evidence that Miss McCrea, who was twenty-four, had been raped. It is unlikely that she was traveling through the woods in her wedding gown, uncertain that she was waiting for her officer, undocumented that they were betrothed. But though he would fight for the King, and she was known as a Tory, the atrocity spurred rebel enlistments vigorously. Burke denounced the murder before Parliament. Countless verses, dramas, and fictions recounted it, as well as etchings, woodcuts, and paintings (one, over ten feet high, was recently discovered in an upstate New York barn). Jane became the most effective legend of them all, the girl who rallied the Patriots to defeat Burgoyne and then the others, the virgin sacrificed that the nation might be free.

Her murder caused the anger, but the misfortune of Charlotte Stanley the anguish—no matter that her tale is shallowly grounded in fact. As chief engineer of the British army in the Revolution, her reputed seducer John Montresor was well known in this country. "Urbane and cynical," he was owner of Montresor's (now Randall's) Island, and the first man to draw an authentic map of New York. He could not have deserted Charlotte in '75 to marry a fashionable New Yorker; the British did not take the city until '76, and he had married a decade earlier. (An extremely handsome woman, as one of Copley's finest paintings attests, Frances Tucker bore him ten children and remained his wife until he died at the end of the century.) The journal he kept throughout his career shows that at the only time he was in England, available for the ruin of the ill-fated Charlotte, she would have been about seven. The Earl of Derby did indeed have a daughter named Charlotte Stanley; she did die young, and during the war. But not in childbirth nor in this country: she was Burgoyne's wife.

The immediate point is not disclosures of mysteries no one cares to have solved. Rather that the American novel, which grew from the shakiest conceivable beginnings to power and world esteem hand in hand with the nation, was born in sin and nurtured in scandal. It started in abject imitation of Samuel Richardson's persecuted maidens, but its plots were taken from the stories of four unlucky women named Frances Apthorp, Charlotte Stanley, Elizabeth Whitman, and Jane McCrea. *The Power of Sympathy* (1789), which has the best claim on First American Novel, exploited the suicide of the girl who could not control her passion for her sister's husband. Published anonymously, and long if unreasonably attributed to the pen of the betrayed sister herself, it was almost certainly the work of a young writer named William Hill Brown, living right across State Street from the Mortons— who bought all the copies they could, only six originals surviving. (Publication of the novel was itself the subject of two scurrilous farces, in one of which it is pointedly suggested that not all of Mrs. Morton's children were Morton's.)

Charlotte Stanley's story—called *Charlotte, a Tale of Truth* (1791), later *Charlotte Temple,* in which she is betrayed by one "John Montraville"—was written by an Englishwoman and first published in England. But since the author, Mrs. Rowson, was raised in this country and spent the greater part of her adult life here, it is counted American; here the novel went through something like two hundred editions and is still in print. The tale of the abandoned Elizabeth Whitman was turned into *The Coquette* (1797) by Hannah Foster, one of her cousins. It was less popular than *Charlotte,* but Elizabeth's gravestone, like Charlotte's, became a shrine.*

---

*The reputed grave of Charlotte Stanley is still a curiosity, a slab of brown sandstone in which is carved not her own but her fictional name. Legends tell how it was long decorated with flowers by an unseen hand, and "the turf over her remains kept fresh by falling tears." The records of Trinity Church were lost in the great fire of 1776, and nothing but tradition tells how a depression in the

The only person who ever claimed in print to know who fathered Miss Whitman's child never told, and the notion that John Montraville, the seducer in *a Tale of Truth,* was in life John Montresor seems easily dismissed. Indeed it has not yet been firmly established that this Charlotte Stanley—perhaps the *grand*-daughter of the Earl of Derby and the *niece* of Mrs. John Burgoyne—actually existed. But Mrs. Rowson never stopped insisting that her story was founded in fact, and the original for Montraville known to her personally. She certainly knew Montresor, her first cousin.*

No one has looked into both *Charlotte Temple* and its historical background without deciding that the novel was a Tale Invented —an easy conclusion if, as everywhere, the implications of its sequel, *Charlotte's Daughter,* are ignored. In his second appearance the same Montraville is a generation older, and his life presented in sharper detail. He is back in England from America where, as chief engineer for the British in the Revolution, he has unaccountably accumulated a large fortune. He enjoys both an elegant house in Portland Place and a great country estate, with handsome equipage, where he lives like a nobleman. By revealing his guilt, he intervenes at the last second to prevent the marriage of his legitimate son to his and Charlotte's illegitimate daughter. He then expires, the girl devotes her life to charity, and the young man takes off for India with the British army.

The comprehensive *History of New York during the Revolutionary War* was published a century after it was written by Judge

---

stone (recently filled in but clearly visible) once contained a silver plate, placed there in her memory by her daughter in 1800—which was stolen, and her fictional name carved in its place. Others argue that the name did not appear on the stone until much later, probably suggested by the tradition that she died very near the church. No one really knows who is buried beneath the stone—or, since another tale tells how the remains were exhumed and returned to England, if anyone is.

*Montraville is a new land's Lovelace in a travesty of *Clarissa Harlowe.* It is hard to think what things might have been like for the American novel if the first really popular one, still working from a relative of the author's, had been based on a model other than Richardson: John Montresor's stepmother was the daughter of Henry Fielding.

Thomas Jones, a Loyalist New Yorker exiled in England. This work tells how John Montresor, an engineer ordered by General Howe to demolish the forts, batteries, and redoubts erected by the rebels at New York, Long Island, and Staten Island, received for the job from John Bull £150,000, of which he pocketed £100,000. Returning to England, writes the angry judge, he "purchased one of the genteelest houses in Portland Place," as well as "a noble country-seat in Surrey," where he "set up his carriages, had a house full of servants in rich livery, and lived in all the splendour of an eastern prince." God knows what happened to Charlotte's daughter in life, if she ever was; John Montresor had a son who died in 1805 while serving with the British army in India.*

Moral indignation and a taste for the sensational also produced a book called *Mis Mac Rea,* which, had it really been issued at Philadelphia in 1784 as the title page claims, would have been the earliest American novel of all—except that it was written in French and published at Brussels, by Hilliard-d'Auberteuil on the heels of his semi-factual account of the atrocity. It was surely, however, the first novel to exploit a Jeffersonian-Jamesian theme that had a considerable future in our fiction: the contrast, in the Frenchman's words translated, of "American innocence with European vices." A subplot is appended, in which the chaste Jane is subjected in French fashion to British corruption until, "steeping herself in a melancholy poison," she is "no longer afraid of love." But when the Englishman has got her flat on her back in a cornfield, she is still American enough to protest that "Your sensual demands are stronger than the fear of making me the most unfortunate of maidens." And this time when the Indians have

---

*What seems likeliest is that when Mrs. Rowson wrote *Charlotte Temple*—out of moral indignation, she said, at the sexual irresponsibility of young British officers—she did have in mind some unknown, tragic indiscretion of her cousin, whom she called Montraville. With Montresor alive, well, and married, she changed the circumstances until they were unrecognizable, retaining only the similarity of names. Then when the villain was three decades in his grave, and she herself dead (*Charlotte's Daughter* was published posthumously in 1828), she did everything but fingerprint him.

got her completely naked they argue who shall rape her first until suddenly she is dead and hairless.

THE FOUR FEMALES who achieved a tenuous immortality in the birth of the nation's fiction all died and were buried in the country where they came to grief. Revolutionary Ladies did not—not irrevocably—come to grief here at all; these were lives headed in another direction. Their American years and dénouements are dimly foreshadowed by a victim of scandal and the war who was forced from this country to die in England, a woman no writer ever celebrated.

Dorcas Griffiths was born in Boston of a Massachusetts family that was already old. She lived in a house overlooking the harbor on Hancock's Wharf, where she sold spirits, tea, linen, and groceries. She had married at twenty-two and was raising a daughter. Mr. Griffiths was nowhere about, and although she was getting along in years, Dorcas was the mistress of her much younger landlord, John Hancock. In 1775 he "turned her off" (which at the time meant dismissed her) and married. In the same year she changed allegiance too, and after Bunker Hill she "humanely assisted the Sick and Wounded Officers of the King's Army at Boston; which drew the resentment of the Rebels upon them, and obliged them to leave their Country." When the artillery placed on Dorchester Heights forced Howe to embark for Halifax, Dorcas and daughter went along—the mother now the mistress of Captain David Johnston, one of the wounded she had assisted. After three years she emigrated to England and, with the endorsement of Johnston plus Generals Gage and Howe, petitioned for relief for herself and child. She lacked, however, the support of Thomas Flucker, who had been royal secretary of the Massachusetts Colony. Perhaps father Flucker was bitter; his own daughter, over his violent objection, had married Henry Knox, who supplied the cannon which drove him from his home, never to see either it or her again. In any event he testified that Dorcas in Boston had been "a Common Prostitute & bred up her Daughter in the same way. She was kepd by the famous Handcock." He said more, which the court did not choose to commit to paper, and the Griffiths lost the £50 a year they had been allowed.

On the same day that Captain Johnston was wounded at Bunker Hill and taken in by Mrs. Griffiths—but for which, he testified, he would have died in the street—Lady Agnes Frankland watched the battle from the top of her four-storied mansion. The tale of how, while still the mistress of Sir Henry Frankland, she had rescued him in more dramatic fashion than Dorcas's was once well known. Sir Arthur Quiller-Couch related it in a fatuous little novel, Oliver Wendell Holmes in a long ballad with "very strict adhesion to the facts," and there were many other tellings. Closer to the figure of a Revolutionary Lady than Mrs. Griffiths, Lady Frankland is now well enough forgotten that the most recent account of her has it "Franklin" throughout.

She was born Agnes Surriage, in 1726, and at sixteen was a serving wench at the Fountain Inn in "a Dirty, Erregular Stincking Place"—fish a'curing everywhere—called Marblehead. It was at the inn that Henry Frankland, a wealthy and dissolute young Englishman, Collector of the Port of Boston, direct descendant of Oliver Cromwell, and unmarried father of a boy named Henry Cromwell, first saw her, barefoot and scantily clad. Struck by her extraordinary beauty, so goes the tale, he gave her money for shoes. Next time he saw her she still lacked them, explaining that they were saved for church. Frankland was now so smitten that he persuaded her parents to let him take her to Boston as his ward, and there she was educated in the fashionable accomplishments. In 1747 he became a baronet, and by now, if not long before, Agnes had become his mistress. ("Ah!" cries Holmes, "the gift her mother gave, / Its beads are all unstrung!") A servant was not supposed to pluck a plum; Boston society was outraged. Sir Henry responded by building a great estate far out of town at Hopkinton, with pillars from England, marble from Italy, and extraordinary gardens. With their "son," young Henry, they settled in and lived "in Regal splendour."

Then, still a young woman, Agnes sailed with Sir Henry for England. When, as in Boston, she was spurned by his family circle, the couple sought out a more permissive location—the "sensuous and dissolute city of Lisbon." It was 1755, the year of the earthquake. The Portuguese Sodom was punished for its vices—such was the church view—and Agnes's lover, with thousands of others, entombed in debris. Holmes tells most dramatically how in a superhuman effort she "bruised her tender breast / Against the crushing stone" and unearthed him. (He said only that he was "buried in ruins" and "most providentially saved"; a contemporary letter says he saved himself.) It was then, perhaps in providential thanks, that he finally married the woman (and next, according to one story, remarried her in the Church of England to make sure). Back in Boston the following year Lady Frankland found herself this time a leader in society. Sir Henry bought her a town house—a showplace, itself once celebrated in literature—to complement the Hopkinton estate. He also took to writing verses lamenting his profligate youth. He was not well; with Agnes he journeyed repeatedly to a spa near Lisbon to improve his health; he finally died at Bath. His widow inherited all his American properties and a large annuity. She retired to Hopkinton, and lived there until in May of '75, with many other Loyalists, she took refuge in besieged Boston, was let into the city by Dr. Benjamin Church, prominent Patriot, and escorted to the mansion from which in June she witnessed the first great battle of the war. Later that year she retreated to England and settled in Chichester, reputed home of the original "Charlotte," where Henry Cromwell was apparently living. She was fifty-five and looking older, but there are yet clear signs of former beauty in her portrait, and she was not ready for solitude. In a bailiff, and subsequent Mayor of Chichester, she found a new husband with whom she lived for two years. Then one day she signed her will and died. The stone in the churchyard reads "Dame Agnes Frankland" and is good as new. An accurate forecast of Revolutionary Ladies, except in the matter of Birth, she had lost her "good name," defied gossip, made the most of ostracism, sprung from her back and landed on her feet before the English earth at last received her—a full generation in advance of them. Richard Brinsley Sheridan's timing was perfect. In 1775, with no thought for America, he wrote: "Love gilds the scene, and women guide the plot."

ᴘ II

THE SPECIFIC WOMEN whose loves fashioned their lives in the distinctive shape taken on by Revolutionary Ladies are those who finally succeed in Casting the Mold. Three colonial girls closer to the type than Lady Frankland now appear— beautiful and wealthy, Loyalist and Anglican, grown to womanhood in scandal and war, driven into exile and long obscurity. One was not profoundly affected by the struggle and did not have to leave the country. Another, her disrepute more political than sexual, is not really forgotten. With Hannah Van Horne, whose tale has never been told, the pattern is complete and perfect.

In 1771 Sir John Johnson, oldest of the uncounted natural children of Sir William Johnson, Superintendent of Indian Affairs and "Baron of the Mohawk Valley," was in search of a bride and a legitimate heir. Major Thomas Moncrieffe with rare enthusiasm suggested that the pilgrim come to town:

the finest race of Young women I ever saw are at present at New York Polly Watts, Hannah Van Horne, Betsey her sister, an angel, Sukey Van Horne, if I was two and twenty I would not wish for more than her and six thousand bottles of her fathers old wine   make me the Capt. of the Guides and I will lead him. . . .

It was, as touted, a superb list. Sir John, the child of his father's housekeeper and himself already sire of a son and a daughter by his teen-aged mistress, married the first girl on it. He took Polly Watts back to the Valley, where he soon inherited Johnson Hall. There, until driven out by the Patriots from the "farthest outpost of civilization," they lived very grand.*

---

*A forgotten Loyalist heroine, Lady Johnson was taken hostage for her husband's good behavior. At Albany she boldly escaped for New York with three small children, two of whom died as a result; it is said that Sir John was bitter. He

Hannah, Betsey, Sukey. Counting their cousins, the "Van Horne girls" were eight in all, and known to many officers besides Moncrieffe for their apolitical charms. "They bestowed their favors on friend and foe alike." Sukey and the six thousand bottles already had a Tory admirer, on whose arm she graced the streets of Flatbush. Betsey the angel was the cousin of another Betsey Van Horne; a third married James Rivington, newspaper publisher and himself at one time or another on both sides of the conflict. Mary Van Horne would soon be wife to Washington's aide, the colorful Stephen Moylan. She had an unnamed sister who much bemused the visiting Marquis de Chastellux by her uninhibited behavior in his and Mary's presence. As for Hannah, first-cited Van Horne, no American girl of her time is known to have lived a fuller life; except for the fraction of it that impinged on the Baroness von Riedesel's, her story is wholly unknown.

She was, to begin, a native aristocrat, the descendant of a Dutchman of Hoorn, who was in New Amsterdam by 1645. Her great-grandfather, a merchant of New York, made a fortune and bought lands in New Jersey. Her grandfather established the great house, still standing, that became widely known during the Revolution as Phil's Hall, a large estate overlooking the Raritan about eight miles northwest of New Brunswick. Despite the fact that his indentured tutor had long before taken off with an indentured maidservant, Hannah's father went to Harvard and "ran with the wealthy crowd"; he was fined for his part in "an Extravagant drinking Frolic and afterward making indecent Noises, in the College Yard." He married Seleya Hardt, who bore Hannah and the two younger girls. Equally with his brother Philip, John inherited their father's financially encumbered estate. They apparently shared the mansion and together operated rich copper mines in the region, importing men from abroad to work them. But in April of '74 John was jailed for debt, and that December, probably still in prison, he died. A spiritual precedent for his

received the largest compensation for his material losses of any New York Tory, including considerable land in Canada, where Polly, mother of eleven, eventually died.

daughters and nieces was an aunt of his who had married William Burnet, Royal Governor at different times of New York, New Jersey, and Massachusetts. It was said that "Caresses of a young wife" had so depleted him that his power fell into other hands, and he was finished at forty-one.

During the Revolution, Phil's or Convivial Hall resembled "a hotel . . . constantly filled" but free and never out of anything. Its politics, like the girls', were adjustable. On a single day Phil served breakfast to Lord Cornwallis and dinner to a Continental General. Washington wrote an associate, "I am sorry you did not keep old Van Horn under restraint," but he was so kept—paroled on his own estate. When the British raided the house in hope of capturing the rebel Governor Livingston, who was not there, they found some American officers in residence, though Phil professed his Loyalty. "The reason for this leniency," it was explained, "is that the Van Horne's house was rather neutral ground he having three or four very attractive daughters." It was said that on occasion officers of both sides would bump into each other attending them.

In the year that John Johnson came to New York, where Hannah and her sisters then lived, a tall British Captain known as one of the "young heroes of Minden" arrived from England. Edward Foy was secretary to the new Royal Governor of New York—John Murray, Earl of Dunmore, Viscount Fincastle, Baron of Blair, of Moulin, and of Tillymont. The secretary's post was a good one; he was well paid, and his superior—known as "a Jolly Fellow & loves his Bottle"—entertained liberally. Within a year the "bewitching" and somewhat younger Hannah became at Christ Church, New Brunswick, Mrs. Foy. Nine months later, according to the *New York Gazette,* she was "happily deliver'd of a fine Son," named Nathaniel after the Captain's uncle, then Mayor of Bristol, England.

Hannah was soon to be happily circumstanc'd as well. Dunmore, for no good reason, was promoted with a raise in pay to governorship of the more prosperous colony of Virginia. In response to this honor he "took too Chearful a Glass," offended everybody at a feast by proposing the "vilest baudy Healths" (so reported his chief justice, William Smith), "struck Apthorpe & Colo. Fanning," called the new Governor of New York (Tryon) a coward, "& ran about in the night assaulting one & another," while crying out in "a drunken Solliloquy . . . damn Virginia. Did I ever seek it?" James Rivington's explanation for this outburst was that Dunmore was "ill suited to an Anguish Climate," which he thought so little salubrious as to prohibit his bringing over his family. But he moved into his new quarters at Williamsburg, entertained Washington, and made very sure that he retained the services of Captain Foy by adding to his salary "lucrative emoluments" to be taken from fees established expressly for his benefit. Soon acclimated, he dispatched Hannah and her husband to England for the purpose of escorting Lady Charlotte to Yorktown. With six of Lady Charlotte's children they embarked for America on the *Dutchess of Gordon,* and in March of '74 the *Virginia Gazette* announced from Williamsburg that

the Right Honourable the Countess of Dunmore . . . accompanied by Capt Foy and his Lady, arrived at the Palace in this city; to the great joy of his Excellency the Governour.

They had come in at night. Public buildings and private homes were illuminated and the whole town turned out. But one highly placed citizen soon learned that neither the Governor's joy nor his wife's was unconfined. Dunmore, he wrote in his journal, is

a Consummate Rake & does not pay that attention to his Lady that she seems to deserve, she is extremely jealous of a young Lady . . . very dear to him previous to his Ladyship arrival & the scandalous Chronicle says that his Lordship is very great there still . . . (I almost discovered it my self).

The young Lady was certainly not Hannah. A Virginia gentleman who took pains to find fault with everyone he met confessed that Mrs. Foy was "really agreeable"; the only nit he could pick was that she seemed "more fond of her husband Perhaps than the politeness of the day allows of."

It was with the arrival of the Dunmores and the Foys, as Irving explains in his life of Washington, that Williamsburg was restored to its former glory. The brightest spot was the Governor's Palace, in which Hannah and her Captain were magnificently installed with the Governor and his family. Staffed by a dozen indentured servants and fifty-six slaves, with a large library, many valuable paintings, instruments for a full orchestra, and elegant furnishings, it was the center of social splendor. The Virginia aristocracy competed in providing hospitality to the new administration; a court circle sprang up, with regulations determining the rank and precedence of officers and wives. Living at court, with her husband "widely regarded as the power behind the governor's chair," Hannah must have ranked very close to the top. She had not been in the Palace long before Washington came again to dine; there was a great ball, and, given her attractions and his indefatigability on the dance floor, it would have been remarkable if he had not taken a turn or two with her. The inventory of what remained in the Dunmore's cellar when he left the place suggests how they all lived: something like 5,000 gallons of Madeira, nearly 2,000 bottles of other wines and champagne, 480 gallons of old rum, and unmeasured quantities of "common." Recent excavations have unearthed the Chinese porcelain, crested with the Dunmore coat of arms, that they dined on.

Washington thought the Governor very able, an opinion shared by almost nobody. Immediates considered him haughty and "very difficult of access." They liked Foy little better: "watch him," one Patriot leader warned, he is "insolent & arbitrary" and out to "enslave us." The administration was at first treated politely. When Dunmore magisterially dissolved the House of Burgesses it went right ahead and gave, next night, its ball for his lady; Thomas Jefferson contributed 20 shillings (and at Dunmore's request drew a plan for an addition to the College of William and Mary). But the only genuinely popular thing the Governor did in Virginia was to name a newborn daughter for the province. While the colony was moving to give leadership to a revolution, he was proposing—in a letter the *Virginia Gazette* got hold of and published—that the British blockade the colonies and starve them. He commandeered gunpowder, armed his Palace Blacks, and sent out word that "if any insult were offered to

Capt Foy" in his pursuit of duty, *"he would declare freedom to the slaves and lay the town in ashes."* With that what good will was left collapsed, and "in the *dead of night"* in June of 1775 the Foys decamped with Dunmore and family, taking refuge on board the man-of-war *Fowey,* new seat of government. There is no mention of Hannah's son in these scraps of intelligence.

Why Foy at this point decided to quit his post, and America as well, is not, as alleged, very mysterious. He had prospered in both but not got rich. His special fees aroused such hostility that the Governor had been forced to withdraw them. Dunmore's petition for 100,000 acres of land in the western part of the province, plus 20,000 acres for his aide, was unavailing. It was Foy's guess that he was about to "bear more than my share" of blame for the disgrace the administration had fallen into, and he concluded archly that extended service to his Lordship had proved "as little profitable as edifying to me." He got command of artillery in Boston, and sailed for his new job. Lady Dunmore, still beloved at Williamsburg, departed with the children for England, and a few months later the Foys went there too.

Now the Captain, leaving Hannah temporarily behind, sailed back for the New World with "10,000 Brunswickers & british." He had a new post as commissary to their commander, General von Riedesel, whose troops were on their way to reinforce Guy Carleton's at Quebec, restoring British control of Canada. Old acquaintances from Minden, the two soldiers bunked together on the crossing. The commissary displayed an unexpected talent in coping with the privations of seafare. "Again Captain Foy cooked," the General wrote his wife—"this time bouillon, haddock with anchovy sauce, ragout of roast beef, and some roast veal with potatoes." After dinner, two loyal husbands proposed many toasts, never forgetting their absent wives. "As one can see from her letters," Riedesel observed, "Captain Foy's wife loves her husband very much." She is an American, he explained, "hates England and wishes to return as soon as possible and be reunited."

In the spring of '76 the Baroness von Riedesel had left Germany, with three small daughters in tow, to join her husband. But in England she had been strictly enjoined by the Baron not to cross the Atlantic save in the company of "a lady of quality . . . who has already made the trip to America"—clearly Hannah Foy. Frederica's desire to be reunited with Friedrich was excruciating, but after six months she had got no farther than Bristol. What her husband did not know was that Hannah had begun to like England very well, and was not more fond of her Captain than polished manners permitted but of officers as a breed.

In Bristol the Baroness was in for cultural shock. At first she knew no English. One day out walking with Hannah, "with whom I could speak some French," she was suddenly surrounded by over a hundred sailors who "pointed their fingers at me, and cried 'French whore!' " Her new dress, made for her in Germany, she gave in tears to her cook. Before long she decided she'd "gone mad" to put herself in Hannah's care—"but you have forbidden me to go alone. . . . I wish I were dead." The problem was that Hannah was now totally at home in England, uninhibited by the presence in Bristol of Nathaniel Foy, her husband's uncle and son's namesake. While Frederica spent hours in her room weeping for the Baron, Hannah and an unnamed, unmarried sister (Betsey? Sukey?) enjoyed themselves in their "pretty and well-furnished house" entertaining young naval officers of the town. Winter approached; the Baroness could not prevail on Hannah to take passage before it would be too late. Over and over she pleaded with her husband: "if you knew how I suffer," "let me follow," if it is a matter of money "I will deny everything to the children," "Pity me, love me, do not forget me." At one point the Secretary of State for the American Colonies intervened by offering her, her children, and her companions free berths on a packet he owned. Hannah at last consented to travel to Portsmouth and set sail. But the very day they all arrived at the port of embarkation, she and her sister found friends from Bristol. They "passed a very gay evening," and said many things to the young men that Frederica's new English could not handle. It was clear, however, that if the American ladies would consent to winter in Portsmouth they would be welcome. Next morning Hannah—a "very gentle" lady, the Baroness had to admit—came to her room with the news that she was not, after all, going to leave. It was spring of the next year before she did, and the Baroness waited.

It may be that Hannah was finally willing to take ship because she had some notion of what the voyage offered. Arbuthnot, commander of the *Blonde,* was one of her good naval companions; as the Baroness explained it to her journal, her "old friendship with the captain prevented her from refusing him liberties which he had enjoyed in the past." Thus Mrs. Foy plied her way to the New World in tandem with her maid—a "beautiful creature," said Frederica, who had come along "to escape from a country in which she was too well known and in order to find the dissolute sort of friends she liked among the sailors." She found in particular a "sot, who often spent the night with her in my antichamber" —for whom she was caught stealing wine from Arbuthnot, and with whom she sported so lustily that a guard was posted to protect the Baroness from the noises. The traveling arrangements of the "capricious" Miss Van Horne are lost to the annals of the sea, but it is known that the journey ended amicably off Quebec. Every cannon in the harbor saluted the Baroness; Captain Arbuthnot came to apologize for his neglect, explaining that it resulted from his intimacy with Mrs. Foy.* The long-suffering Frederica invited the Van Hornes aboard the tender sent to fetch her ashore. She was met on land by the equipage of Lady Carleton, wife of the commanding Sir Guy, to whose residence she continued, parting company with her long-time escort.

But not, according to the biographer of the von Riedesels, for good. The Baron had left Quebec for Lake Champlain; Louise Hall Tharp believes that Hannah and Frederica met again when the General's wife finally caught up with her husband at Fort Edward. There, the Baroness noted, General Burgoyne in his comfortable farmhouse had established "the wife of a commissary

---

*Surely he was not, as alleged, Captain Marriott Arbuthnot, soon to replace Admiral Howe as commander in American waters. A "coarse, blustering, foulmouthed bully" and an "absurd" tactician, Marriott at the time of the crossing of the *Blonde* was sixty-five; Hannah was beautiful and twenty-four.

who was his mistress . . . a gay lady fond of singing and champagne." (It is elsewhere reported that she had "come down from Canada," and that Burgoyne had "thirty carts earmarked for his own belongings, his traveling cellar, and the extensive wardrobe of Mrs. Commissary.") If the Baroness had it right, it was while Gentleman Johnny drank and dallied that his retreat from Saratoga was cut off. He surrendered to his lady, then his foe; at last the Alliance with France was signed, and history turned a page.

The Baroness thought it would be clear in the context—so argues her biographer—that Burgoyne's sparkling, tuneful bedmate was Hannah Foy. She speculates further that Mrs. Foy's husband, having learned of his wife's adventures on land and sea, had left her. He had, following the defeat at Saratoga and the capture of von Riedesel, landed on his feet again as secretary and adjutant-general to the commander-in-chief Guy Carleton.* He worked closely with Guy's younger brother, Major Thomas Carleton, and as adjutant was given to issuing fire-eating directives; he went to London with dispatches from the General, and had a "long interview with His Majesty at St. James's." During this period Hannah is nowhere to be found.

Separated once more from her prisoner-husband, the Baroness rejoined him finally, and in the summer of 1779, en route from Pennsylvania to New York, they were entertained by a hospitable family in New Jersey. Their hosts were Royalists, they said, and behaved festively as such. Back at the same mansion for a second visit, Frederica suffered a shock of the sort she never grew accustomed to. The place was full of rollicking Patriot officers, who stayed up all night singing "God damn the King!" Worse, they attended an unnamed young lady of the house who, numerous as

---

*General Carleton's other secretary was his nephew Christopher Carleton. Disguised as an Indian—he "dressed like a savage, painted his face, wore a ring in his nose"—he was a celebrated spy who powerfully vexed the Americans, and more particularly Lafayette, who offered a large personal reward to anyone who would bring him in alive; it was never collected. Married to the "very pretty" Lady Anne, Christopher consummated his cover by taking an Indian woman to wife as well.

they were, "allowed them all sorts of liberties." It is clear that the Baroness was at Phil's Hall. It does not seem to have crossed her mind that this was the ancestral home of the missing Hannah Foy, or that the girl who freely distributed her favors—perhaps the one who had startled the sophisticated Marquis de Chastellux— was Hannah's cousin.

NEITHER SO FAMOUS, fashionable, or fortunate as the Van Hornes, "the Browne girls" were daughters of the Reverend Arthur Browne, staunch church supporter of the Royalist state at Portsmouth, New Hampshire. And only the unlucky Betsy, "youngest and prettiest" of them, is still recalled—as wife to the foremost hero of the French and Indian Wars, Robert Rogers of Rogers' Rangers. Even in England his feats in the wilderness were legendary.

The Major was not keyed for wedlock, but the young woman —"hir who so sudenlly made me a prisonar to Love"—accepted him over alleged parental objections. "After tarrying with her six days," as she would herself later tell the story,

he left her, went off to South-Carolina, and there remained seventeen months without making any provision for a house or housekeeping—He then returned tarried four or five months—& went to De-troit where he remained about a twelve-month leaving her unprovided (save by her father) as before—He came back—staid a few days—and then went to England, tarried eighteen months, (she unprovided still) and once more returned.

Whittier would one day compose a ballad in which he tactlessly informs "The Ranger's Wife" that "Some red squaw his moose-meat's broiling, / Or some French lass singing gay . . ." Whichever, the Reverend Browne perceived, in gaining a son he had failed to lose a daughter. He had, further, been receiving "odious reports," so he wrote Rogers, which he "attributed to Prodigality or ye Gratification of unlawful pleasure and Passion." To recover the sum he had expended on Mrs. Rogers and their servants, he sued for £2,500. He never collected, and to his surprise Betsy

played Penelope to the wandering hero and remained loyal. Rogers wrote her that "Every moment My thoughts are with you My
Souls desiar is to be personaly So"; he promised to be a "more
Study Husband . . . more loving there canot be." In an attempt
to collect funds to cover debts he had unavoidably accumulated
in service to the Crown and illicitly incurred in trade with the
Indians, he had already, without telling her, sailed for England.
In London, with the probable help of his secretary, a Princeton
and Harvard man,* he published his *Journals* (1765), which,
though judged "almost incredible," were well received. Even
more popular was his *Concise Account of North America* (also 1765),
which extolled the virtues of the American West, and contained
the proposal that he conduct an extended journey to discover
"whether there is, or is not" a Northwest Passage to the fabled
East. Shortly after he left town a play appeared called *Ponteach: or
the Savages of America* (1766), which was generally attributed to
him. It is still, though he never claimed he wrote it and would
seem to have had little talent for blank verse. It was very badly
received.†

---

*The secretary and Rogers were a likely pair. Nathaniel Potter, who would later
accuse his superior of attempted treason, had been an ordained minister at
Plymouth, "famous for Piety and Gravity," wrote John Adams, who was "discovered to have the most debauched and polluted of Minds, to have pursued a
series of wanton Intrigues, with one Woman and another, to have got his Maid
with Child and all that." (At which point Potter wrote his parish, "I have left
the Sacred work.")

†Reviewers had expected savages exclusively noble, and responded to the blood
and gore with "abhorrence and disgust." If Rogers had no direct hand in the
composition it is apparent that the unknown playwright took material from his
Concise Account. The liveliest part of the drama features a French priest struggling
for the heroine's virtue: "I must, I can, and will enjoy you now." Her Indian
suitor breaks it up:

Have you not told us, holy Men like you
Are by the Gods forbid all fleshly Converse?

The priest, quick on his feet, explains:

I have a dispensation from St. Peter
To quench the Fire of Love when it grows painful. . . .

But a son of the noble Pontiac kills off the love interest, sending her to death
a virgin. (The play was advertised as *A Tragedy.*)

As a step toward the Passage, Rogers was given command at Fort Michilimackinac—the westernmost British outpost, located on a strait connecting Lakes Huron and Michigan. He kissed the King's hand and set out for his new assignment, stopping off at Portsmouth. "No English woman," meaning American lady, "had gone so far west"—thirteen hundred miles into the wilderness. But Betsy Rogers, over definite parental objection, packed her finest gowns and proceeded with him. She was "desirous of doing her duty," she later remarked, and "in hopes of winning him by gentleness and condescension." She wrote her mother that she was "much taken with every place she passed through on her way . . . it is a fine pleasent Country." (Mrs. Browne wished she might "always think so" but feared she "will alter her note when Winter sets in.") On her arrival at the fort, according to the *New Hampshire Gazette,* the Otawars presented her with a beaver blanket: "Here is a Bed we give her, she may sit down upon it quietly . . . and see her Children all round her."

There were no children, nor much use for her clothes. Winter set in. She later claimed that to paint her sufferings at Michilimackinac "in their true colours" was beyond her:

'Tis enough to say that she underwent every hardship and endured every species of ill-treatment which infidelity uncleaness & drunken barbarity could inflict from one bound by the tenderest & most sacred ties . . . to mention all the particulars would neither consist with the modesty of the sex or the respect due. . . .

The fort was a crude pile with some thirty buildings in a stockade, and about a hundred soldiers, some with wives. It was essentially a fur-trading post, cut off from the world six months a year. Were it not for the discovery, in London in 1914, of a "journal" kept there in the tidy, even hand of Daniel Morison, surgeon's mate, the immodest particulars of her residence would be left to the imagination. "Excesses of debauchery & most licentious practices" is Morison's appraisal. "Such is the depraved disposition of this profligate garrison."

What the utterly intimidated surgeon's mate really wished was to record the evidence with which he would one day bring to justice an ensign named Robert Johnston. Johnston watered the rum, then sold it; put a powerful purgative in Morison's punch-bowl, then beat him dreadfully in his bed. A sergeant who discovered Johnston in the sergeant's house with the sergeant's wife was punished for his indiscretion by having his head knocked "into blubber," then "kicked in the private parts" so that one of his testicles was "greatly Swelled, of a hue black as his Hat." Johnston used "uncommon libertys" with another woman, then offered her £100 to "destroy her peace with her husband." For not "suffering his wife to comply with obscene proposit to her," the company tailor was put in the guardhouse. Betimes Johnston was living with the sergeant's wife, and conducting her to dinner at the commander's table in front of everybody. He next charged her husband with disrespect and reduced him to private. Then after six weeks he forced the soldier, who had no more use for his wife, to take her back, and also to write a letter begging forgiveness for her "imprudent behaviour." Frustrated in the rape of a girl "betwixt nine & ten Years of age," he boasted "publickly that he had carnal dealings" with her mother. *Monstrum horrendum Ingens!* observes Morison, correctly recalling Virgil's Cyclops.

It was in this setting, with Johnston already on the scene, that Betsy had lived for two years just before Morison arrived. As for her husband's contribution to social life, her charges were almost surely warranted: others, not she, complained of his "Familiarity with the Non Commissioned Officers and Soldiers Wives." But he had enemies more powerful than these, and was eventually arrested on suspicion of entertaining "Designs of . . . Deserting to the French," and of "Stirring up the Indians against His Majesty." He was put in chains and thrown into solitary confinement; it was December of 1767, and his cell had an open, barred window. When Betsy once attempted to speak to him through it, so it was said, a guard "kicked her Arse away." Among Rogers's chief accusers was Ensign Johnston, who claimed that the commander "had formed a deep and horrid Plot to kill me." It was with Johnston in charge that Betsy and her husband were shipped east that spring for his trial in Montreal—the Major, with a very bad leg, tossed in irons on the ballast stones in the hold. Betsy, who was now pregnant, went on to Boston to gather evidence in his defense. In Montreal the sexual allegations were passed over and Rogers was found not guilty of the heavier ones. He was awaiting release when his wife gave birth to Arthur, named for and baptized by his grandfather at Portsmouth that winter.

Rogers's creditors were still after him; if he had stayed in this country they would have jailed him for his debts. Again he sailed to England to seek redress. He received some, but not enough, and stayed on trying for more. Rumors of his mode of existence evidently reached his wife, since he wrote to "Show you how Villenious those persons are that has Set you on your High Hors about my Extravagant Living. . . ." He spent twenty-two months for debt in the Fleet Prison, but in the spring of 1775 was granted retirement pay and funds to take him to America. He had been gone six years, and when he met up with Betsy it was for but one mysterious moment: just as "he was in a situation which . . . forced her *then* to shun & fly from him so Decency *now* forbids her to say more upon so delicate a subject." Rogers then offered his services to the Patriots, but Washington had good reason to think he was a British spy and arrested him. He escaped, and raised a battalion of Rangers for the English. By now his talents had fallen "prey to Intemperance"; he was captured, and when New York was evacuated he returned to London for the last time. After a long confinement in the King's Bench, another debtor's prison, he died "in the most miserable state of wretchedness."

After shunning & fleeing, Betsy never saw him again. He could not return to Portsmouth, which was in Patriot hands, and in 1778 for the reasons she gave, plus "others which might be mentioned some of which your Honors own minds will readily suggest," she petitioned the New Hampshire Legislature for divorce. Finding that the Major had "in the most flagrant manner . . . violated the marriage contract—but especially by *Infidelity to her Bed*," that body granted it.

IF YOU WERE LUCKY ENOUGH to be a beautiful girl, well-to-do and better positioned than Betsy Browne, there never was a season like that of 1777–78, when the British took over Philadelphia and its women. Blond and perhaps frivolous, the toast of their officers was Peggy Shippen, best remembered of all Revolutionary Ladies. An expert in these matters pronounced her the prettiest girl he had seen in America. She appeared to care for little but society and fashion, yet was subject to occasional fits of hysteria—"paroxysms of physical indisposition," said a friend, "during which she would give utterance to anything . . . on her mind." If as claimed she remains somewhat enigmatic still, so does the most exciting of the young officers, perhaps the handsomest and most charming in the whole British army. All the girls were crazy about Major André and none could land him. Where the others wenched, drank, and gambled, he devoted himself to music, art, and literature. But he found time to "flirt with an intense blonde of seventeen, the moody Miss Shippen." Among many other things he designed the Turkish gown she would have worn to the "Mischianza"—a gigantic farewell party for General Howe—if her father had allowed her to appear in it. And he sketched her picture, with particular attention to the coiffure. Later on he would write her that the extravaganza for Howe had made him a "complete milliner."

The American officers who replaced the British on their departure were a considerable comedown to Peggy, except for their thoroughly masculine commander Benedict Arnold. By that time he had proved himself the best and bravest General in the war, and if his blindness to politics, and insensitivity to human relations generally, had already begun to get him into trouble she ignored or was unaware of it. He lived as lavishly as Howe had done, attended the same ladies the British had favored, and was suspected of being a Tory—perhaps under the influence of Miss Shippen. He was a gimpy widower exactly twice her age with three sons larger than she. And though he had once and perhaps twice failed to win a new lady with the line, he asked Peggy in

a letter to let her "heavenly bosom . . . expand" to accept him
and she did. His leg was so badly wounded that he could not stand
for the ceremony unaided, but some dream of glory was already
filling her head.

For over 150 years those who had any interest in it debated the
question of whether or not Mrs. Arnold knew about her husband's dealings with John André for the delivery of West Point
to the English army. Great attention has been paid the mad scene
she either pitifully suffered or brilliantly staged at the time of her
husband's exposure. Washington and Hamilton, among others,
witnessed it, took pity, and believed Arnold when he wrote that
in his treason she was "innocent as an angel." Aaron Burr had
reason to think she was acting. Either way, the plot backfired.
Arnold was despised for life by the British who bought him,
André adored for his grace and courage by the Americans who
hanged him as a spy. Given a choice between joining her husband
in New York or returning to Philadelphia, Peggy chose home.
She had retained, perhaps as a keepsake, the letter in which André
remarked to her that he had become a milliner, and it had fallen
into the hands of suspicious Patriots. She was forced to leave
town, and had little choice but to sail with her husband and child
for England. There she was welcomed with great cordiality. The
King pensioned her, not her husband, for life; the Queen asked
the court ladies to pay her "much attention." She was called "the
handsomest woman in England." George III frequently consulted
Arnold, but he was reviled in the Whig press and hissed at the
theater. When the Tory government fell, he realized how poor
were his chances. His wife was pitied for the man she had married, and he went along with the notion that she was a guileless
girl who had joined with a villain. On the other hand she never
told him about the lock of André's hair she cherished to the end.
They were once observed together, silently visiting the spy's new
resting place in Westminster Abbey. The depth of her involve-
ment in the treason was not known until 1941. Since that time it
has seemed more and more likely that she was the instigator
of it.

Despite the energy that has gone into searching out every detail in the highly publicized lives of Peggy, Arnold, and André, a few odd lines of the story still hang loose. One of them concerns the possibility of the heroine's sexual rather than political fall from grace. When Peggy was a girl her father worried ceaselessly over the fact that with the British in Philadelphia a young lady had, as Peggy wrote a friend, "an opportunity of raking as much as you chose. . . . I've been but three evenings alone." Still there is no sign that she raked her way into anything beneath the surface pleasures of the season. If, as is not really known, "she made advances to Major André," it is agreed that they were repulsed. There is no evidence that she wore her bit of his hair "in a small gold locket that hung between her fair breasts." The only scent of trouble that ever arose came later from Arnold's spinster sister, when she wrote her absent brother about his wife's behavior in Philadelphia, warning him of "the presence of a certain chancellor who . . . is a dangerous companion for a particular lady in the absence of her husband. . . . I could tell you of frequent private assignations . . . if I had a mind to make mischief." But nothing more is known of the matter, if ever there was anything to know.

The biggest question about Mrs. Arnold relates to the crucial scene of her life: she either went mad on learning that the plot to deliver West Point had been discovered or she summoned her physical charms to disclose her innocence in it. "I heard a shriek," wrote Richard Varick,

ran upstairs and there met the miserable lady, raving distracted. . . . Her morning gown, with few other clothes, remained on her, too few to be seen by a gentleman in the family, much less by many strangers. . . . She seized me by the hand. . . . "Colonel Varick, have you ordered my child to be killed?"

She fell at his feet with "prayers and entreaties"; three men carried her to her bed "raving mad." Washington was brought to see for himself; Peggy claimed he was not the General but an aide to Varick in murdering her baby. Convinced by the spectacle and Arnold's protestation that she was sinless, Washington let her be. Hamilton visited her hours later. "She received us in bed," he wrote his fiancée, "with every circumstance that would interest our sympathy." But he too was a believer. "It was the most affecting scene I ever was to witness to."

Peggy had gone into hysterics when it momentarily appeared that Arnold would not be assigned to the installation he had agreed to hand over. The next attack, when Varick and Washington saw her, may have been genuine—though if so, as Varick came to doubt, she uttered anything but what was "on her mind." By the time Hamilton got there she had probably cast herself in a seductive role and played it heavily. So—according to Theodora Prevost, the widow of a British officer—she said herself, remarking that she was "heartily sick" of her "theatrics." (Further that she had brought Arnold to the plan only "through great persuasion and unceasing perseverance.") Mrs. Prevost repeated this to Aaron Burr, whom she later married, and he—with little reputation for this sort of gallantry—kept the secret until both Arnolds were dead. The Shippen family then countered with the claim that he had made it all up, because although they were together and had the opportunity, Peggy refused him.

Chief among the innuendoes that have arisen out of the Shippen-Arnold-André triangle is a modern rumor that after the departure from America of Howe, André "advanced himself in Clinton's esteem as a homosexual." It is true that the new commander found close friends in a succession of junior officers. Also true that the Major wrote for the General's pleasure a fairly long erotic poem. But the verses are addressed to "Sally":

Thy limbs from his Limbs a new Warmth shall acquire;
His passions from thine shall redouble their Fire
'Til wreck'd and o'erwhelmed in the Storm of delight
Thine ears lose their hearing, thine eyes lose their Sight. . . .

Clinton had already fathered six children, one by a mistress before he married, five in five years by a wife who then died. He would father "many" more, by his own admission, on Mrs. Baddeley. After the war he was a family man in London with two families, between which he divided his time.*

———————

*Mrs. Loring, alleged mistress of General Howe, Clinton's predecessor in com-

Although his life has been searched thoroughly, André is not known ever to have been intimate with anyone. Possessed, according to a friend, of "nearly womanlike modesty and gentleness," he was in the judgment of another source "a dilettante, not a lover." But dilettantes may fall in love, and millinery is as odd an occupation for a soldier of any age as dress designing. The sketch André made of Miss Shippen lavishes care on her monstrous hair-do, fails to give any hint of the beauty her face was said to possess, which a later portrait confirms, and anticipates the modern notion that male designers for women at bottom dislike them. Most striking of all was the Major's attempt, made during his internment at Lancaster, Pennsylvania, to take with him first to Carlisle and finally to England a boy in whose "childish drawings" he professed to find genius. If only the lad's father would consent, he would educate the youth at his own expense and give him "all my attention." It seems entirely possible that André, whose unrevealed secret is unrevealable, was at once a very brave man and no man at all.

As for Peggy Shippen Arnold, the dénouement remains. After her initial and unsustainable triumph abroad, the woman who had

---

mand, caused endless comment; the story of Clinton's mistress, which he wrote for the edification of his legitimate children, is very little known. Mrs. Baddeley was the daughter of an Irish country gentleman; curiously, she married a sergeant major and came with him to this country. Because his wife, according to rumor, had refused his commanding officer, Baddeley was demoted to private. Clinton heard of this in Boston, noted Mrs. Baddeley's "very interesting appearance and history and situation," and hired her as housekeeper of John Hancock's mansion, in which he was installed. He was "tempted," but she so "discreet that I never dare hint it." And she was pregnant. A year later she arrived in New York with husband and child, "a poor wretched being; and I took her in." It was now clear to Clinton that Baddeley wished his wife to enjoy "a certain degree of intimacy" with his General; for his part, Clinton could not "gain an inch." Things gradually improved, but "though she admitted me to certain liberties I could never prevail on her to grant the last." Finally "she detected her h[usband] in an intrigue with a common strumpet. She came to me directly, told him she would, and surrendered." Over the strenuous objection of Howe, who was said to be amply rewarding the husband of his own mistress, Clinton promoted Baddeley, who eventually became a captain and called down blessings on the union that made it possible. He soon died, and Clinton was with his widow till he died too.

gone rapidly from girlish innocence to worldly knowledge moved into a state surpassing both. In spite of the continuing misadventures of her financially desperate husband, she held the family together. She guided Arnold's three sons as she cared for three children of her own. To promote their futures she kept "appearances" high with a fine house, a carriage and footmen, and expensive wines she could not afford. She personally procured pensions for four of them, an education for another, an army commission for his brother. Arnold turned out to be, as people had believed, her cross, but she never admitted it. While she was for a long time ill after the birth of a child, he was running a store in St. John, New Brunswick. He neglected to write and, as Peggy knew, fathered a child on some nameless woman. When he died he bequeathed her £6,000 in debts, exactly the sum for which he had sold his services to the British. Frequently writing that her reason was "despaired of," his widow for a while feared that her wretchedness was affecting the lives of her children and considered suicide as a means of freeing them. Instead she moved into a small house, went without the carriage, and through a series of complicated financial maneuvers at home and abroad paid off every debt. She pronounced herself if not happy, contented. Even while dying of cancer of the womb she never stopped writing her father, whom she credited for her business acumen. She never referred to "the General" as anything but "the best of possible husbands," never complained, never repented the acts that sent her into permanent exile (if she had returned to America she would have lost her pension), never regretted, and expired in agony, believing that she had lived out her destiny exactly as the Lord had planned it. At forty-four her ravaged body was laid to rest at Battersea. She had become the Valiant Woman of Proverbs, who lookest well to the ways of her household, bringeth food from afar, considereth a field and buyeth it. Her children rise up and call her blessed, her works praise her in the gates.

PROSPECTS FOR THE DIVORCED Betsy Browne at thirty-eight were not good. Her father had died an invalid dependent on charity; all she had was a house in Concord, New Hampshire, which Rogers in one prudent move had long ago deeded the Reverend Browne for her benefit. But in the year of her legal separation from him there arrived an Irish sea captain by the name of Roche (frequently Roach), who was said to have sailed from Quebec for London by "dead reckoning" and landed "most *unaccountably*" in Portsmouth with a great load of furs, which he sold. He was, nonetheless, given a proud new command, and suddenly the lady who had shed the Ranger married the man who captained the *Ranger*—until, that is, he was relieved by a Scotsman who signed himself JN° P. Jones. Except for his arrival in this country, Roche is remembered for little but the quantities of rum he took aboard at the tavern and the vehemence of oaths he discharged. His barratry—selling the cargo that belonged to people in London—caught up with him just as he was about to take the *Ranger* on her maiden cruise. In quick successive actions, Congress removed him, replaced him with John Paul Jones, and adopted the Stars and Stripes as the national flag. Betsy lived out her days in Concord with Roche and raised her son to be a lawyer. According to her death certificate she expired there a couple of years after her husband—at the age of seventy-two. No gravestone can be found for either of them. It is supposed they died poor.

Betsy's true nature has remained as little known as her last thirty-five years. Even her feelings about Rogers are not absolutely clear. Far from having married him against her parents' wishes, she did it, she claims in her petition for divorce, "solely in obedience" to them and her friends. On the other hand if she had not carefully saved his letters they would not now exist. Her extended treatment in Kenneth Roberts's *Northwest Passage* (1937) is unsympathetic, based on a "tradition" the novelist says he picked up that she was a bit of a shrew. If there ever was such a tradition it is hard to locate now; Roberts, further, was unaware not only of gossip that is warmer but also of circumstances that alter everything. Without these contributions to the story she might forever be remembered as the slender, prim, and not especially pretty young woman of Joseph Blackburn's portrait, who married an undomesticable warrior only to realize her mistake and marry a faint imitation of him. With them, the picture is softened.

Robert Rogers of the Rangers (1959), the only full-scale biography of him, offers the facts which blur the image of his wife's chilly chastity without ever recognizing how. John R. Cuneo, a lawyer, has examined the record carefully. Rogers was thrown into solitary confinement at Michilimackinac in December of 1767; he remained there until May 21, 1768, when, still in solitary and irons, he was stowed in the hold of a ship which was headed for his trial—Captain Turnbull in command and Betsy aboard. He had been held in "Confinement . . . so severe," as she protested in a letter to Gage, "that no Person was permitted even to speak to him." On February 12, 1769, her son Arthur was baptized by her father at Portsmouth. Assuming that the child on this occasion was no more than two weeks old, and that he had gestated for nine months, what has escaped notice is that he would have been conceived about May 1, 1768, by which date Rogers had served between four and five of his six months in total isolation. He was not present at Arthur's christening, and it would not have been easy for him to have been present at his conception.

While he lay on the ballast stones of the ship *Gladwin,* "the bone of my right leg was split," as Rogers would later testify, "and the marrow forced its way out of the skin." No less painful, he suffered "the utmost Tortures" of the mind. Both Captain Turnbull and Betsy must have understood. Three months before the Major was arrested, Turnbull had written Gage that the brutal Ensign Johnston, who claimed that Rogers was out to kill him, was "returned to Michilimackinac"—despite the fact that "Major Roger's I hear was somewhat jealous of him with his wife. . . ." If this was so while Rogers was at liberty to keep them apart, the state of his mind during the months when he was immobilized can be imagined. By the time he was permitted Mrs. Rogers's company—June 29 at Fort Niagara—she was two months pregnant. And if Rogers's jealousy was mistaken, so was the consensus of opinion at Michilimackinac. High on the list of charges leveled at Johnston by surgeon's mate Morison was that the Ensign "used uncommon freedom" with Betsy—"common fame says to the extent of carnal conversation with her."

Rogers's letters to his wife after the birth of the child extend to the boy little more than perfunctory affection; once he calls him "Your Son"; on another occasion he submits a whole list of people to be greeted, never so much as mentioning Arthur. On the other hand he did sometimes refer to "our Son" or "Arty" as if he thought himself the father. What this would mean for Betsy is that during her husband's crude, cruel imprisonment she experienced the embarrassment of paying conjugal visits to him, as could not have been kept secret at the little post—or of sneaking past or bribing the guard to get to him. Such details may have been among the "particulars" mentioned in her petition for divorce that "modesty" would not allow her to describe. In any event, if Rogers sired the child, Arthur was started less in love than squalor. If he did not, then for over two hundred years, dead and alive, Betsy has kept a secret—especially from the boy whom the Major appears to have seen only once and the Ensign never. On the back of a sheet that evidently wrapped the packet of Rogers's correspondence, the son who had not received any of them wrote in a firm hand, "Fathers Letters."

THERE IS NOTHING to show that Hannah Van Horne was ever faced with this problem. Nor do sober historians, like General von Riedesel's wife, attribute Burgoyne's defeat to his mistress—a woman whose identity has never been discovered. Mrs. Foy qualifies in every way but one: if it had been Hannah, Frederica would have named her as she had done many times before. It is probable, as suggested, that the short-suffering Captain Foy would have abandoned his wife if he had heard of her activities. What is more probable is that in her travels abroad she was in the process of shedding him. In any event, after going ashore at Quebec in the summer of 1777 on the tender sent by Lady Maria Carleton, Hannah drops out of sight. It seems certain that she did not go home to New

Jersey. Although he had been very friendly with her family, Governor Livingston refused Loyalists who had fled to New York permission to return; in this connection he specifically included "the children of Mrs. Van Horne."

On May 2, 1783, Colonel Thomas Carleton, the brother of Sir Guy and the associate in Canada of Edward Foy, walked through the pillared portico of St. George's, Hanover Square, Mayfair, past the iron dogs and into the church. It is chiefly known for weddings. Here Emma Lyon would become Lady Hamilton; here would be married Shelley, George Eliot, Disraeli, Theodore Roosevelt. With Carleton, to witness his marriage, was his sister-in-law Lady Maria. The bride was Hannah Foy, whose Captain, estranged or no, had died in Canada of cause unknown four years back. She and her son had been chief beneficiaries of the will of Nathaniel Foy of Bristol. For a period unknown, they had been living on the outskirts of London; the *Gentleman's Magazine* identified her as "Mrs. Foy of Blackheath." Well over half her life lay ahead.

Colonel Carleton was another widely traveled soldier who had served at Minden—also with the Russians, fighting the Turks on the lower Danube and wintering in St. Petersburg. At "our court of St. James's," announced George III about a year after the wedding, "our Trusty and well beloved Thomas Carleton, Esqu'r" was appointed Governor "in and over our Province of New Brunswick in America," newly created. Thomas kissed His Majesty's hand; now her own Governor's Lady, Hannah sailed yet again for the New World. On board was Jonathan Odell, terrible poet, secretary of the new province, and former secret agent for the British at Philadelphia, where he helped handle André's correspondence with the Arnolds. Aide to the Governor, though still a boy, was the resurfaced Nathaniel Foy. In November they all arrived at St. John, and were warmly welcomed to the "Loyalist Province" by the exiled Americans who had settled it. It was known as the emptiest, most forbidding part of Nova Scotia, with everything short or lacking save for a rudimentary social hierarchy. Hannah moved into the best house available and nearly froze to death.

It still bemuses New Brunswick historians how little they know about the ruler of their first twenty years. He was, in the early part of his reign, active. At fifty, his brother Sir Guy seriously ill at Quebec, he made his way there and back on snowshoes, passing eight nights in the forest. He was affluent, and continued to advance in the army, eventually becoming full General. Infuriating the people of St. John, he moved the capital to Fredericton. There Government House, a large and handsome mansion in which his Council sat, was built for him and his family. He is most remembered for personal rectitude. It was remarked, indeed—astonishing claim—that he was so "dignified and correct" that he "rendered morality fashionable."

Thus Hannah became a lady of an entirely new style, so proper as to escape notice almost entirely. She did, in New Brunswick, have three children: Emma, Anne, and William. She once took them to see a man dance on wire; once she visited Quebec with Nathaniel. Aside from these events only two things are recalled of her full two decades in the province. She was thirty-six when a belle of the capital wrote that "Everybody's dancing this winter"; to emphasize the point she added "even Mrs. Carleton." Another woman posed a riddle: "Do you know why Mrs. Carleton doesn't like to ride in a sleigh with two horses?" And solved it: "She thinks two horses looks sociable and she hates everything that looks sociable."

In 1803 Hannah and her family paid a visit to England, intending to return to Fredericton. They took a house in a "pleasant spot on the seashore" at Ramsgate, a socially desirable resort on the Isle of Thanet. For his daughters, Carleton explained, there was a ball every Tuesday, and three a week at Margate. They never went back to New Brunswick.

Old friends of Hannah's named Dunmore had retired to the same watering place. The ex-Governor of Virginia—not his aide, as Foy had feared—was blamed not only for the maladministration at Williamsburg but also for having done more "to work an eternal separation between Great Britain and the Colonies than any other expedient which could possibly have been thought of." Yet a few had a different opinion. The usually temperate Thomas

Jefferson, looking back on that period, came to believe that the disaster was not Hannah's host but her husband:

Capt. Foy was private secretary to Ld. Dunmore, lived with him at the palace, was believed to be the chief instigator of all his violences, and being very ill tempered, haughty & presumptuous, was very obnoxious.

William Smith, chief justice of the province of New York, had arrived at that conclusion before his Lordship had ever left for Williamsburg. "So helpless a Mortal," he wrote of his superior in his journal, "utterly ignorant of the Nature of Business of all Kinds . . . such a blockhead." Long before Dunmore's débâcle in the south, Smith in the north was convinced that the real power was "Foy . . . his Guardian." From his "silent Modest & seemingly unconcerned Behaviour" this was not easy to detect, he admitted. But "his art in concealing it . . . is a Proof of his Capacity."

In any event, the Carletons like the Dunmores died in Ramsgate. Still Governor of New Brunswick, Hannah's second husband expired fourteen years after he left it. What if anything he knew of his wife's past is undiscoverable. The Baroness von Riedesel's revelation of a part of it had been published long before he died, and the fact that it appeared in German would have been no matter to him; he had acquired German, French, Spanish, Italian, and presumably a little Russian. Nor can it be known if Hannah's friends, acquaintances, or children—or Hannah herself—learned of her featured role in that published journal, which was widely issued in English eight years before she died.

Few American girls if any had survived more scandal, and two problematical marriages, to achieve greater respectability. By the end, Phil's Hall, New York, Williamsburg, Bristol, Portsmouth, the crossing of the *Blonde*—America itself—must have seemed to belong to someone else's life. The present belonged to her children. Nathaniel Foy had married a woman of whom Carleton wrote, "by all accounts there is not much beauty or fortune." The others lived as if to expunge their mother's adventures. Her son William was at Trafalgar with Nelson, and lived to be the oldest survivor of that engagement; though married he died without issue. Despite the balls at Margate, neither of her daughters—who were hitting fifty when she died—either wed or bred. The world of the Van Horne girls was nearly sixty years gone when in 1835 Mrs. Carleton died at eighty-three. By that time she had long been both harbinger and embodiment of a revolution that transformed eighteenth-century Fashion into a spirit the nineteenth would name for Victoria. She was two years in her grave before the Princess, who grew up in Ramsgate as Hannah declined there, succeeded to the throne.

Chapter Two

∽

MRS. LORING, AND HOWE

A CHILD'S INTEREST in genealogy is limited. If an interest develops later on, chances are both parents are gone and there is no book to deal with questions they could have answered in a minute.

So with me. My paternal ancestors seem to have been yeomen. I clearly remember my great-grandfather, John Philip Young, a New York State farmer as distinguished looking as any President unless Harding, who was President. He sat me on his knee and gave me a quarter. His great-grandfather, according to tradition, as a Young Man Went West, reached Ohio, got the picture, and returned to upstate New York, where he ran an inn all through the Revolution. Now that was my kind of ancestor.

Mother's people were gentry, no question. Her father was a Pratt and her mother a Loring. Around our house there was virtually no talk of family, but I got an impression anyway that the Pratts were brains, as a shelf of deep books by her uncle James suggested, and the Lorings class: her uncle Harry bred spaniels, collected antiques, and never worked a day in his life. My idea of aristocracy.

And that was it until not so long ago when my wife was going through my mother's desk. It had never been really cleared, and in it we found among other relics some old D.A.R. papers. Zealous to provide our small daughter with a notion of her paternal forebears (there *is* a book on her maternal ones) we seized on these, whereby Mother's descent is traced back through the Lorings to John, born in England in 1800, who came here and married Lydia Parker, whereupon the line goes back through her family to Deacon Thomas Parker, the founder of it in this country, who arrived in 1635. It was gratifying to learn, in a quick trip to the library, that our child is related to Theodore Parker of Concord—Emerson called him one of the three great minds of the age—who traces directly back to that same Deacon Thomas. Also to the Parkers of Lexington, one of whom is supposed to have said: "Stand your ground; don't fire unless fired upon; but if they mean to have a war, let it begin here."

But why the switch to Parkers? Surely the Lorings had arrived before the Revolution. Did I recall a boyish thrill of faint criminality in that ever so respectable line? I thought I did, and the same trip to the library confirmed it. Deacon Thomas Loring settled in Hingham, Massachusetts, in 1634, and two of his descendants, the Joshua Lorings Senior and Junior, were prominently involved in the Revolution—as Loyalists, who eventually had to flee the country. The D.A.R. doesn't take you from the wrong side.

And that would probably have been the end of that if a short time after I had not found myself having a drink in Corvallis, Oregon, with an air force Colonel by the name of Pratt. Having established the likelihood that we were in some remote fashion related, I mentioned to him the Tory Lorings. Oh yes, he said, I've heard of them. Freneau has a poem called "The Battle of the Kegs," where General Gage is "In bed with Mrs. Loring." The next library visit lasted a little longer. The poem is Hopkinson's, not Freneau's, and the General is not Thomas Gage but William Howe. The poem, however, turns out to be familiar to every student of our literature but me—especially the stanza in question:

Sir William, he, snug as a flea,
   Lay all the time a-snoring;
Nor dreamed of harm, as he lay warm
   In bed with Mrs. L———g.

A typical printing of this verse will asterisk the lady as the wife of Joshua Loring, Jr., Commissary of Prisoners under Howe, commander-in-chief of British forces in America. And I do believe, though a link is missing in the chain, that the lady is my daughter's great-great-great-great-great-great-grand *some*thing or other.

But to register the national force of Hopkinson's quatrain, and its implications for our history, you have to remember how strange was our War for Independence—from one angle a protracted struggle, clearly won by the British, to see which side could lose. Neither side had any great enthusiasm for its cause, or really wanted to fight. Few colonials were willing to do much for Independence; many prominent Englishmen were openly sympathetic with it; New York furnished more soldiers to George III than to George Washington. But the strangest figure was Howe. Hamilton wrote that no rule could be found to "unravel his designs"; John Adams remarked that it is "impossible to discover the design of an enemy who has no design at all." It is hard to calculate exactly how many occasions there were—very many have been cited—when he could have wiped out the Patriots by simply giving an aggressive order. But he never did. If he had just taken up all his prisoners on Brooklyn Heights, for instance, Washington's army would have been his, and Congress could not have raised another. It was on this occasion that Israel Putnam decided that General Howe was either a "friend of America or no General." General Lee summed him up a little differently: "He shut his eyes, fought his battles, drank his bottle, had his little whore." One man, Washington, held our forces together and one man failed to defeat them.

If Howe remains a mystery it is because history has insufficiently credited the revelation of that "shrewd social observer" John Bernard. This British actor and traveler, in his *Retrospections of America, 1797–1811,* explained the whole thing. In New York, he tells us, he met "survivors of the Revolution" and through them learned

proof of how ignorant is the world of the little causes of many great events. American independence, for instance, everyone supposes was owing to George Washington, with some support. . . . Nothing could be more erroneous, according to these worthies, by whom it was attributed to a female patriot, the beautiful and fascinating Mrs. Loring. Seeing the affairs of the Provincialists veering . . . she conceived the noble enterprise of their rescue, by exerting all her arts and charms to entrap the affections and influence the counsels of Sir William Howe.

Whereupon Bernard cites a key instance of this entrapment, an occasion when if Howe had pursued Washington's army by land he could have wiped it out "like so many mosquitoes" (an opinion in which his successor, General Clinton, absolutely concurred). But he moved his troops by ship instead and blew it.

What could have led the general to the above perverse and fatal preference has been a matter of speculation to statesmen and soldiers. It need be no longer, when they learn that Mrs. Loring, being at this time in as critical a condition as the country, required the benefit of sea-air, and her wish was law!

There is no real evidence that Mrs. Loring had issue during the war, or that in her intercourse with Howe she had any other motive than pleasure. But the affair was notorious. Howe's chief biographer points out that one British officer didn't even need to name her, in telling his brother that Sir William is "on Long Island in the old way," while another Englishman wrote that there would be fighting whenever Howe "shall think proper to leave Mrs. Lorain." Historians tell how "drawing rooms began to titter and taverns to guffaw" over the "blue-eyed flashing blonde," whose "contribution to the American cause . . . defies measure." Even Mercy Warren, too much the lady to supply the name, remarks of Howe in her 1805 history of the Revolution: "few scrupled to assert, that the man . . . was lost for a time, in the arms of a handsome adultress." He was "too much engrossed by his bottle and his mistress."

A full generation before that, Judge Thomas Jones, a prominent New York Loyalist, wrote his compendious *History of New York during the Revolutionary War*—a work which "from a feeling of delicacy" for living children of participants was not published for nearly a century. Whether to quote, paraphrase, or plagiarize, Jones is the contemporary that later historians flock to. He was an embittered Tory who found a scapegoat for his lost cause in Howe, the explanation for Howe's failures in Mrs. Loring, and the bare bones of the story in what he thought he knew about it.

The Lorings—Jones's editor, Edward F. de Lancey, explains— were Bostonians Howe had met during the British occupation of that city. Joshua Junior was a Boston merchant who had a comfortable post from General Gage. When the British evacuated the town he and his wife went with their army to Halifax, where, "for his marital complaisance," he was appointed Commissary of Prisoners. At this post, according to Jones, he appropriated to his own use "nearly two-thirds of the rations allowed to the prisoners." To Howe's use of his wife he "made no objections": he "fingered the cash, the General enjoyed Madame." Mrs. Loring (de Lancey explains) was born Elizabeth Lloyd, whom Joshua had married at Dorchester, Massachusetts, in 1769—"a very handsome woman, and noted for her love of play." Indeed it was said that in New York "the favorite sultana lost 300 guineas at a single sitting." The "famous and celebrated Mrs. Loring," Jones intones with his dander up: "as Cleopatra of old lost Mark Antony the world, so did this illustrious courtezan lose Sir William Howe the honour, the laurels, and the glory, of putting an end to one of the most obstinate rebellions that ever existed."

He cites two striking instances, one when British "numbers were sufficient to have driven Washington out of Jersey with the greatest ease. But orders were wanting. . . . The Commander-in-Chief . . . was diverting himself in New-York, in feasting, gunning, banqueting, and in the arms of Mrs. Loring." The other in the fall of '75 in Boston, when "nothing seemed to engross his attention but in the faro table, the play house, the dancing assembly, and Mrs. Loring." On Howe's transfer of the revenues of New York City to its Mayor, the judge comes up with a nice comparison: he "might with as much propriety . . . have presented Mrs. Loring with Rhode Island."

Word really got around. In *The Baroness and the General* (1962) Louise Tharp reports a conversation General von Riedesel, who commanded the German mercenaries here, had with George III himself, in which he was surprised to learn how much the King knew about his commanders, and "the scandalous stories . . . going the rounds in the army, especially in the time of Sir William Howe." The reputation of "the beautiful golden-haired Mrs. Loring," Tharp concludes, "was international." Indeed it was, far more than she realized; in March of 1778 all members of both Houses of Parliament were delivered a handbill (originally an anonymous letter from "New-York, Jan 25. 1778") concerning Howe's failures to squash the rebellion—once "a contemptible pigmy . . . now . . . become a giant." All the time that Washington's army was in its "wretched condition" at Trenton, says the letter, "General Howe was at *New-York* in the lap of Ease; or, rather, amusing himself in the lap of a Mrs. L———g, who is the very Cleopatra to this Anthony of ours." She is, it goes on, "beyond compare the Greatest Woman in the world; to whom all men must pay their court, if they hope for Preferment."*

It was only a few months after receiving the handbill that

---

* Risky, perhaps, to put a name to a letter written two centuries back, but surely (Egypto-Roman associations aside) our correspondent is the same Judge Jones whose special blend of outrage and irony identifies him as unmistakably as a signature. "Evidence" that he is not descending to "little scandal," as he calls it, that we will "at some time hear," would be in the book that he planned to write. What he couldn't know is where he would be writing it. Later in the year of his letter Jones was taken off to Connecticut a prisoner, although at the time he was already a prisoner on parole, the reason being that the rebels held no one important enough to exchange for their captured General Silliman, his old friend at Yale. The judge was still a prisoner when Joshua Loring in New York turned a man out of his rented "house" and installed a new tenant named Roubalet—"Loring's pimp," Jones calls him. If so, he had other talents; Roubalet's became perhaps the best of New York taverns. In 1782, while Jones was in England, his considerable estate was confiscated and it was declared that if he should set foot in New York he would "suffer death . . . without benefit of clergy." Thus exiled and next to himself with indignation he wrote his book in England and died there.

Parliament would investigate Howe's militance, or the lack of it; there is no mention of the world's greatest woman in the proceedings. But her name is to be found in practically all other investigations of the Revolution, whatever their persuasion. Only the words change: "the profligate courtesan," "the femme fatale of the War of Independence." Or do not: "the blue-eyed handsome blonde, but very gay and reckless . . . 300 guineas in a single evening," and so on. A modern historian informs us that when Ben Franklin in Paris was told, "Well, Doctor, Howe has taken Philadelphia," and famously replied, "I beg your pardon, Sir, Philadelphia has taken Howe," he was thinking specifically of Mrs. Loring. Long ago a more sober authority conceded that there is "no question" but that the General "wasted much of his time, his strength, his opportunities and his fortune" on her, his "baneful influence." This is the summary of one inspired historian:

Howe fell in love with her blonde loveliness, and she fell in love with glory. . . . They used to drink all day and all evening, and what they did the rest of the night was never held secret by anybody. . . . The success of American arms undoubtedly owed a heavy debt to the success of hers.

Given such notoriety, it is no surprise that poets other than Hopkinson should have made merry with her and Howe, though most of their efforts are easily forgotten. Hopkinson himself did not write a play that he once advertised as "The amorous Hero and contented Cuckold, by Gen. Howe and Mr. Loring." But he probably did write:

Howe with his legions came,
In hopes of wealth and fame.
   What has he done?
All day, at Faro play'd
All night, with whores he laid,
And with his bottle made,
   Excellent fun.

The Loyalists were not silent on the subject. Joseph Stansbury, a British agent in Philadelphia, portrayed Howe as a "Carpet

Knight" who rejects even Venus for the mortal Mrs. Loring. But he is easily outdone by nameless Patriots, one of whom composed a scene in which the General, with some help, addresses his troops:

Without wit, without wisdom, half stupid and drunk,
And rolling along arm in arm with his punk,
The gallant Sir William, who fights all by proxy,
Thus spoke to his soldiers, held up by his doxy . . .

The speech is a disappointment. Besides, Hopkinson's "Kegs" puts such verses in the background. First printed in the *Pennsylvania Packet* on March 4, 1778, "It flew," all twenty-two stanzas of it, according to Tyler's *Literary History of the American Revolution,* "from colony to colony . . . like some merry messenger of glad tidings . . . in many a camp, and along a thousand highroads, and by ten thousand patriot firesides . . . in very scorn of the enemy." It was worth perhaps as much, he estimates, "as the winning of a considerable battle."* The ballad was based on an actual incident of the British occupation of Philadelphia, when David Bushnell filled a number of wooden kegs with gunpowder, and sent them drifting down the Delaware above the English shipping— the first attempt, it is said, to use mines in warfare. No great damage resulted, although a couple of the things exploded and one blew up a small boat; but they "occasioned among British seamen the greatest alarm and consternation": they panicked and made fools of themselves, firing "small arms and cannon at everything they could see floating in the river." The ballad was not read or recited, however, but sung—to the tune of "Yankee Doodle," a song of complex origins which rebel troops had appropriated after Bunker Hill from the British, who had been

---

*Its author, a Renaissance man of the Rebellion, deserves remembering for more than this. Francis Hopkinson was a musician, composer, artist, and the probable designer of the American flag; a lawyer, politician, and judge; an inventor, writer of prose and verse, recipient of the first diploma from what became the University of Pennsylvania, member of the First Continental Congress, signer of the Declaration of Independence, and father of the man who wrote "Hail Columbia."

singing it in derision of them. It fits the tune well, as in the stanza
following the famous one where Howe

Now in a fright, he starts upright
    Awak'd by such a clatter;
He rubs both eyes, and boldly cries,
    For God's sake, what's the matter?

The real question, however, is what was the matter with him?
Even Parliament couldn't decide. A man of great personal bravery, he was either too cautious, or indolent, or sympathetic with
his foe—no theory held up as unquestionably superior to the Mrs.
Loring explanation. But it does seem safe to say that for at least
two years the British command did more to lose the war than the
Americans to win it. England was the most powerful nation on
earth, with a large professional army, a tremendous navy, money
to hire foreign troops, and cooperation from passionate Loyalists
already on the scene. But Howe, Joseph Galloway observed,
"pursued the very measures which Washington himself would
have advised," and by the time he was relieved the French were
on their way and things were turning around.

William Howe came naturally by some of his bad habits. Born
in 1729, he was a grandson of George I, "that coarse, vulgar,
vicious little profligate," in the words of Winthrop Sargent, and
one of George's German mistresses, the Baroness Kielsmansegge
—an "ogress," according to Walpole: "two acres of cheeks spread
with crimson, an ocean of neck, that overflowed . . . the lower
parts of her body, and no part restrained by stays. . . ." Howe did
make a respectable marriage in 1764 to a member of the distinguished Wentworth family. But it was alleged that he was also one
of the numerous lovers of "a singularly beautiful Italian opera
dancer . . . and of other demi-mondaines," as well as the keeper
of a London mistress.

His military record was sound. He had honorable service behind him in the French and Indian War, and under Wolfe in
Canada. An anti-Tory, however, he had told his constituents he
would never accept a command against the colonies, and when he
eventually took it one Whig told another, "he is one of us and

will do the Americans no harm." He did a lot less than he might have. Horribly mauled at Bunker's Hill (an unaccountable misnomer; it was Breed's Hill, adjacent), he shrank from frontal assault ever after. During the ensuing siege of Boston, to Washington's immense relief he went into his first period of hyperinactivity. As everyone knows, he had a closed mind on campaigning in the winter, hibernating in New York in '76 and Philadelphia in '77, ignoring an utterly vulnerable enemy barely a day's march down the pike. As fewer know, he frequently found the summer too hot "for active service." Six months before their Declaration of Independence he suggested that it might be best to "withdraw completely . . . and leave the colonists to war with each other."

The famous Battle of Long Island, or of Brooklyn, was his triumph, and he was knighted for it. It was the sort of victory that lost the war. He struck, the rebels crumbled, and it would have been easy to have killed or captured all of the Patriots on Long Island. But he held back so long that Washington had time to round up a bunch of Marblehead fishermen, who ferried the troops to Manhattan. When Howe learned of this maneuver he had taken fewer than eleven hundred prisoners and it was too late. Right away he had another chance, for Washington's soldiers were not only sitting ducks, they were deserting "by companies, almost by regiments." For over two weeks he refused to move. Then, after he took possession of New York, he left his foe undisturbed on Harlem Heights for near a month. And so it went, right up to Washington's retreat across the Delaware—when, as the American commander was to remark himself, it would have been easy "to dissipate the remaining force which still kept alive our expiring opposition." Not that Washington was covering himself with military glory. After the battle at Germantown an anonymous journalist summed things up: "Any other General in the world than General Howe would have beaten General Washington, and any other General in the world than General Washington would have beaten General Howe."

Then came the best remembered part of the war: Howe at Philadelphia with his officers playing in the drawing rooms, ballrooms, gaming rooms, and bedrooms of the city; Washington's army at Valley Forge, half-frozen, half-armed, half-clad, half-starved, and out of liquor. But, as Howe informed his superiors, at this point unassailable. That spring his resignation was accepted and he went home. Not, however, before his grateful officers had thrown him the biggest bash the New World had ever seen, "the most splendid entertainment," according to Major André, who designed much of it and wrote it up, "ever given by an army to their General." It was called a Mischianza, meaning a medley or mixture of entertainments, a twelve-hour extravaganza that included a regatta of three divisions (each with band) so big it clogged the river, triumphal arches, a tournament with jousting officers championing the cream of Loyalist girls in Turkish costumes and fantastic hair-dos, elaborate fireworks, a midnight banquet served by costumed slaves in a saloon over two hundred feet long, dancing till four in the morning—all in celebration of it was not clear what. A few days later Howe, recovered, went back to England, and faced Parliament, which neither condemned nor exonerated him. He lost his seat in that body but remained in the army until 1802, and became Viscount on the death of his brother Richard, the Admiral. He expired at eighty-five, having long outlived Washington, whom he somewhat resembled in both face and figure. They both had rotten teeth and died without heirs.

SOME TIME IN 1778 Elizabeth Loring also withdrew to England, where at the end of the war she was joined by her husband, who received a small settlement for the loss of his properties here. They settled at Reading, had more children, and there Joshua died in 1789. In the same year, Elizabeth's petition for a pension was signed by "Wm. Howe," among others; it was granted and paid until 1831. No one knows what memories she had of the war, or how she would have felt about an old question if she'd heard it: "What do you think of the favorite sultana losing 300 guineas in a night at cards, who three years ago would have found it difficult to have mustered as many pence?"

She'd probably have said nothing, but could have said Nonsense. Three hundred guineas were not far from a year's pay for her husband, but it does not appear that she had ever cause to worry about pennies. In the first place she had married into a family that was not entirely obscure. Thomas Loring, the one who came here in 1634, has been traced back to Robert, a poet, mathematician, and architect who built Hereford Cathedral and was made Bishop of that see in 1279. Over two centuries before that Sir Pers Loring, knighted under Henry III, who did battle in Lorraine where the name comes from, sired Nigel Loring, who is the heroic leader of the White Company in Conan Doyle's novel of that name.

Joshua Loring, Sr., was born in Boston in 1716, went to sea as a young man, privateered against the French, then rose in the Royal Navy to become commander of England's ships on the Great Lakes through the French and Indian War—whence his title, Commodore. His son Benjamin, Joshua Junior's brother, went to Harvard when the college still listed students in the order of "family prestige"; he appears second. For a long time the Commodore prospered, and his holdings were extensive. He had an elaborate estate in Roxbury, plus an elegant mansion in Boston which was a showplace in the city well into this century. But for his Loyalty he lost nearly everything. Mobbed and otherwise ill-treated, he had to flee into Boston as early as the summer of '74. He is the man who announced, on the 19th of April in '75, "I have always eaten the King's bread, and I always intend to." Thus he abandoned Boston when the British did, went like Howe to Halifax, thence to London, where he died at Highgate at 1781. His widow was compensated by the Crown for his losses, and died at Englefield, near Reading, in the same year and place as her son Joshua Junior.

Captain Loring, the future commissary, had been born November 1, 1744, in Roxbury, and nothing seems known of him until at seventeen he became an officer in the British army, from which he retired at twenty-four and was given twenty thousand acres of land in New Hampshire for his services (unknown). The next year, on October 19, 1769, he married Elizabeth Lloyd at the great house—which belonged to his bride's stepfather—of Colonel Hatch in Dorchester. As one of her relatives wrote another at the time, he was an "agreeable young Gentleman of a Good

Disposition with an unspotted Character & in good circumstances. . . ." It was probably true. The Lorings were among "the noblesse of Boston society." Henry Pelham's 1777 map of Boston identifies only five houses in the whole region of Dorchester by name; one is Col. Hatch's, another Capt. Loring's. And he was on the way up. In 1771 he took over as Comptroller of the Port of Philadelphia (Elizabeth went there with him), and he traveled a good deal between Boston, New York, and Philadelphia—also to New Hampshire and north to Canada—in pursuit of his other interests. In '75 General Gage commissioned him sole auctioneer for Boston, and in the same year he became Sheriff of Suffolk County. He was in business as well; Loring & Company sold spirits to both Howe and Clinton, and, in Halifax, wine to Howe, who saw to it that he was well paid. In addition he was, under Governor John Wentworth of New Hampshire, Deputy Surveyor of the King's Woods in North America. These were lucrative positions and he worked at them.

He might have gone the other way in the war, for he had, according to his wife, "most flattering overtures from the disaffected party." Many Lorings were of that party; the massive volumes called *Massachusetts Soldiers and Sailors of the American Revolution* list several other Joshua Lorings, all rebels—including a private who "marched on the alarm of April 19" and served for one day. But Joshua Junior ate the King's bread to the end like his parent, and took refuge in Boston on the same night that his father made that declaration of Loyalty. He and Mrs. Loring were still in Boston on the night of March 4, 1776, when Washington's work party placed some cannon—courtesy of Henry Knox and his oxen, who had dragged them all the way from Ticonderoga —on Dorchester Heights, very near their abandoned home.*

---

* A poet at the time placed Mrs. Loring in Howe's bed that night. So did John Trumbull in his popular *M'Fingal* (1782), an imitation of Samuel Butler's *Hudibras*. Butler wrote: "The sun had long since in the lap / Of Thetis, taken out his nap," and Trumbull inserted the lovers: "Great Howe had long since in the lap / Of Loring taken out his nap." That morning the General first sees "th' encircling hills around, / With instantaneous breastworks crown'd" when Joshua arrives early to collect the rent.

The installation appeared to the English "like majick," the work of "15 to 20,000 men." Howe ordered an attack by sea, which was prevented by a violent gale, then decided to evacuate the city instead. The Lorings, and eleven hundred other Loyalists unwilling to risk the mercy of the Patriots, went along to Nova Scotia. Most of them continued into exile; but on June 10 Joshua and Elizabeth sailed for New York with Richard Howe's navy and William Howe's army—on the *Crawford,* an "easy voyage generally."

There, according to a recent writer, having shown "a remarkable talent for mistreating the prisoners" taken at Breed's Hill, Loring was made Commissary of Prisoners—with, as an English historian put it, "much opportunity for the pursuit of what the Americans call 'graft.' " It was regarded as a very good job—he had 20 shillings a day, a house, coal, candles, and rations—and he kept it until June of 1783. The matter of a house was not trivial. For seventeen months at New York it was the Beekman mansion (a mile from town then), occupied previously by General Howe and subsequently by General Clinton. The Lorings had survived their losses, as per two quick notices of them at the time from the journal of Ambrose Serle, secretary to Admiral Howe. In October of '76 Serle entered the fact that he had dined with Sir Peter Parker, commander of the British fleet off New York, on the *Bristol* (the fifty-gun flagship aboard which Sir Peter had his "Britches . . . quite torn off" at Charleston). Present at the table were "Col. & the celebrated Mrs. Clarke, Mr. & Mrs. Loring . . . &c." (Colonel George Clarke was for many years secretary of the colony of New York; Serle does not say what his wife was celebrated for.) In the following June he notes that "The Genl. . . . dined at Commissary Loring's near Haerlem."

But it is in connection with other people's meals, or the lack of them, that Joshua is remembered. An early historian remarks soberly that "it is not easy to ascertain the truth or to determine his personal responsibility in the treatment of prisoners," but his reputation as a villain has become secure as his wife's as a doxy. He is generally described as the man who—in charging rations for prisoners deceased—got rich by "starving the living and feeding the dead." Judge Jones accuses him of doing away with "about 300 of the poor wretches," and, with a few other "bloodsucking harpies," of swallowing up some *"twenty millions sterling"* in the course of the war.

Loring's deputy, Captain William Cunningham, keeper of the Walnut Street Prison in Philadelphia, "executioner of Nathan Hale and torturer of Ethan Allen," has the blackest reputation of all Revolutionary jailors. It is widely reported that he would kick over the kettle so as to watch his charges lick soup from the stones; even the most temperate historian takes satisfaction in reporting that this "brutal sadist," back in England after the war, was found guilty of forgery and hanged. But there is an exception to the opinion that Cunningham was the chief villain: Ethan Allen, leader of the Green Mountain Boys and himself a British prisoner. The famous *Narrative* of his captivity (1779) contains a graphic picture of what things were like in the New York churches that had been taken over as prisons where, as a result of the constant "fluxes," the stones were covered with more than soup, and some of the dead lay in it. Cunningham, says Allen, was "as great a rascal as their army could boast of"—

except one Joshua Loring. . . . This Loring is a monster! . . . There is not his like in human shape: He exhibits a smiling countenance, seems to wear a phiz of humanity, but has been instrumentally capable of the most consummate acts of wickedness . . . (cloathed with the authority of a Howe) murdering premeditately (in cold blood) near or quite 2000 helpless prisoners . . . (at N. York). He is the most mean-spirited, cowardly, deceitful, and destructive animal in God's creation below. . . .

A different witness was Ambrose Serle again, who entered in his journal Loring's revealing report on Patriot morale as of June, 1778. He writes that Joshua showed him a "List of Rebels taken between the Landing upon Long Island & the End of Decr. 1777, of which the Total was near 6000." The commissary then told Serle of a conversation he'd had the day before, while negotiating an exchange of prisoners with Alexander Hamilton, General Lee, and "a Col. Morgan," who took some letters addressed to Washington. Loring said the Patriots "behaved very well; though they all seemed very dull, & wished very much for Peace." Daniel Morgan said that "99 in a 100, were of the same Sentiment & wd. be glad to give up Independency . . . and that none but a few low dirty Rascals . . . were for it." "Follies and Blunders without End!" concludes Serle, incredulous that the war was not over.

Not a lot more is known. Joshua was in New York in March of 1782, left for England in November, and kept his post until June of the next year, having joined his wife and family in Reading, where they had three more sons. In spite of his four-star references—Howe, Gage, Clinton, and Cornwallis—his request for a pension was turned down, probably because it was felt he didn't need the money. A letter of June, 1789, from London to his wife's family on Long Island fears that he "will not remain long with us." He remained three months, then died and was buried at Englefield. According to a letter from the rectory there, a stone tablet on the wall of the side chapel bears this inscription:

> *Near this spot lies the body of Joshua Loring, Esq.*
> *British Commissary General of prisoners in North America*
> *Who died at Englefield much lamented*
> *on the 18th September 1789*
> *being only in the 45th year of his Age.*
> *An honest man's the noblest*
> *work of God.*

Five days later, according to the records of the same church, Mrs. Loring baptized their last child. She was apparently reunited with her mother, for it is recorded that near Englefield her once wealthy stepfather, depressed by the loss of his cause and his property, did away with himself. Almost nothing is known of what happened to Elizabeth through the rest of her life. Famous at twenty-four she virtually disappears from history at thirty-seven.

Where had she entered it? The time and place were long as obscure as her exit. But it is certain that she had not married above her station, for she was, in the manner of birth, to the manor born. She was a Lloyd, that is, of the Manor of Queen's Village, which constituted the large peninsula reaching out into Long Island Sound immediately east of Oyster Bay—three thousand acres of choice land with many miles of shoreline. Once known as Horse Neck (in outline it much resembles the head of a horse), it became Lloyd's Neck; a road map of the area still shows Lloyd Point, Lloyd Lane, Lloyd Beach, Lloyd Harbor Road, the town of Lloyd Harbor, and the harbor itself. There is a state park in the middle of the area called Caumsett, the Indian name for both Sound and Neck. A short tour of the history of the place affords split-second glimpses of what things were like long ago in a privileged quarter of the New World, and for Elizabeth in an exposed part of it.

The original deed to this land exists, whereby on "September the 20 1654" the Sagamore of Cow Harbor sold "my neck of land" to some Englishmen for "Three Coates three shurts two Cuttels three Hatchetts three howes two faddom of wampum Six knifes two payer of Stockins two payer of Shooes." The whites signed; the Sagamore and fourteen other Indians affixed their X's. Twelve years later a man named Sampson, who had become principal owner of the land, made ready for a voyage to the Barbados, and wrote a will leaving everything to his betrothed, Grizzell Sylvester of Shelter Island, in case he should not survive the trip. He did not. Then in 1670 an English descendant of a Lloyd who had been "Dr. in Physick" to Elizabeth the Queen married Grizzell, and later bought the rest of the Neck, becoming sole owner of it. In 1685 the Manorial Grant was awarded, under which the village became a nearly self-sufficient community, with slaves, domestic animals, crops, and an enormous stand of fine timber—also a distinct political entity with its own little government—for nearly a century.

Henry Lloyd, Elizabeth Loring's grandfather, succeeded to the estate. And her uncle Henry intended to—but as a Loyalist lived instead in exile to become so distinguished looking an old gentleman that one night at Drury Lane the King asked for his name. Her uncle James was the eminent Boston physician, a Loyalist who stayed. After the war he went to England to seek compensation for his losses, and being told it would be granted if he would declare himself a British subject, he refused, returned to Boston, and practiced medicine unmolested until he died and was buried under King's Chapel. But as with the Lorings, many of the Lloyds were Patriots, and since the Manor was occupied by the British throughout the war they withdrew to Connecticut. The English plundered the place and built a fort on it. After they left, New York confiscated it; then another Lloyd bought it back. The Manor as such was gone, but the second manor house, 1711, is there still: a modest mansion overlooking Lloyd Harbor, to which it was once connected, according to a tale, by a secret tunnel. Just off the edge of the original property is the spot where Nathan Hale, according to another tale, landed on Long Island and was later taken prisoner, shipped to Howe at the Beekman estate, and then, regretting his but one life, was hanged the next morning at Cunningham's order.

The *Papers of the Lloyd Family, 1654–1826,* generations of correspondence, are preserved and published. There is endless notice of births, deaths, and healths; also of pirates ("Some of the men they rip't their hearts out and made their relations eat"). And Negro slaves—such as Jupiter, aged nineteen, who in 1730 took sick with "pains in his Leggs, Knees, and Thighs, ascending to his Bowels, which in my esteem is a Gouty Rumatick Disorder." There is a steady preoccupation as well with suitable marriages. "Mr Fitch is Gon over to pay Betsie a Visit. He is a likely man but is worth nothing but his learning. . . . She stands as Good a Chance to make her fortune by Matching Well as any Young Lady allmos without Exception." (Betsie married Samuel Fitch, who became a prominent Boston lawyer and later wrote Henry Lloyd, "we were obliged to you for the fruit you was so good as to send us: tho most of it was rotten.") "Brother Nat has engaged . . . to Miss Betty Davenport . . . a young lady of Sixteen educated in a very prudent sober Family. Her Father gives her by Will Twenty five hundred pounds sterling. . . ." They were married, too, the groom's pleasure mitigated by a wedding that cost him "4 or 5 hundred pounds, let me manage ever so prudently."

The Gouty Rumatick Jupiter is never mentioned again in the *Papers,* but in spite of everything that could be done for him he survived. The lords of Queen's Village are pretty well forgot, but there are two books on the slave—who might as well announce his full name himself, as Walt Whitman, born just down the road, would do a century later:

Believe me now, my Christian friends,
Believe your friend call'd Hammon:
You cannot to your God attend,
And serve the God of Mammon.

A Lloyd property from birth to death, Jupiter Hammon had special talents. The first of his several published poems, a broadside called "An Evening Thought," is dated December 25, 1760. Phillis Wheatley, "America's first Negro poet," was in Africa at the time without a word of English.*

---

*Born at the Manor on October 17, 1711, Jupiter was educated there. One schoolmaster was a graduate of Harvard; the family library, which was an exceptional one, was available to him. He published among other things a call for Abolition, which at seventy he didn't want personally as he'd "hardly know how to take care of himself." And he had had, as he also wrote, "more advantages than many white people have enjoyed."

The Lloyds were of course Anglicans; they had to sail clean across the Sound on Sundays to worship. But among Hammon's advantages was a wave of Methodist fervor that swept Long Island in the mid-eighteenth century, inspiring in Jupiter a Wigglesworth of evangelism—with a hint of spirituals to come:

Salvation comes now from the Lord,
Our victorious King.
His holy name be well ador'd,
Salvation surely bring.
Dear Jesus give thy spirit now,
Thy grace to every Nation,
That han't the Lord to whom we bow,
The author of Salvation.
Dear Jesus, unto thee we cry,
Give us the preparation;
Turn not away thy tender eye:
We seek the true Salvation

—a word that occurs in the poem nineteen more times.

Hammon would have been around forty when the future Mrs. Loring was born. Her parents were Nathaniel Lloyd, he of the expensive wedding, Yale '45, and Elizabeth Davenport, sixteen, the girl of sober family and twenty-five hundred sterling. They were married on September 17, 1751, at New South Church in Boston; and on October 15 of the next year they took the new-born Elizabeth from Lloyd Manor into the town of Huntington to be baptized. It was probably the only excursion the little family ever made. In November the infant's grandfather Henry Lloyd received a letter from Boston reporting genuinely

Malancholy News, this awful striking affair. . . . Nat just past (happily) thro the Smallpox . . . here preparing to sett out to you and his Deare Wife . . . was by a sudden & violant Gust in an Instant drowned . . . in full bloom of life. . . . Oh Sir I need not say to you to be tender of his young wife and little one as they were deare to your Son, they will be to you. . . .

The infant's father, married little over a year, had gone down in Boston Harbor a month and a day after the christening of his daughter on Long Island. His body was not recovered; his estate "of right descends to the Child."

"I can scarce hold my pen in my hand," the baby's great-aunt wrote the grandfather from Boston two weeks later. "I pity the poor little Creature his Widow who has mete with a pridigious loss . . . he is gone." Next June the same lady wrote again: "the little babe you sent us is a fine Child and puts us much in mind of its father who was a lovely creature but he is gone. . . . I have received ten pounds . . . for the Child"—who had been brought to Boston by ship, her mother perhaps incapacitated.

When the baby was three the mother married the wealthy and prominent Nathaniel Hatch, who, when she was six, wrote of "the arrival of Our little Daughter safe & well at Dorchester. You may depend on our exerting Ourselves for her good always. . . . Bets . . . don't know I'm writing her Grandpapa." By then the girl's mother, who was to have seven children by her second husband, would have been living at "Col. Hatch's," the estate that was now her husband's, the Colonel's son. (Joshua Loring,

Jr., by now fourteen, would have been living in Jamaica Plain, Roxbury, nearby.) When Bets was nine she wrote Grandpapa herself (it is her only known letter):

Honoured Sir

I received your kind letter by Capt Wimble and am very much obliged to you for taking notice of a little girl and if you Please to write to me often it will encourage me to try to improve in learning more than anything else, besides I shall know by your letters how you do. . . .

Pray give my duty to aunt Woolsey and Uncle Joseph. . . . I am Dear Grand Papa

Your Dutiful Grand Daughter
Elizabeth Lloyd

There are more gaps in the record than entries. And a small mystery. Not long after Elizabeth's letter, the doctor who had diagnosed Jupiter's ailments wrote her grandfather from Boston out of "Anxiety" for her in connection with the "Ruin" of a girl named Cate Smith. Mr. Smith also wrote him: "I am heartily grieved that my dear Child Cate's Conduct Should give you So Much Uneasiness. . . . I shall do all that is in my power . . . to prevent any more Correspondency between my Dear Child and them Wicked Scandalous people. . . ." It is conceivable that this is why in July of the same year Grandpapa received a letter saying, "Hope Wimble has delivered Betsey . . . safe at Queen's Village." Apparently he had, for soon there is a bill—for over £40, another mystery—for her "Mourning Gloves." Grandfather had died, leaving her £1,000 at twenty-one if "she marries with Consent of my Executors & her Parents."

It was also payable on the occasion of such a marriage, and nothing more is known of Betsey until at seventeen, on October 19, 1769, she married Joshua at Colonel Hatch's "elegant Mansion house," and had a "Right to Demand her Fortune"—unless "it will be full as agreeable to Mr. Loring" to keep it at "Interest of 6 per cent." In 1771 she and Joshua visited the Manor, and were "extreamly pleasd with Queen's Village & the kind Reception you gave them, they Say they Left you with reluctance & would gladly have Spent more time with you but for special reasons which you can gess." Their first child, the third Elizabeth in a row, was born in due course.

By then they were living at "Capt. Loring's," very near Hatch's in Dorchester. But with the outbreak of the war they fled into Boston, occupied by the British and surrounded by Patriots, where they probably stayed with Joshua's father. It is easy to conjecture where they met Howe, for on his arrival the General had sought out "his former physician," Elizabeth's uncle James, who had treated him at Castle William in 1755 "so successfully that they became firm friends." Howe lived for a while with the doctor, and then next door. The Lorings could hardly have avoided him.

The rest of the story is mostly told, though uncertain details can be added. Various sources report, for instance, that outside Philadelphia, a couple of years after Boston, Mrs. Loring was established at Stenton—Howe's elegant headquarters near Germantown. And she is frequently mentioned as having attended the Mischianza as the General's lady. On the other hand, the letter that wound up a handbill says that she did not go to Philadelphia at all: "She is . . . far advanced in her pregnancy, and was left at *New-York.* * But then the General has found another Desdemona, even the pretty Miss ———, who is now his excellency's flirt."

The belief that Howe had two mistresses is flimsily founded in rumors of the time. On July 30, 1778, a Philadelphia newspaper reported that:

Last Saturday an imitation of the Mischenza . . . was humbly attempted. A noted strumpet was paraded through the streets with her head dressed in the modern *British* taste. . . . She acted her part well; to complete the farce there ought to have been another lady of the same character (as General Howe had two). . . .

---

*The notion that Mrs. Loring was in Philadelphia with Howe is widespread, but there appears to be no real evidence to support it. If the General expected her to leave New York with him, it seems unlikely that he would—on May 1, 1777—have turned the Beekman mansion, which had been his headquarters, over to the Lorings, who were entitled to the place until long after he returned to England. (There was even less reason for her to leave town if, as John Bernard also claimed, Elizabeth was pregnant at the time.)

If so, the second was probably no Miss ————. Years later the writer Du Ponceau remembered having once stayed at a boardinghouse in Philadelphia kept by a Mrs. Clarke, "who was said to have been the mistress of Sir William How." (There was such a place on Chestnut Street, facing the State House.) Is this the "celebrated Mrs. Clarke," wife of George Clarke the secretary, who had dinner that night with the Lorings and Peter Parker aboard the *Bristol?*

Nobody knows. The Clarkes are forgot, the Lorings remembered—in literature as well as history. Even in the annals of the American drama, for according to the record Joshua is a character —listed in the dramatis personae as Commodore Batteau, and identified by John Adams among others as Joshua Junior in life —in Mercy Warren's satire of the Boston Loyalists called *The Group* (1775). It would be impossible to make too little of this. In the first place it is clear that Joshua Senior, the commodore, is meant; in the second this has got to be the least rewarding role in the history of our theater: not only does Batteau never get to speak a line, or get mentioned by anyone who does, it nowhere appears that he is on stage.

In fictions of our own time his daughter-in-law has been less obscure. She appears prominently, for instance, in Kenneth Roberts's very best-selling *Oliver Wiswell* (1940), which was carefully researched. Oliver, Roberts's mouthpiece, blames the loss of America squarely on Howe, the "Duke of Dally, Lord Lingerloring," who saw ability in Joshua "right the first glance" at his wife. Elizabeth is promisingly arrayed in a gown that would become embarrassing "if she'd coughed unguardedly," and she has "a suggestion of indecencies in her voice." But when we get to know her it is as a pouty, baby-talking flirt totally incapable of the accomplishments other characters credit her with. Further, having prepared both Lorings for great roles, the author lets them linger, then disappear, as he follows Oliver to London. But not before one excited fellow has placed the blame for Howe's neglect in taking up those prisoners on Long Island directly on his lady's blue eyes, her lips, and her "fat little switch-tail." But for them "the war'd been over. . . . Nobody else ought to have a statue":

The truth is, Oliver, that . . . Mrs. Loring's done ten times as much for the rebels as all their generals and Congresses and regiments put together! . . . There wouldn't *be* any rebel generals or army except for Mrs. Loring! If there'd been *two* Mrs. Lorings, the rebels would have King George in a cage on Boston Common. . . .

E. Irvine Haines's *Exquisite Siren* (1938) is Peggy Shippen, the future Mrs. Benedict Arnold, but Mrs. Loring figures in it vitally. A worse novel than *Wiswell,* it is also more interesting, for this time the author's "quarter of a century of painstaking and exhaustive research" into "original letters, documents, and other authentic data" has turned up some genuine revelations. The chief one is that Howe's mistress, that "haughty beauty . . . Jane Lloyd Loring," is "the trusted and faithful agent of Washington!" Howe refuses to take up his Long Island prisoners because he has trouble enough already with Jane. Major André complains that "we sleep while the rebels march to safety," then glides off to his desk and flawlessly turns out "Sir William, he, snug as a flea, / Lay all the time a-snoring," et cetera, which Clinton calls a sonnet. Indeed André soon produces another poem (he was in life an amateur poet, but has suddenly lost his touch):

Your question don't think me a moment ignoring
How long she has honored the surname of Loring

and so on.

Peggy is a Loyalist spy, and to punish her and André (on account of his "slanderous sonnets") Jane devises a little intrigue to deprive Miss Shippen of her maidenhead. It is a game in which a Colonel gambles—and wins—a diamond necklace against Peggy's garters, which turn out to be a Symbol. The officer goes hotly to his reward; André breaks up the party at the very moment of penetration. But the real damage is done and Peggy changed into a woman who will one day betray her country. Both women attend the Mischianza, Peggy as Queen of it, Jane as Howe's lady. André says Jane can't go to England with the General, though, because the government blames her for his failures. "Mayhap," says Mrs. Loring, "I shall retire to the manor house on Long Island." That she does, in dishonor and disrepute for her dalliance. "But I ruined Sir William Howe," she says, "and lost England her Colonies."*

Clearly this woman is a bit of a legend, and it is one that can be placed in line with a larger tradition. As everyone familiar with American culture knows, we long subscribed to the notion of two categories, or symbolic types, of women, the Dark Lady and the Fair. The Dark was erotic, sensual, irresistibly seductive; the Light chaste, delicate, undefilable, and though apparently sexless, to be married, in rejection of dark temptation. Blond Betsey Loring reverses both concepts. Eminently defilable, she prefigures a type that was neither known nor recognized until our own era: the Blonds that Gentlemen Prefer, especially to fighting in the winter. Never grimly sexual, she is joyously so, and born of a cultural discovery or belief that the fair are just as much fun in bed as the dark and more fun out of it: guiltless, playful, or downright reckless—champagne drinkers. Mrs. Loring was 150 years ahead of her time, the virginal fair lady become vaginal.

Oliver Wiswell's friend is not the only one to think of some sort of sculptured or modeled immortality for her, or the first. Rupert Hughes wrote of her in 1930:

How long must she wait for her statue to adorn the Hall of Fame? She is still exiled from the knowledge, not to say the gratitude, of her countrymen, while Betsy Ross, who did nothing worth mentioning, smiles down from innumerable walls.

Perhaps a drive should be got up to erect a monument to be placed, say, off Coney Island, near where Howe landed in Brooklyn, and across the harbor from Liberty's Statue—especially if it could be conveyed, as the phrase used to be, that she is blond all over:

---

*In 1976 Betsey Loring finally became herself the heroine of a novel, Hugh Best's *Red Hot & Blue,* which is memorable for the way the author captures the flavor of the period. After she and Howe have first been together, Mrs. Loring moans, "Oh God you're marvelous . . . I never had it like that. . . . It's like two comets streaking across the sky and suddenly colliding together, fusing into one brilliant star."

Give me your tired, your poor,
Huddled few yearning to breathe hard . . .
I lift my glass beside the golden door.

Legends have traditions, too. The archetypal account of the victory of a chosen people over its enemies thanks to the wiles of a beautiful woman is Judith's, whose calculated sexual attractions drove an enemy commander beside himself with passion and into a drunken stupor, thence to his bed where she joined him and cut off his head, thus saving her country. But Judith was a widow: what to do with Joshua while his wife works her magic and he starves his prisoners, polishing his golden horns?

Straighten the picture a little, perhaps. No one has explained, for instance, how if he owed his position to the gift of his wife he continued in it for five years after she had taken herself from the scene. Ethan Allen is not the most reliable of witnesses; a better one might be the American Commissary of Prisoners, Boudinot, who in New York in February of 1778 investigated Loring's performance and pronounced himself well satisfied with it. After General Silliman was exchanged for Judge Jones, he wrote that while he was prisoner of the British Loring treated him "with complaisance, kindness, and friendship . . . never to be forgotten by me." There is no question but that the captured on both sides suffered horribly, but it was often because supplies were hard to come by. And if rebels in Loring's hands suffered too, as there is no doubt, it was partly the fault of their own Congress, which was supposed to "provide certain necessaries, as custom required," and did not. One man who denounced the "heartlessness" of our government was Loring himself, who protested for his prisoners that "your superiors are cruel enough not to suffer the men who fight their battles to be exchanged." He was right. At that point Washington and the Congress refused to exchange prisoners according to the convention because they didn't want to give up the British regulars they held for rebel soldiers whose enlistments were up.*

---

*No one made the point more emphatically than Loring himself. In the archives of the Historical Society of Pennsylvania is a long letter of November, 1777,

As for Joshua as husband and father there seems to be no record until now, when two letters from his pen may enter the vacuum. Here is the complaisant commissary writing Howe's mistress (Loring is apparently in New York; his wife at the Beekman mansion outside it, or in Harlem) at the very time when her long embrace was most fateful:

11 °clock

My dear Betsey

Don't be alarmed at a report of the Rebels being landed on Long Island which prevents my returning to night as I promised the General I would not go out of town, should it prove true I shall be obliged to go to Long Island in the morning to take up all the Rebel Officers, in that case will send you word   my Trunk of Papers & your plate you will bring to town with you should I send out for you to come to town, let Othello come back with Cornelius on one of the Generals horses, & I'll send him out to you early in the morning when I have seen the General—keep everything I have wrote you a profound secret—

Yrs most affectionately J. Loring

Some years later, shortly before returning to England, Joshua wrote his daughter Elizabeth, then eleven, chiefly about his wife:

New York 24th March 1782

My dear Daughter

How could you think I had forgot you who I know possesses one of the best hearts & most excellent understanding of any little girl on Earth, cultivated improved in the highest manner by the abilities and great attention of a fond Mother, who is entirely devoted to you & your brothers good . . . do honor to the Pains she is bestowing on you; you will not only lay up a treasure of knowledge of Virtue & Relegion but you will secure the affections of a fond father . . . as to your education I have entrusted it intirely to her care . . . follow strictly her commands in all things & you cannot fail of possessing a warm share in my

---

in his elegant hand, pleading with his Patriot counterpart for a general, not a partial, exchange of prisoners as the means of saving many lives, and protesting the disregard of "repeated applications of our side" for such a transfer. In regard to graft, it is virtually certain that Joshua profited from his post; a commissary was expected to.

heart   love advice & assist your brother and be assured of the regard
of your affectionate   Father J. Loring

The brother here is John Wentworth, age nine, who was to have
three brothers, as yet unborn.

Sons are a gift from the Lord, says the Psalm, whose parents will
not be put to shame by enemies in court. Nothing is known of
Elizabeth (1771–), and Joshua III died an infant in Dorchester.
But William Loring (1785–1812) became a Captain in the Royal
Army before dying at Tenerife at the age of twenty-six. Robert
Roberts Loring (1789–1848) became a Colonel and had command at Halifax in the War of 1812. Henry Lloyd Loring (1784–
1822) became a Fellow of Magdalen College, then an Anglican
Bishop at Calcutta. John Wentworth Loring (1773–1840) became an Admiral of the Royal Navy and was knighted. Nor did
sons renounce mother. She was thirty-seven when Joshua died,
and she lived a long time after him. Did she remarry? Disappear?
We might never know but for the inscription at her grave which
reads:

Sacred to the Memory
of Elizabeth
Relict of the late Joshua Loring Esq.
who died Oct 2nd 1835
full of years and honour
and of the faith in the Mercy of God
through the merits of her Redeemer.
She fulfilled the duties of life to all
with exemplary constancy
especially to her children
who in grateful remembrance of her devotion
to them during forty six years of Widowhood
have erected this record
of her Virtue, and of their affection

It is entirely possible that the conventional rhetoric of the period, tombstone and epistolary, has overwhelmed the truth, as
rhetoric and hypocrisy have been known to do. But who's to say?

How much do we really know, and how much do we know that isn't true? Could it be the muse of history that's a doxy? How, as an instance, could General Howe have gone so long uncomprehended? In the gratuitous assumption that he was out to win the war, of course. Empowered to make real concessions to the colonies if they would lay down their arms, he was in fact fighting for peace. He would have to do a lot of damage before the enemy would consider his terms. But if he completely suppressed the rebellion it would cost England more to garrison troops here and keep it suppressed than the colonies were worth. Thus the finishing stroke was never delivered.

Similarly, given the nature of human nature, of the time, and his own track record, there is no doubt that the General had a mistress or two. And there is no leading candidate but Betsey Loring. But of all the people who have ever described her not one could ever have seen her. The idea that she is a forecast of the modern dashing blonde gives way to the suspicion that she is the modern product of that stereotype, the creation of twentieth-century historians who could not picture a reckless champagne mistress with anything but golden hair. It is hard to say who was first to paint her that way, with the blue eyes, but it apparently happened in our time.

There ought to be a portrait, specifically by John Singleton Copley. Joshua had the money and the station. He and Copley seem to have been friends; in his travels between Boston and New York he carried letters from the artist to his half brother Henry Pelham and from Pelham back. There are well-known Copleys of Joshua Loring, Sr., and of his sister. And there are portraits, alleged to be by Copley and to show Elizabeth and Joshua Junior, held very privately by descendants in England and unknown to any inventory of Copley's work.

These paintings do not look at all like Copleys. But whoever the artist, they are without question portraits of the commissary and his wife. Joshua presents, as Ethan Allen conceded, a "phiz of humanity"—gentle, affable, fine-featured, an eerie, plumper duplicate of his father. But it is Elizabeth's likeness that is compelling. Different people looking at the same picture see different things, even under a realistic brush. Yet it is safe to say that the lady, although regal, was not conventionally beautiful: nose and chin a little prominent (that is the Lloyd look, exactly my mother's), mouth a bit too wide, forehead very high with a great crest of hair *à la mode* above it. She is viewed from the hip up in profile, chin in graceful hand, dressed in a jacket with lace blouse and cuff that leave only hand, face, and throat exposed. She is looking off to the left for what appears to be a long way, but with an eye that seems to permit a long look in. The look about the eye is truly beautiful: gentle, vulnerable, compassionate. The eye itself does not seem to have any dominant color. The hair is brown.

Chapter Three

LADY FRANCES,
SIR JOHN

AROUND THE FOOT of a mountain, where Governor's Road dwindled to a bridle path, the guest came side-saddle. Past the head of her horse, like a white mirage off a blue lake in the brown greens of a forest, was a mansion. Wentworth House—Wolfeborough, New Hampshire, population only yesterday zero—was not quite finished. But in the din of a ballroom in progress, Frances Wentworth was in residence with her husband, John, Royal Governor of the Province and Surveyor General of the King's Woods in North America. Betsey Loring dismounted. It was 1770. Her husband was Deputy Surveyor; she had come for a visit from Dorchester, Massachusetts, where she lived quietly. It was different, she knew, with Frances. Back at her official home in the gilded little dukedom of Portsmouth, its first lady was famous: beautiful, brainy, stylish, and sexually disreputable.

"Dancing, Writing, Reading, Painting on Glass, & all sorts of Needle Work"—the curriculum for well-to-do females of Boston when Frances was born there in 1745, the daughter of Samuel Wentworth, merchant. But the girls were taught things never advertised, and when John Singleton Copley painted her as a young woman he captured some of them. Elegant, fashionable, quick, Frances is robed in a satin gown of pewter hue, liberally bestrung with pearls, and seated at a table; she holds a small flying squirrel by a dainty chain. The hair and eyes, slightly slanted, are dark brown; the nose a little turned up but classic, the lips perfectly bowed. It was an occasion; the artist, early in his career, would never paint anyone more beautiful. But just as memorable as beauty is the look on that face: self-possessed, aloof, vaguely smiling but faintly disdainful—at the same time very bold and alluring, as if conscious of décolletage cut broad and perilously low. Copley's best portraits are startling. "You can scarce help discoursing with them," John Adams remarked, "asking questions and receiving answers." But the question about Frances Wentworth—splendid lady or aristocratic tart?—the painter left hanging. Her life, inextricable from Governor John's, can be recovered in more detail than any other Revolutionary Lady's, but after two hundred years there is still no sure answer.

ᦇI

DOWN FROM PORTSMOUTH and living across the river at Cambridge, her cousin John Wentworth is the first man on whom Frances is supposed to have turned that ambiguous eye. But after college, according to family tradition, when his father sent him to watch over business interests in England and he sailed off without marrying her, she spun about and seized on her other first cousin, Theodore Atkinson, Jr., whose bride she is in the portrait. Frances's uncle, Theodore's father, was chief justice of the province just to the north, where he served under another of her uncles, Benning Wentworth the Governor. The post of Secretary of the Province was arranged for her husband; the newlyweds made their way to Portsmouth and moved into the Atkinson mansion where, it is reported, two days were required to polish the silver. The Atkinsons were New Hampshire's second family, the Wentworths its first.

Portsmouth offered its little aristocracy luxury and festivity, but in the full enjoyment of them Frances may have felt handicapped.

Copley's portrait of the groom shows a slender, diffident young man, "utterly unlike his fiery cousins" Frances and John, "mild and obliging in his disposition . . . and devout in the exercises of religion." Living with him, and with Uncle Theo and Aunt Hannah, she must have felt a little constricted. She remained childless, and as the years went by it became obvious that her husband was not well enough to keep up with her had he wished to.

Cousin John stayed on in England. Uncle Benning, in his rambling residence just outside town at Little Harbor—complete with council chamber, fifty-one other rooms, and a stable in the cellar for thirty horses in case of emergency—continued high-handedly to rule the province, having already done so longer than any other colonial Governor. A great-bellied old fellow crippled with gout, he had also got rich at a job he'd taken on bankrupt—chiefly by granting lands for new townships and reserving a piece of each for himself; he held in the neighborhood of 100,000 acres, some outside his jurisdiction, it turned out, as in Bennington, Vermont. At exactly the time his sins finally caught up with him, and it became apparent to the Board of Trade in England that he would have to be removed from office in America, John was at Wentworth Woodhouse, Yorkshire, the guest of Charles Watson-Wentworth, the Marquis of Rockingham. A Whig of some influence, Rockingham had first noticed the young colonist for his heavy betting on the horses, and had been pleased to discover that conceivably they were relatives. It didn't hurt that John was New Hampshire agent for the Stamp Act Congress to petition the King for repeal of the Stamp Tax, that "cursed act" which Rockingham had opposed. And he had a reasonable suggestion for his Lordship. When Benning outlived his welcome as Governor, as he had both wife and children, John defended the "good old gentleman" as though he meant it, then pointed out to the Marquis that if his uncle really must be replaced, the graceful way to do it would be to permit him to resign in favor of his nephew and apparent heir. It was done, and at twenty-nine he inherited Benning's titles: Surveyor General of the King's Woods in North America, "Captain-General, GOVERNOR, and Commander in Chief, in and over HIS MAJESTY'S Province of New-Hampshire, and VICE ADMIRAL of the same." Oxford awarded him a prognostic Ll.D. He accoutered himself for his posts and set sail.

There is no record, but even Charleston, South Carolina, must have been impressed on that day in March of 1767 when a vigorous young gentleman disembarked there with a stable of the bluest blooded horses of England plus a whole retinue of trained Yorkshire servants. And astonished, if anyone watched, as he proceeded to take his forest duties seriously. Accompanied by his deputy, Joshua Loring, and journeying northward like a prince, he inspected the great yellow pines of North Carolina, stopped off at Westover to pay his respects to the Byrds of Virginia, and at Chatsworth, the seat of Randolphs; finally reaching New York, he shipped for Boston. The Stamp Act had been repealed, and New Hampshire was of a mind to receive him. Met at the border by his Troops of Guard and Horse, his entourage was escorted all the way to Portsmouth, where he was saluted by cannon, the militia, and local dignitaries, and publicly dined amid the general rejoicing of the people. It is doubtful that any other Royal Governor in America had ever been greeted with such enthusiasm, and if Frances did not have her eye on him now, it was out of focus.

"A Small Hut with little comfortable Apartments" was the Governor's description of the seventeen-room mansion provided him. But he hoped to turn it into a Lilliputian Wentworth Woodhouse, where "we endeavour to make everyone as happy as we can." The intent was general, the energy inexhaustible, the dedication absolute. He tended to all interests of the province, shaped great plans, and watched all details. Hearing that royal pines were being cut in Vermont he rode across the mountains in the middle of winter, captured the guilty, got them convicted and jailed, then recommended release. Warned that men threatening to kill anyone who interfered were up to the same thing in Maine, he moved in unarmed and stopped them.

Life at the Governor's court did not go on foot or horseback; to dignify the occasion and his province, he required for traveling to Boston accommodations for twelve horses and eight servants. Horses and music were his passions, both shared by his companion and resident guest Michael Wentworth—another putative relative, who had introduced him to Rockingham. A retired Colonel in the British army who had distinguished himself at Culloden, and was famed for having ridden from Boston to Portsmouth in ten hours, Michael would fiddle till dawn at Stoodley's Tavern. The administration was Royalist, Anglican, and spirited. To avoid "the pomps and vanities and ceremonies of that little world Portsmouth," John Adams, republican and Congregationalist, on a trip to Maine from Boston made a long detour and regretted he could not take the same route back, feeling bound to pay his respects to his Harvard classmate (for "he is my friend and I am his"). Meanwhile Wentworth had discovered a deficiency in the way he was served, and wrote to England for two more footmen who were good on the French horn. If possible, one of them should double on the violin.

With the first families of Portsmouth, John and Frances worshipped at Queen's Chapel, communicants of the Reverend Arthur Browne—said to have been as a young man in Dublin secretary to Jonathan Swift, and occasionally remembered for having officiated at some curious weddings, the first of which had the town talking for a long time. In 1760 Benning Wentworth, still Governor and a widower, had invited Browne and select members of the flock to his sprawling mansion for a dinner in honor of his sixtieth birthday. In the midst of the toasts at the end of it, so goes the story, Benning ordered the minister to marry him— to consternation general, there being no bride in sight until the host pointed to one of his servants: Martha Hilton, aged twenty, a "dirty slute of a maid," according to some, and previously notorious as a tavern wench at Stavers's, where she went about scantily clad. One did what Benning said, never mind. Martha was suddenly the Governor's lady, mistress of her own servants and a great house.

In the fall of '69 Portsmouth had something richer to savor, though at first it was only a matter of rumor. The trouble with Theodore Atkinson, Jr., was tuberculosis, and the trouble with his wife was that she was not keeping watch by his bed but leading a social life of her own. Copley was in town, now painting the Governor, and this fine-featured but confident and rugged young patrician (as he appears) was calling with increasing frequency on his Atkinson relatives. There was nothing to block the view of the Governor's house from Frances: gossip had it that signals were exchanged for the arrangement of more private occasions. In the midst of this, poor Atkinson died, and his widow lit the last lamp —or waved the last handkerchief—in her window. On November 1 Reverend Browne performed the funeral at Queen's Chapel. Frances entered her period of mourning, but in exactly ten days was back at the same church before the same minister with John at her side. "A lady adorned with every accomplishment to make the marriage state agreeable," rejoiced the *Gazette*. "All the bells in town are ringing. . . . The day is spending in innocent mirth." Some thought the portly rector's response more fitting; on leaving church he fell down the steps and broke his arm. Whatever the circumstances, Michael Wentworth, companion of the Governor's bachelorhood, moved out of the Governor's mansion—mysteriously attaching himself, according to John, "to some very wretched low people"—and Frances Wentworth moved in. The question posed by Copley's portrait was of great public interest, but the lady rose up and stared it down. The months went by, and if there was a child at court to embarrass the newlyweds the secret was marvelously kept. That fall Frances had an unexpected problem.

Her uncle Mark, the Governor's father, was rich. Her husband, whose tastes—let alone hers—outran his two salaries, was not. The way out of this dilemma appeared to be through their uncle Benning, who was now old, had long been ailing, and was expected at his demise to bequeath the greater part of great wealth to his political heir. But before she had been married a year the old man died, and created an explosion that would reverberate for years by leaving his widow not the anticipated retainer, nor a fortune, but "my whole estate, both real & personal, whatsoever and wheresoever"—the lands, extraordinary house, and 10,000 guineas cash. Now "tho't to be the richest widow in New-England," Martha Hilton Wentworth was little older than Frances, and physically attractive. The precedent was clear. Only a few weeks passed before Arthur Browne was back at Little

Harbor, as Michael Wentworth formed a new attachment by marrying the heiress who'd been the maid and become the mistress of Wentworth House.

Money could always be borrowed. Frances looked to the pleasures of society and her Marital Accomplishments. John, for his part, was powerfully drawn to the frontier and already pursuing what he called his Designations in the Wilderness. Modeled on the baronies of England, particularly on Rockingham's, his country seat at Wolfeborough—fifty miles northwest of the capital, two long days through the forest—was nearing completion. Its design was ambitious: an estate of over four thousand acres set on a "pond" four miles long by three across, connected by river to Lake Winnepesaukee, with a mall thirty feet wide lined with elms that extended from mansion to water. Built of white clapboard and dominated by a huge central fireplace, this Wentworth House was dignified and graceful. John himself was its architect, but the interior was by Peter Harrison, who had to his credit King's Chapel in Boston and the Touro Synagogue at Newport. Hanging inside were the portraits of the young Mrs. Atkinson and the young Governor, and the King George and Queen Charlotte that the owner had also commissioned of Copley. The furnishings, "superabundant," were "rich & elegant." The servants, save for Hagar and Remus, wore the Wentworth livery—green with gold lacing. Down by the lake was Mount Delight, a very special little hill where refreshments were served the bride under a giant pine John exempted from the mast laws and would never cut. In the lake, connected to the mainland by causeway for dining *alfresco,* were Turtle Island and Tea Rock. It was a happy estate. When a housemaid married a farmhand, John in scarlet tied the knot; Frances was all in blue; the feast for devoted servants, neighbors, and guests went on all night. The Governor had already spent £ 20,000 on the place, money advanced by his father.

But his design was also serious. "Better built and equipped, at that time, than Mount Vernon," the estate was a working plantation, carved out of the wilderness with such energy and skill as to dazzle the province without offending it. John joined in all labors himself—clearing, building, and plowing, he gave thanks, "with equal avidity." The mansion was the center of a whole community, population unknown. In addition to an enormous barn, "two large stables and coach houses," there were, in his own inventory,

One large dairy with a well . . . smoke and ashes house, etc. etc. One blacksmith shop. Joiner and cabinet-makers do. . . . One garden walled with stone . . . about 40 acres. A park of 600 acres substantially enclosed. . . . One saw mill and one grist mill . . . various boats and gondola for conveyance of goods, produce, and cattle. . . .

He did not mention other livestock, his orchards, the two-masted *Rockingham,* some other outbuildings, or Dr. Cutter, resident physician.

His hand was in everything. Anxious to employ his mind as well, he urged Deputy Surveyor Loring, on a trip to Canada, to watch for "curiosities, natural or artificial"; he had a large library. From England he imported pheasants, which were promptly devoured by predators; he transported cusk, a species of cod, from the ocean to his lake, where, to the astonishment of everyone but himself, they thrived.

Frances did not; she would never "prefer a grove to a Ball room." And her Governor worked so hard, "I am most turned hermit." Travel frightened her: John, if he could, would "ride over the tops of the trees on Moose Mountain . . . I tremble at Passing through a road cut at the foot of it." One thing she did enjoy was her billiard room, and her ballroom was ready for flooring. She had frequent guests. Only one tale of marital friction survives, relating how one night she proposed to attend a husking bee with the farmers. John forbade it (country matters; the finder of a red ear was entitled to a kiss). She went anyway, and returned late to discover herself locked out. Screaming hysterically that she was throwing herself in the lake—or down the well—she ducked into the house as he rushed out of it, and he was the one locked out.

Portsmouth was her realm, with its round of teas, dinners, receptions, levées, and entertainments at the sign of the Earl of Halifax, where John Stavers kept his tavern, and society raised glasses to her and her Governor. She flirted, it is reported, with the handsomest of the young gentlemen, and placated their wives, perhaps, with clever compliments. It helped that her husband was a triumph. He had the colony explored and mapped, backed the writing of its history, got roads built, canals planned, and dreamed of the day when water would connect Winnipesaukee with the sea. A road would connect it with Quebec; the interior of the province would open; Wolfeborough, then central, would be the seat of government. He promoted agriculture (neglected because of New Hampshire's success in trade), worked for a new college, granted its lands and charter, smiled at the suggestion that it be called Wentworth, and wrote Dartmouth into the papers. He plotted to advance the Church of England there and throughout his domain, instructed Eleazar Wheelock on how to feed the students, was banquet host to everyone at its first commencement, and presented the institution—which had little else —with an engraved silver punchbowl. In the forest he was a democrat, as many stories attest—a candid and comfortable guest in many an isolated cabin.

Loyal as he was, Wentworth's understanding of the conflict with England was acute. He warned his superiors that force, fact or threat, could only work against them, that the colonies could be kept dependent only by reforms, and that the next great crisis would bring rebellion. They would have done well to heed him. He had kept a grumbling province perfectly in line while Massachusetts was totally out of it; he had personally prevented a Portsmouth Tea Party. He even explained how it was done: "be steady, open, and resolute without any mystery or intrigue. . . . It is impractical to raise a great dangerous mob if all the business is understood." The King commended him, but did not listen.

A growing number of New Hampshire colonists, including some Wentworths, believed that the Governor and his hand-picked Council should be under, not over, the Assembly. But the autocracy was so benevolent and skillful that it took Massachusetts and the violation of his own principle to bring about its collapse. In the fall of '74—winter approaching, no barracks in Boston for the occupying British troops, no carpenters willing to build them—General Gage sent to him for help. He saw it as an order, his duty, and arranged secretly for fifteen workmen to go down from Wolfeborough, where things were quiet; Portsmouth Patriots learned of the move and pronounced him an "enemy of the community." The lid he had held on a simmering pot was blown. In December "one Paul Revere," as he put it, rode into town with the alarm: the Redcoats were coming, specifically to secure the munitions at little Fort William and Mary just outside town. His orders no longer had any effect. A mob overran the decrepit bastion; arms and a hundred barrels of gunpowder—which would be fired, tradition has it, at Bunker Hill—were carried off. Rebels had taken a British post by force; Lexington and Concord were four months away.

The Governor did what he could: ordered the arrest of everyone involved in the plunder, then informed higher authority that no jail would hold them; no jury convict. "Peace, my dear friend," he wrote to Boston, "has by unwise men been driven out. God forgive them." His wife was deeply concerned about his worries and his safety; he was more anxious about her. "Much frighted" in the "late confusions," she "summon'd all her fortitude" in vain, frequently in tears. The crisis could not have come at a worse time; by the end of 1774 she was expecting every day the arrival of a "young friend." But it was not until January 20 that she was delivered of a "sturdy, healthy boy," and then only after the "severest natural labor Dr. Hall Jackson remembers"— seventeen hours long, during most of which the attending physician, a distinguished doctor but dedicated Patriot, spent his time in "the jolly laughing servant's hall . . . entertaining the circle" with obstetrical anecdotes. Thus entered the world what a descendant called John's "only legitimate child," christened Charles-Mary, the Governor explained, "after Lord and Lady Rockingham at their request." Frances did not much participate; but, as her mother remarked, "had a young prince been born there could not have been more rejoicing. . . . For one week, cake, caudle, wine &c. passing." Sire approved son: "He will do to pull up stumps at Wentworth House."

It was the last hurrah in a truce that lay under the guns of two

British ships sent into the harbor from Boston. The troops which
the Governor had requested never came from Gage, who in April
sent them to Concord instead. That expedition shattered the fragile peace at Portsmouth, and destroyed the dynasty. He could "no
further than to arm my house well," John wrote Lord Dartmouth,
and give any who moved against it "a very warm and serious
entertainment." But no talent he possessed would divert the mob
he'd said could not properly be raised.

Frances was just as understanding, and more realistic: "har-
ass'd, distressed and confused. . . . Not a night . . . since Lexington
have all my family been in bed, but one or more sit up to watch
lest we are in our sleep surprised and taken." She was eloquent
in her grasp of the situation: these provincials, she warns, "are
content to die." (Frances is sending thanks to Lady Rockingham
for the sponsoring of her son, "a sweet hansome boy . . . my
delight in him is inexpressible.") She was philosophical: "Providence frowns on our land. We were growing too fast. A Frost has
cut off our Grass." And her timing was perfect. It was afternoon,
June 13, 1775, and even as she wrote, "the Governor came to my
room and beg'd me not to be alarmed, for the House was about
to be attacked.

The street was full . . . they stove with Clubs, brought a large cannon
and placed it before the Door, and swore to fire through. . . . It was
Sun-down and damp air . . . no time to get a hat or blanket for him.
. . . We got into the Boat with our poor Child. . . . We have frequently
heard . . . if they could get him they would split him down the Back and
broil him. This affected us. . . .

Still in danger, she was now writing two weeks later from a
"miserable house . . . confined for room and neither wind or
water tight" at Fort William and Mary, itself "a ruinous Castle
with the walls in many places down." If the "prevailing madness
of the people should follow me hither," John informed Gates,
and if it should be in his power, he hoped to retreat on the
Scarborough. It never came to that; the ships were worthless, and
the officer in command, unable to put ashore for food and water,
decided at the end of August to return to Boston. The little family

was helpless. Wentworth wrote Atkinson Senior, second in the
fallen command, that he found it necessary to go to sea "for a few
days," and off they sailed. If Frances looked back across the water
she saw that her ramshackle house was torn to the ground before
she was out of sight. Her mansion had been sacked ten weeks
earlier, even of her rouge. And "a few days" were forever.

"It is impossible for many of us to hold much longer," Joshua
wrote at Boston. What concerned him was food and fuel for
Betsey and their infant son, John Wentworth Loring. The city
was under siege, jammed with Loyalists from nearby towns like
themselves. It was fall and getting cold; there was danger everywhere, plus privation and smallpox. Even to the sanguine Wentworth, "things wear a most gloomy prospect indeed." He was
completely balked. What he wanted was a frigate on which he
could return to Portsmouth and lay down the law with force;
when he failed to get it, he also failed to convince General Howe
that they should invade New Hampshire together. But he had
invitations from England, from old friends—the Rockinghams,
and especially Paul Wentworth, another wealthy relative with
whom he had once lived in London. In January he shipped
Frances and the baby abroad for safekeeping. It was not much too
soon; in March Howe sailed for Halifax, abandoning such Loyalists as he could not take along. John hired a schooner, put fifty of
them on board, and went with him. He then went too to Long
Island, and at Flatbush organized a company called Wentworth's
Volunteers. Optimistic bulletins to England kept issuing from his
pen: G. Howe (whose lady's mother was yet another Wentworth)
"has the American rebellion in his Power." But the General's
failure ever to take advantage of that strength exasperated him,
and with the news of Saratoga he despaired. A letter in which he
announced that "20,000 Russians and 12,000 Witenbergers &c."
were on the way to reinforce the British was intercepted and
published to his discredit; he was accused of being the fount of
the counterfeit money that was flooding the colonies. Every scrap
of his property had been confiscated, and virtually all of it sold;
the New Hampshire legislature had forbid him ever to set foot
in his province, and a second offense meant death. He was not

angry with those who had stripped and outlawed him, but he must have been hurt: "God knows my heart sought and indulged its greatest delight . . . in their comfort and growing prosperity." Two years had passed since he had sent his wife to England, and now sick at heart he sailed himself.

Frances had not been suffering from discouragement, deprivation, or neglect. Scarcely had the refugee debarked with her child than the *London Chronicle* announced: "Yesterday, the Lady of Gov. W———th, of N— H———, lately arrived in town from that Province, was introduced to their Majesties at St. James." It was only a little less regal at Wentworth Woodhouse—set in a private park of twelve hundred acres, over two hundred yards from tower to tower, stocked with Titians, Guidos, and portraits of Strafford, greatest of all Wentworths—where she was set in the splendor of Rockingham's palace. For livelier times she paid extended visits to Paul Wentworth on Poland Street in London; she had known him in New Hampshire, and John called him "my near relation and most intimate, dearest, and confidential friend." He owned plantations in Surinam, qualified as "the first American cosmopolitan and international speculator," and was much away from home. (Mysteriously; on one occasion he went *"secretly* to Paris," leaving Frances with odd instructions—that "if she had any letters to send to me . . . to send them to Amster-am. . . . That if L. or Ly R. tryed to find out my reason for so sudden a journey to be backward, but if they insisted much to tell them . . . my Factor in Amsterdam . . . I did not know what Effects he may have lately received from my Estates in the West Indies.") Things were more regular at Wentworth Woodhouse. And privileged; when John joined her there in the spring of 1778 he found Charles-Mary installed in the regal apartments the Marquis had himself occupied as a child.

In 1780 Paul bought an estate of his own known as Brandenburgh House, an early seventeenth-century mansion overlooking the river just outside London at Hammersmith. Here he entertained nobility, and "as one family" until the summer of '83 the American Wentworths—Frances, her husband and son, her mother, and the growing brood of her brother Benning. King

George distrusted Paul, as he did all speculators; because of
John's pessimistic view of the war he rather disliked him too,
though he is said to have used him on "special missions." The
displaced governor—described as "very much dejected and pin-
ing for his native country"—also worked in London on behalf of
Loyalist refugees who did not have rich relatives. The city was full
of them, and the government loath to find them positions since
it expected them to return to former ones as soon as the rebellion
was quashed. Then, at the end of 1781, things began happening
fast. Cornwallis surrendered, the colonies were almost gone, and
next, at fifty-two, Rockingham died, his estate passing to Lord
Fitzwilliam, a nephew. The King's Woods in North America
were radically shrunk, but there were great pines in Nova Scotia,
which then included New Brunswick; the Whigs were returned
to power, and Fitzwilliam had somehow inherited the American
Wentworths along with Wentworth Woodhouse. Frances was
again wife of the Surveyor General, with a new patron.

"SHARPERS, TROLLOPS & CUTPURSES," German, Scottish, and
Hessian Troops, Indians, slaves, press gangs: Halifax was over-
run. It had been a small base for the British fleet, which Washington had said it would be easy to "overawe" could he have spared
an ounce of ammunition. But by the time Frances arrived in the
fall of 1783 it had been twice inundated—first by Howe with his
army and the Loyalists from Boston, then at the end of the war
by the army again, and twelve thousand new Loyalists from New
York. They called the country Nova Scarcity; it was expensive
and short of everything but women and rum. Halifax was "dark
& vile as Sodom": one regiment of artillery, according to an old
saw, two of infantry, and three of whores. Sandwiched between
the brothels and grog shops of Barracks Street on one side and
the "Beach"—the same resorts for sailors—on the other, was a
thin slice of gentry. For the first time in her life Frances was not
of it. The Governor's lady was Mrs. Parr.

Not long after landing in the stewy capital, John Wentworth
left his wife for an extensive survey, by foot and birch canoe, of

his new territory. It was better to be at work he loved. For Frances it was a disaster, the start of a life as full of ups and downs as her first forty years. Yorkshire, London, Hammersmith—suddenly she found herself in a house, rent exorbitant, with no quarters for servants, and "not one room papered or painted until we came into it." She felt her Change of Fortune—this aimed at her new target, Lady Fitzwilliam—"with a poignancy almost insupportable." As they drove by in their carriages, she found herself looking up to ladies transformed from "nurse Maids and cooks." She "never felt the want of rank" in England; in Halifax "I keep mostly at home." And home alone, Charles-Mary having been left at Westminster to be educated, John "absent on his duty more than two thirds of the time since I arrived." She "plumes" herself with hope of "a short exile," and, "freezing by the fire . . . which will continue necessary until July," plots her escape. "Breathe to your Lord," she writes his Lady, "a thought of your absent but humble dependents—the time will come when you can by a word make us happy"; the reins of government "will rest with or about you—bear in mind the solicitation I have ventured to suggest." She was never more candid: "I would venture anywhere to better my fortune."

The plumes wilted; she was left to deal with fortune at Halifax, and within a year it was changing again. "The last Assembly," wrote Penelope Winslow, "was amazingly brilliant, the Ladies Dress superb. . . . Mrs. Wentworth stood first in fashion and magnificence . . . a train of four yards long, her hair and wrists ornamented with real Diamonds." By 1787 Frances was writing cheerfully herself—about a moose she sent Lord Fitzwilliam which, if addressed as Jack, would follow him around. The clear reason for her ebullience was the recent visit of a "most charming Prince, who did us the honor to call on us every day, and once dined here." She rejoiced that he was expected back in a month, and regretted that the people of Halifax "do not at all know how to treat this Royal Visitor."

William Henry, the Sailor Prince, third son of George III, arrived at Halifax in command of the frigate *Pegasus*. Feared but respected as an officer, he was better known for debauchery.

Nova Scotia he found bleak, but its capital congenial: "a very gay and lively place," he wrote the Prince of Wales late in 1786, "full of women and those of the most obliging kind." Ten months later he wrote his brother again—summoned home, he said, to receive a "family lecture for immorality, vice, dissipation and expence," chiefly because of "a certain affair likely to take place. . . . These damn women cause me more uneasiness than enough." It is not certain what affair he referred to, but possible that Mrs. Wentworth had learned in England how a Prince was to be treated, had earned during her husband's absences in the forest the reputation Portsmouth gossip would have foretold, and was now ostracized by the ladies of Halifax she sniffed at. So at any rate has it been rumored, and so believes Philip Ziegler, who in 1971 turned his talents to a biography of Prince William. The King, thinks Ziegler, recalled his son to prevent a royal scandal with Frances, his "handsome and sophisticated mistress." Her fame "was that of a trollop who never hesitated to cuckold her . . . husband if she thought she could get away with it." Thomas Raddall, foremost historian of Halifax, had in 1948 thought the same: the town was "full of naughty women . . . from the unwashed sluts of Barracks Street to the elegant wife of John Wentworth." But according to Raddall she knew very well she could get away with it: "she exerted her shapely self . . . for the pleasure of their royal guest," and with her husband's "obvious knowledge and consent. Whenever the Prince was in town Mr. Wentworth conveniently left for the country to pursue his duties. . . ." A lesser authority goes further: "beautiful, intelligent, wanton . . . she delighted to share her bed with any man in a position to further her social ambitions."

Though aging, John did not relax in his job; in the same month that William reported to Wales on the women of Halifax, the Surveyor returned from a trip of fantastic distance and "repeated shipwrecks," terminating with the "total destruction of my sloop . . . thank God I saved all my men." If tradition be trusted, Frances, now forty-two, did not cut back either. In the spring of 1787 William returned with a companion in dissipation, and Dyott, a young subaltern, also became her admirer. The two men would occasionally visit the brothels, apparently to watch. The women would perform with each other; William's passions aroused, he would "head straight for the arms of the pretty Mrs. Wentworth." He was twenty-one.

Frances had a sister at Halifax—Mary Brinley, wife of the commissary general—"whose habits," it was remarked, "are Equally pliable." But if the town deplored the Wentworth females, Frances's lot was much improved. John had bought them a modest country home on Bedford Basin, six miles out of town, which he named Friar Lawrence's Cell; though the scene much resembled Wolfeborough, his wife was very fond of the place. Fortune had other smiles in store. At last, in 1791, Frances had the opportunity to revisit England and her son, now sixteen. By this time William, now Duke of Clarence, had found a mistress who would last him twenty years; a famous actress called Mrs. Jordan, she had borne at least three bastards by the time she met him and would produce ten more. Frances hunted him down anyway, so it is reported, and "enticed him into a resumption of past pleasures." He presented her with a "Damask Sopha," and "they tried the length of it on the Queen's birthday." Thus Frances was in England at the moment she had been waiting for; back in Nova Scotia Governor Parr expired in an epileptic seizure. It is possible that at this point Clarence paid off a sexual debt; it is certain that Frances had never stopped reminding Lady Fitzwilliam that her ambition "rests in your favor." But this time she made clear that Halifax was where she wanted to be: "my situation would be so different going out with some rank to what it was before." The people of Nova Scotia, further, wished her husband in Parr's old post "with a solicitude you would scarce believe." Either way, royalty or nobility, she was once again a Governor's lady. On May 12, 1792, the H.M.S. *Hussar* sailed into the harbor, the guns boomed, and "the gaudiest era in the history of Halifax" had opened.

VERY LIKE PORTSMOUTH REPLAYED. The Governor built roads and defenses, France and England being at war again; he raised a regiment and commanded it, started a flour-milling industry and began to mine coal. There were new problems with minorities—sullen Acadians to be conciliated, Indians to be fitted into the economy, five hundred Maroons (Negro rebels deported from Jamaica) to be housed and cared for. But the Governor was as popular as he had ever been: "Around his chariot crowding numbers throng/And hail his virtues as he moves along." Frances still hoped that one day they would return to England and "lay our bones in quiet"; meanwhile she too was back in command. Shortly after her arrival she staged "the most brilliant and successful entertainment," thus read the gazette, "ever seen in this country." At Government House, "every room illuminated and elegantly decorated," there was dancing with two orchestras—cotillions upstairs and country dances down—until four in the morning. "Ease, elegance, and superiority of manners" gain Mrs. Wentworth the admiration, so the reporter runs on, of "the whole community." Not, it would appear, quite: the party "was only for the friends of the Governor and lady." Revenge was hers, and she got away with it. Social correspondence of the time is speckled with references to this "really wonderfully charming woman," or "hostess marvelously Gay." The first historian of Nova Scotia (1865) remarks that with her "personal beauty, graceful manners, intellectual attainments and ready wit," this first lady of the province "sustained her position in a manner that has never been equalled."

Thus it was precisely when she did not need it that her status got a sudden boost: Edward, a Soldier Prince and the King's fourth son, arrived and for six years added royal dignity and weight to an already splendid reign. As commander-in-chief he was convinced the French would try to retake Canada, using Halifax as a base, and he turned it into the strongest fortress outside Europe. There were not even rumors involving "the Circe of Government House"; Edward did not wench and was never drunk. He was twenty-seven, Frances forty-nine. And he had brought along the fabled and lovely Julie de St. Laurent, half Frances's age, who according to report had deserted her husband and child at Gibraltar to live with Edward in Quebec, whence they came. Frances immediately conformed to his rectitude, and the two couples became close friends; they often dined together, she at the Prince's left. For a time at Government House they all lived together. Evincing "a desire to promote social enjoyment and festivity," said the newspaper, Frances and John offered "scenes of gaiety and splendour" with "strains of Music." In one period of ten months the number of people dining with the Wentworths came to 2,437. Distinguished names were missing from the list. The chief justice at Halifax refused his invitation; his counterpart at Quebec was sympathetic, remarking that Frances as "first Female . . . in the Settlement" was making "matters unpleasant" by publicly entertaining the royal mistress. It was a neat reversal, and she scarcely suffered for it. In April of 1795 George III got around to making her husband a baronet; there was another gala, the Prince and all officers paying her a "special visit to congratulate her on her new title." As one in attendance observed, "The Baronet takes it very cooly, but her Ladyship is all smiles & joy."

When Edward and Julie wanted a house of their own, the Wentworths offered Friar Lawrence's Cell, which Edward completely rebuilt, setting little pagodas about the place, erecting a rotunda for band music, and a large barracks for his guard. For themselves the Wentworths constructed yet another country estate on a hilltop outside Preston, staffing it with servants white and black, and installing cannon to welcome guests. It was at that time, according to persistent rumor, that John "took revenge on the woman who had so often sent him forth from her bed to make way for other lovers" and fathered a child on "the most beautiful young virgin" among the Maroons who worked for him there. He also purchased a luxurious galley, rowed by many oars, for getting Frances and himself about the harbor. And in town at staggering cost a new and magnificent Government House was built for them. When Edward was recalled to England and returned to the Wentworths a Prince's Lodge, now quite grand, that had been a Cell, Frances had three splendid establishments where once were unpainted walls.

It is said that she cruised about the harbor "on her amorous quests" like an ageless Egyptian Queen; she was in fact fifty-three by now, and often too ill for that. In the spring of '98 she was anxious about her son at Oxford, also ailing; the *Indian Prince* was outfitted entirely for her comfort, and she sailed, took the waters at Bath and Bristol, and remained for a year and a half with the Fitzwilliams. She was presented at court, on July 5, 1798, by Lady Dorothy, and it has everywhere been reported that Queen Charlotte was so taken with her beauty and bearing that she made her "Lady in Waiting with a pension of 500 a year and permission to live abroad." Her son Charles, now recovered and a graduate of Oxford, where he had performed with distinction, was appointed to his father's Council and granted the same permission. He did visit his parents when they returned to Halifax, but soon departed for a tour of America and a call on President Adams. A couple of weeks after he left, Frances had unexpected visitors. "I hate Frenchmen," she wrote—but not "three very fine young Princes": the Duc d'Orléans, an old friend of Julie's, and his brothers. Edward asked that they be entertained; she gave a ball for three hundred; their Royal Highnesses were pleased. Thomas Moore ("Believe Me If All Those Endearing Young Charms") also paid a call and enjoyed it.

But "I move, crack goes my dress." She was putting on weight, and by 1801 steadily deploring her health: painful Spasms, "weakness and sad agues in my head that affects my hearing and eyesight." In semi-retirement at Bedford Basin, she no longer ruled over society. By 1809 the retirement was full, and all rule ended. "Dreadful illnesses," she writes Lady Dorothy, have rendered her old and feeble, sight and hearing "shockingly bad." She is fit only to "tend poultry—and feed my dogs." John, further, is "treacherously stripped" of office. Once again the Wentworths had remained monarchists in a society that no longer wanted them. There was opposition to his old practice of dominating the Assembly and stacking the Council—with specific objection to his having replaced, on his death, Frances's brother Benning as Secretary of the Province with his son Charles in England, the work to be done by a deputy. At the same time, forces in the States were hoping to grab Canada while England was busy with Napoleon;

in a show of strength the British dismissed and pensioned Sir John and replaced him with a military Governor. Next year he and Lady Frances returned to England on a leaking ship in the dead of winter. They "lay in a salt bath almost all the way"; the animals they brought with them all drowned on board. Frances's exile had lasted a quarter century.

The story ends, much as it began, with houses. In June Prince Edward writes Mrs. Fitzherbert, morganatic wife of the Prince of Wales, that her establishment is "too large for my friends," who are staying on at Nottingham Place. In April of 1812 Frances writes that there is to be a court on the thirtieth, but she is not inclined to attend, nor well enough, and would not be, she was sure, again. In July she reports that she and Sir John have driven out in search of a country house, and stopped at Castle Hill Lodge, Edward's estate at Ealing—a great columnar mansion he preferred to his Kensington Palace—to call on him and Julie. They found their house, and on February 14 of the next year, attended by Catherine Moody, her sister Mary Brinley's granddaughter, Frances died in it. She was buried at Sunning Hill, hard by Ascot in the long shadow of Windsor Castle. At the Church of St. Michael and All Angels the inscription on her tombstone announces

> *The remains of Frances Lady Wentworth, wife of Sir John Wentworth, Bart., are here deposited. . . . She encountered the tempest of a furious revolution, until driven by the rage of civil war from the land of her nativity, she found refuge with her only child in the bosom of the parent country. . . .*

John did not remain to lay his bones with hers, nor to accept an invitation to become a permanent guest at Castle Hill. He returned to Halifax, and where once he had been monarch of all he could survey he now moved like a wraith. Only Prince's Lodge still belonged to him, and that more than he could handle; he lived with the once pliable widow Brinley. He had a standing invitation to visit the States, and must have ached to see his old province, which over a generation before had expressed "kindness" toward him—particularly, after forty-five years, Wolfeborough. It was not out of bitterness that he stayed away. "I do most cordially," he wrote,

wish the most extensive, great, and permanent blessings to the United States. . . . If there is anything partial in my heart in this case, it is that New Hampshire, my native country, may arise to be among the most brilliant members of the Confederation; as it was my zealous wish, ambition, and unremitted endeavor to have led her to. . . . For this object nothing appeared to me too much. My whole heart and fortune were devoted to it.

But he was old and, according to Charles, suffering from a "paralytic disease." Mary Brinley died, and in January of 1820 so did Prince Edward. That news did not reach Halifax until April, where it was explained that the Governor

had been failing very gradually through the winter past . . . till the melancholy and unexpected account of the Duke of Kents death was confirmed when Sir Johns spirits sunk, his mind failed and he expired on the evening of the 8th Instant at half past Ten o clock.

He was eighty-three, and had been living on Hollis Street in Mrs. Fliegher's boardinghouse.

⌒II

HAUNTED HOUSES. Across the street from the Atkinsons' in Portsmouth, Thomas Bailey Aldrich grew up a *Bad Boy,* and long ago mused

Ah, that old house might tell a startling tale . . .
A curious legend, rather wild withal,

but he never got around to it. And that, for poets and the Wentworths, is just about the size of it. Sarah Wentworth Morton—Frances's niece, known in her day as the American Sappho—unsuccessfully invoked "The Shades of My Ancestors." A jingle, once popular, about the hasty remarriage (" 'Shame!' cried the gossips far and wide") died a natural death. In 1970 the late S. Foster Damon set to rhyme an old story telling how Frances and John, fleeing Wolfeborough in the spring of '75, took along a chest of silver too heavy for the horses and had to bury it in the woods. Benjamin Shillaber, another Portsmouth boy, had long before written out the same tale.

Frances in fiction has figured a little larger, beginning with an acid tale by one Adeline A. Knight in which "My Lady Wentworth" (1891) is a bad girl and the ruin of her husband. Cooling on him early, warming to his youthful secretary, she tolerates "freedoms" from the farmers at the husking bee, announcing that the Red Ear is "what all the maids want." When the setting shifts to the court of Queen Charlotte, the Duke of Queensberry ("Old Q, the Rake of Piccadilly," who in life preferred nymphets), joyfully observes "this little Wentworth hath spirit . . . reminds me of Coghlan" (Margaret Moncrieffe Coghlan, American-born courtesan). "Behaves like her too." Aroused by the association, he takes after Frances as the Governor, drunk and resigned to her "usual triumph," looks numbly on.

A promising start led to nothing, until of a curious sudden two novels called *The Governor's Lady* and *The Last Gentleman* appeared in 1960. Pointing with their titles to the fact that the heroine's story can only be told with the hero's, both books pronounce her "immoral" and provide her with a child, who dies seven months after her second marriage. Shirley Barker's *Gentleman* has a curious dream in which he hears a voice announcing "My doom is in Strafford," but in the novel it lies again in his wife. When another woman catches her with John's young aide, and sees "where your prying fingers went!" the question is if the Governor knows; it turns out he does.

Thomas Raddall's *Governor's Lady* is much the same woman but a different matter. Fiction, it also purports to present the historical Frances—a Siren who dominated the "best of the royal governors," who became ruler of Nova Scotia chiefly through her indiscretions. She seduces John in Portsmouth, signals him for repeat performances, marries him, and bears the child who dies. Living in London with Paul Wentworth, she is exposed to fashionable vice and easily embraces it, leaving a party to enjoy an anonymous young lover (who shows up later as Lieutenant Dyott, Prince William's companion at Halifax) and to return without being missed. In Nova Scotia she remains beautiful, wicked, and forever young. While John is in the forest she entertains the junior officers of Halifax; when he returns she sends him back to promote their affairs by conducting one with the Prince; when William leaves she takes on Dyott, who is then sent off when his Royal Highness comes back and surprises them together. This favor is repaid in England when the Prince secures for John the appointment as Governor. Predicting that he will be knighted, and she Ladied-in-Waiting, they sail for the New World to prepare for the arrival of Edward and Julie.

Raddall claims historicity; faced with his parade of Frances's lovers—anticipated by the unsubstantiated allegations of his history of Halifax—the reader is left to wonder where they came from. It is a problem old as the story: the fictionalization of reality is not peculiar to novelists. Anyone can play, as gossips do. And long have done with the Wentworths—from the start the subject of rumors, which at first circulated according to the workings of what might be called Instant Folklore. This concept, unknown to the trade, says that given certain circumstances people will improve on them. If it is believed that lovers meet clandestinely, and known that nothing blocks the view of one's residence from the other's, it is virtually inevitable that signals—if in fact there were none—will be invented. If a woman was close to her second husband before she married the first, it tidies things up to claim she meant to marry him originally, or wanted to. Someone will say such things, others repeat them, and we have "oral tradition," which is the definition of folklore (until it gets written down, which is its fate).

So, when reality fails, it is natural to supply what fiction—or anyone's sense of the fitness of things—demands. Frances's whole existence points to its climax, and no one since 1865 (when the event was apparently first recorded) has given her more than a couple of lines without telling how the Queen was so impressed at court that she was made Lady-in-Waiting. Doubtless Charlotte should have been, but it never happened in life. Folklore corrects its mistakes.

Other parts of the tale have been subjected to what is well known to folklore as the Law of Contrast. According to its operation, stories of the likes of Benning's marriage to Martha Hilton will heighten the difference in age and social station—and point up the first by placing the event on his birthday. Benning was born in July; the wedding was in March. He was sixty-three not sixty. Three to one obtains; Martha was twenty-three not twenty. Her family was older in Portsmouth than his, Hiltons having founded the place; the reason for servitude was that her father had been killed at Louisbourg, leaving his children without means.* Such is the power of the Law that Martha's subsequent marriage to Michael Wentworth has been mostly ignored. When Michael left the Governor's house at the time of John's wedding, and fell in with the Wretched Low People, he had a happy secret: as signed witness to Benning's will, made out a year before the old man died, he knew the destination of the money he was going to marry.†

Twists in Contrast. More in accord with the old Law, it is natural that if a mulatto child is born to a black Maroon on a plantation outside Halifax, gossip will assign paternity to the great white owner. And understandable that child and descendants will choose to believe. There was such a child; in 1947 Thomas Raddall visited a small house next to a depression in the ground—all that was left of the Wentworth mansion at Preston, Nova Scotia

---

*The whole story of that famous dinner party, standardized as one of the *Tales of a Wayside Inn* and endlessly repeated, is probably specious. Thomas Wentworth Higginson dismissed the poet's version of it by citing a niece of Benning's who protested Longfellow's "making it appear that any others than the family were present to witness what they considered a great degradation"—Martha being, after all, a maid.

†Also ignored is the fact that Michael and his old friend John had a bad falling out; not long after his marriage to Martha the groom was assisting the Governor's two chief enemies, Peter Livius and Woodbury Langdon, in an attempt to unseat him. John believed that Benning, "extremely debilitated with Infirmity, was prevailed on to destroy his will . . . to the utter disherison of myself & every other Relative he had." It is also possible that Benning was coolly arranging his wife's future.

—and found an aged Negro who introduced himself with pride as John Wentworth Colley, great-grandson of the Governor. The novelist had been led to the spot by a little 1893 history of the place, in which the daughter of a contemporary there of John and Frances remarked that the house had fallen forty years back, but that "George Colley, an illegitimate coloured son of the great governor, is still living" there, with descendants. A recent claim is that the line started with an Irish workman on the estate. But it is unsupported, and Nova Scotia historians have chosen to agree with the Colleys about their progenitor. Rightly, perhaps, but without the contrast they have no story.

Spontaneous folklore can repeat ancient. Hero Returns and Marries First Love, Unfaithful Wife Signals Lover When He Must Come—many such Wentworth motifs are officially classified. All very well, life being at liberty to imitate folk art equally with formal. The tale of Frances locked out at Wolfeborough, however, is plagiarism; Type K, #1511, in the *Motif-Index* reads

Adultress returns home late at night and her husband refuses to admit her, she threatens to throw herself into the well. The husband goes after her. She enters the house and bars him out

—and has been traced immemorially from India across Europe to a Boston chapbook of 1794.

Wentworth folklore is otherwise of origin miscellaneous and unknown. The tale of Frances and John burying the silver in the forest has occasioned a great deal of strenuous digging, but rightly found its way into Skinner's *Myths and Legends of Our Own Land*. The cherished tradition which says that Frances wed her second Harvard cousin because the first had left for England has forever eluded the record; she may have had her eye on John when he was at Cambridge, though she was ten when he graduated, or in Portsmouth later on. But she married Atkinson at King's Chapel in May, 1762, and Wentworth didn't take sail until the fall of '63. Cusk are still being taken from what is now called Lake Wentworth: no great ichthyologistical surprise, since these cod are indigenous to fresh waters of the region. (If the Governor transplanted some to his pond, the incumbent Chief of Fisheries suggests, "he stocked them on top of a resident population.") Jonathan Swift never had a secretary named Arthur Browne.

From such traditions we have the character of Frances Wentworth herself. Her affair with Prince William was long simply Halifax gossip vaguely remembered; the notion that the relationship was resumed in England rests on nothing but a letter which reports the gift of that sofa "they tried the length of" (it actually reads "she tried") on the Queen's birthday. If back at Portsmouth she was bedding with the Governor while Atkinson perished, and hurried the wedding because she was pregnant, there is no published evidence of it. "Most aristocratic ladies of the day were snobbish," and "not very scrupulous sexually," so it has been argued. It would not be surprising if Frances were the same. But that is from a British viewpoint, born of familiarity with English fashion; if it pertains to American ladies there has been remarkably little demonstration of it. And if she were not different in kind, there would still be the matter of degree. But mostly there is the matter of separating her from legend.

The ultimate meaning of an eye "full of promises and denial," as another lady long ago read it, has a formal interpretation. Chiseled in stone, it is an unequivocal one, forever to be seen at her grave in Sunning Hill, where her epitaph concludes:

> *A most affectionate mother and unblemished wife, she rendered up her soul to God through Christ, in the principles of the Established Church of England, MDCCCXIII.*

If that is even roughly valid it follows, item, that Frances was no American Ninon de Lenclos, fabled courtesan who drove men wild with desire in her old age. Her health would not have permitted such a role had she chosen it. Still beautiful in her forties, she began complaining about her weight, and after she reached fifty she was often and seriously ill. In addition to the unexplained failures of sight and hearing, the dreadful headaches and Spasms, she was reported by a doctor, shortly before she journeyed to England for the baths, to be dying—"after an illness of three days, supposed a pleurisy." Later on she herself describes a case of what was evidently not as she called it the "water Brash":

one night as she retched in the dark and John brought a candle, they were "Horror Struck . . . to see a Bason half full of clear blood with a number of large clots floating and swiming in it." (In three weeks she was improved, but "kept wild by anodynes.") Long half an invalid, and completely one before she died at sixty-eight of cause unknown in a rural parish of Windsor, Lady Wentworth had for some time been waiting for little but her demise.

A snob she was, classic. She knew her place, viewed all beneath her from a height, and on those above looked with awe and fawned. During a visit to Brussels in 1781—meeting princes, breakfasting with one, and sitting "a whole evening" at a concert next to Marie Christine, sister of Marie Antoinette—she was in ecstasy. At London she would issue bulletins from court—the "great *Personage* is very ill indeed . . . his mind is *disturbed*"—and exult in all news of the royal family. Thrust into the English aristocracy, many provincial ladies would have reacted this way. But snobbery with Frances was a pursuit; she had early discovered her talent for the obsequious and learned its uses. After the birth of Charles-Mary she wrote Lady Rockingham that she nursed the infant herself out of gratitude for his name and sponsorship. Nobility like royalty expected this sort of thing and readily accepted it, but in her tireless zeal to promote her status Frances achieved a sycophancy as pure as could be found this side the ocean.*

Most affectionate mother she was not, having virtually given up an only child at eight so that he could attend a fashionable school, and never living with him for any extended period again. As a young man she found him superior and dogmatic; when she hopes that Prince Edward will support him, she is quick to point out that Charles does not deserve it, never having shown a proper respect for the Duke's station. "I can never make out that boy," she writes; "a strange creature and his opinions, no per-

---

* She had also a taste for melodrama, beginning the letter about the water Brash: "in all human possibility I shall be at rest before this reaches you." She had asked Lady Rockingham to believe that in escaping Portsmouth she hadn't a moment to grab a blanket for the baby but managed to carry along the letter she was writing to her.

son on earth but Lord Fitzwilliam would make him deviate from."

Unblemished wife: that is the question, and she herself threw little doubts on the claim. When she first rejoices in the presence of Prince William at Halifax she also observes that she is not fit "for this cold climate where one ought to be as frozen as the seasons." Her "steps," she admits in another letter, are "often giddy"; in still another, "I can't govern my feelings, they are so quick and irresistable." Portsmouth had certainly been skeptical of her chastity. At the peak of her social triumph there, the Governor had noted "oblique insults" (which she regarded "with pity and contempt"). What their nature may have been was suggested by Woodbury Langdon, a political foe of John's but well acquainted with Frances, whose guest he had been at Wolfeborough. When the Governor sailed to join his wife in England, Langdon wrote that "on his arrival there, he will . . . be presented with a pair of GOLDEN HORNS, which will . . . fit as easy on his pate, as those he formerly wore at Portsmouth," and published his prediction in the newspaper.

But it was for straying into his bed that Frances was chiefly known in that town, and for the sudden wedding that gossip said resulted. Completely overlooked in that oft-told tale is the question of her condition at the time. Atkinson was dying a wretched and protracted death, about which nothing could be done, and she may reasonably have felt that if she was to live herself she had best seize the day. Her father had died; so very recently had her cousin Thomas, John's brother, leaving five children. Her brother Henry—rusticated from Harvard for Confessed Drunkenness—had gone to sea and, not yet twenty, drowned in the wreck of his ship; at Oxford her brother Samuel, recently "prohibited, banished from" the company of his beloved Miss Lane (which caused his cousin John to "fear some rash act from his despair"), had on his nineteenth birthday taken poison and died with the girl. Nor did people know about a letter, buried over two hundred years in Yorkshire, which flatly contradicts the rumors about the circumstances of her second marriage. Cited here with permission of the present Earl Fitzwilliam, proprietor of the muniments, it is addressed to Rockingham on November 2, 1770, by Wentworth himself, who had announced a year before "my domestic felicity completed, by an Union with Mrs. Atkinson." Now he gives the "full state of this alliance," rehearsing for the first time the innocent events that speeded it.

His parents, he explains, were first to know, two days after the funeral, of his intent regarding his cousin. Their "satisfaction in it . . . beyond expression," they "insisted on the earliest completion thereof, that circumstances and Custom would permit." Next he told "the good old governor," who "pray'd me it might be directly done, lest he might not live to see it." Then he "resolved to mention it to Col Atkinson & wife," who accepted the death of their son as his relief from misery ("the last two or three years . . . his reason impaired by violent fits"). Atkinson promised John that Frances would make him happy, and

There I expected the affair would have rested, until the mourn.g weeds were something rusty: But the old Gent. says to me

Sir, as you are determin'd upon the matter, I wish it may be directly:
I am an old Man . . . there need be no delay.

I suggested to him, that perhaps a proposal might come unexpectedly.

Sir—my Daughter is a Woman of Sense. I will undertake to communicate your intentions to her, and . . . obviate all ceremonial difficulties.

He was sure of success; and therefore invited me . . . the same Day to Tea, & he would settle the matter.

On this occasion Frances was allowed to speak, and

I was frankly told

Sir your proposal is eligible. . . . I give you my Heart and will ratify it with my Hand, in proper time.

Col Atkinson replyed

You are both agreed—Why then delay, for what you call a proper time —the old lady beg'd her daughter wd. sacrifice her forms . . . to her Age and exhausted life . . . almost expir'd.

The betrothed gave way, the Atkinsons fixed the date. And then John supplied the one fact that remained to be reported of the allied state in requesting that offspring of the union be named for his Lordship or Lady: "We are still in hopes, the Loss we sustain'd from Mrs. Wentworth's being frighted by an attack of a large dog,

which caus'd her miscarriage, will be one day repair'd; and per-
fected. . . ."

It is possible that no one was ever pleased with Wentworth's
drawing room comedy but the author of it. Old Mrs. Atkinson did
expire within a month, and Benning a year, but the large dog is
no clumsier than the rest of the script; encountering the beast the
scribe's pen, normally slanted and fluent, stilts in amazement.
There was no miscarriage; the reason for haste was that he had
got his cousin with child—as "The Parish Record of Queen's
Chapel . . . during the Rectorship of Rev. Arthur Browne, 1738–
1773," under Baptisms for 1770 makes clear:

Portsmouth June 9th John son of John & Frances Wentworth P.B.

That date is seven months less two days from the date of the
marriage, baptism then normally following birth by one to four
weeks. There was no celebration, such as that which would greet
Charles-Mary; John Junior apparently died soon—clearly before
his father wrote that letter; there is no record of burial, or a
funeral.*

What Frances Wentworth was really up to in Halifax during the
absences of the Surveyor, whom she still called the Governor,
would be lost to history save for the fact that the lieutenant who
was partner to Prince William's carousing there kept a diary
(published early in this century and the tacit source of Raddall's
allegations). William Dyott was chiefly impressed with the drinking. When anyone lagged in refilling, the Prince would bellow:

---

*The chapel burned down in 1806; its records and silver service survived the fire,
and St. John's now stands on the site—over Benning's tomb, in which Arthur
Browne, though he died in Cambridge, is appropriately installed. The original
record turns out to be missing, but had been painstakingly copied by a subsequent rector. Thomas Raddall knew of this entry, but thought P.B. signified
premature birth, leaving the matter theoretically in doubt. It is not plausible that
a cleric would pronounce on the development of a newborn infant. In the
records of King's Chapel, Boston—which were returned after Rev. Caner carried them off when he fled to Halifax on John's schooner, and show Frances's
baptism—the term Private Baptism is spelled out. The fact is that where there
was "great cause and necessity" (as appears to have been frequently), the Book
of Common Prayer for the Church of England provided—still provides—a special ceremony for "The Ministration of Private Baptism of Children in Houses."

"I see some of God Almighty's daylight in that glass, Sir; banish it!" He gave extravagant shipboard parties; Reel Britannia, the celebration of the King's birthday, was so intense that a frigate ablaze only five miles off, firing signals in all directions, went down without the rescue of a hand. As for the wenching, Dyott is more reticent—about himself.

The royal William had become acquainted with obliging women of Halifax late in 1786; Dyott arrived the next year and in October met the Prince, who had returned from the West Indies. The two got "literally drunk almost every day" and cruised the town, visiting appropriate females. The diarist first mentions his companion and a specific lady when on a Sunday morning

I met him after church at Mrs. Wentworth's, Governor Wentworth's lady. He was gone up to the country on business, as he is surveyor-general of the woods of this province. . . . His Royal Highness used to be there frequently.

So did Dyott, and not, apparently, for tea. On the following Wednesday the pair of them went to

dinner at Governor Wentworth's, or rather Mrs. Wentworth's, the Governor being away from home. Mrs. Wentworth is a most charming woman, but unhappily for her husband, rather more partial to our sex than her own. But he, poor man, cannot see her foibles, and they live very happy. I believe there was a mutual passion which subsisted between his Royal Highness and her. She is an American, but has lived a good deal in England and with people of the first fashion. As I was pretty intimate at the house she desired me to dine there.

Frances's disrepute in the capital, it then becomes obvious, was not the result of this princely passion but had so far preceded it that William thought better of appearing with her in public. After dinner, to prepare for a ball,

RH dressed at Mrs. Wentworth's and went in her carriage, but not with her, as the ladies of Halifax are a little scrupulous of their virtue and think it in danger if they were to visit Mrs. Wentworth. For my part I think her the best-bred woman in the province.

The next Thursday evening he and William "strolled about the town, went to some houses of a certain description, and to be sure had some pretty scenes." What goes in between these entries must be inferred, but the following morning, "I met him at Mrs. Wentworth's." That evening was another ball, and RH dressed there again. He sailed off at the start of 1788, but next August returned most unexpected:

I . . . was engaged to spend the evening at Mrs. Wentworth's. When we had done supper . . . in came the Prince. I had the honour to light him to his chamber, as he had a bed from Mrs. Wentworth.

A week later the men were together with Frances again; Dyott mentions dining at the Governor's four months later, and with him a year after. By then the Prince was long gone, having left his friend thinking: "I shall never spend three months in that way again, for such a time of dissipation, etc., etc., I cannot suppose possible to happen."

Thus Dyott did not believe that the Governor facilitated his wife's adultery by taking to the woods, but was lost in a pastoral innocence where the lieutenant profited as much as the Prince. But his Highness, who yearned for females who "would not pox or clap me every time," was capable of being shocked by one his companion admired. After the night he discovered Dyott with Frances, he is recorded as having visited her only once more— for reason unknown, until a letter in his own cramped hand turned up in some musty Maritime Archives in London. Writing at Halifax on September 13, 1788, to a fellow officer named Keats, William muses on "the comforts of matrimony":

Your friend Wentworth is inspecting the woods of New Brunswick and is not expected back till the middle of November. in the mean time Madam is amusing herself with an officer and has I am sorry to say thrown off all remaining decency.

He doesn't name Dyott; from the look of the diary it was someone else.

◈III

BLOSSOMING LILACS. Out at Little Harbor by the water's edge the shrubs Benning was proud of are enormous; the mansion, a noble old pile, looks much as it must have to Frances. So do many of the houses she knew in town, including the one she lived in with John. A fragile gown and some chairs that have had their legs shortened suggest a small woman; there are few other relics. But the dark maroon paper she had on the walls of her drawing room has unaccountably not faded. Looking at the only sample of her intricate needlework that survives, a Portsmouth matron can still be heard to remark, "Her sewin' was better'n her morals."

She has only the vaguest idea why she says that, except that others do. Told that the same woman—child in arms, newly arrived in London from the provinces—was received by the King and Queen of England, she would have no idea what to make of it. The relations of Frances and John to people of the great world are a story little known to Portsmouth or anywhere else, discursive but to a point. Their history, punctuated with names unavoidably dropped, is exactly as they saw it: their stature can be roughly measured by taking the size of their connections. Even a forgotten girl in the cast of characters is worth notice. Catherine Moody, Frances's grandniece who attended her in her last illness, grew up to be Mrs. Gore. The wife of an army officer retired to stud, she turned out ten children and some two hundred volumes of fiction, drama, and verse to support them by; before she went totally blind, there was no more popular writer in England.

Many a titled English lady went through life without a close relation to any member of the royal family; Frances had connections with two princes—whose fates would be linked after her death in ways she could never have foreseen. No one could have predicted the future of William the debauched. After fathering a family on Mrs. Jordan, he married properly, settled in as King William the Fourth, reigned through the greatest period of reform in England's history, and be-

queathed to his heir "the securest throne in Europe," which
he had inherited "in tatters." Meanwhile Dyott had become
an entirely circumspect full General.

From the time they met until the last visit, the closest friends
the Wentworths had were Edward and his lovely mistress. Julie
"of an hundred names and titles," as John called her—it was
Alphonsine Thérèse Bernadine Julie de St. Laurent de Mont-
genêt, Baronne de Fortisson—was already gathering legend. Of
noble blood, she fled France with husband and child and left both
for Edward, by whom she had seven children (hidden by him to
escape his father's notice); gently dismissed by him after twenty-
seven years, she married an Italian Prince and lived out her days
near Quebec, where she died at the age of one hundred and six.
That, until recently corrected, was a typical account; Julie was in
fact a middle-class beauty, mistress of three men and never a wife
or mother. After leaving Edward she went to Paris, where she was
watched over by the Duc d'Orléans, her friend for forty years,
whom Frances had entertained long before at Halifax. She died
just short of her seventieth birthday; within twenty-four hours her
Duke was Louis Philippe, King of France.

Wentworth lived to see the end of the royal liaisons, occasioned
in 1817 by the death in childbirth of Princess Charlotte, heir
presumptive to the throne. The government instructed the Dukes
of Kent (Edward), Clarence (William), Cambridge, and Sussex to
wed promptly and reproduce legitimately. Edward had laid eyes
on his bride exactly once; he and William married in a double
ceremony in July of 1818, and Yoicks! wrote Peter Pindar,

The Royal sport's begun
I'faith but it is glorious fun
For hot and hard each Royal pair
Are at it hunting for the heir.

By Christmas both Clarence and Kent were expectant fathers, and
so was Cambridge. But William's heir was premature and died.
Shortly thereafter Sir John—"one of my best and oldest friends"
—received a letter from Edward: "You will, I am sure, be pleased
to know that the Duchess has been able to suckle her child from

the first." The infant's name, to the satisfaction of neither parent, was Victoria.

Frances and John could trace their ancestry no further back than to the first American Wentworth, who came here as a dissenting churchman in 1637. It would have pleased them to know that they were twenty-seven generations in direct descent from the first known English Wentworth, Rynold of Winterwade (fl. 1066, etc.). The belief that they were somehow related to the Second Marquis of Rockingham was sound; for twelve generations they were in the same line. And it was reasonable that they regarded Charles Watson-Wentworth (1730–82) as a figure of importance. When in 1765 John resided with him at Wentworth Woodhouse, deplored the Stamp Tax, and became an admirer of his private secretary Edmund Burke, he was Prime Minister of Great Britain; it was his government that repealed the Act. By the time Frances and Charles-Mary were established with him he was long out of power, but a considerable force in opposition to the war and, as he said, the "ministerial imbecilities that had provoked it." He awaited the day when it might be ended; and in 1782, with the surrender of Cornwallis and the resignation of Lord North, that day dawned. On condition that there be "no veto to the independence of America," he accepted the government again—then died without having found a spot for the Americans whose fortunes most concerned him.

Rockingham's estate in Yorkshire—the product, over the centuries, of various strategic marriages—was very great; when his nephew William Wentworth Fitzwilliam added it, and an extra £40,000 per year, to his own magnificent estate in Northamptonshire his wealth was immense. The Earl had the finest stables and kennels in England, and was himself sometimes suggested as a Whig Prime Minister. That is what Frances had in mind, but he had to settle for a stint as Lord Lieutenant of Ireland. Paul Wentworth, the most intriguing man in her life, settled for less.

Shortly after Frances was joined by her husband in England, John Adams in Paris attended a performance of Voltaire's *Brutus* at the Comédie Française. As he left his box a man seized him by the hand:

"Governor Wentworth, sir," said the gentleman. . . . I knew not how to behave towards him. As my classmate, and friend at college, and ever since, I could have pressed him to my bosom. . . . But we now belonged to two different nations at war with each other.

Adams was also nervous at the thought that John was surely "watched by the spies of the police, and our interview would be known the next morning at Versailles." Wentworth was perfectly at ease, inquired after the health of Benjamin Franklin,

and said he must come out to Passy, and pay his compliments. . . . Dr. Franklin and I received him together; but there was no conversation but upon trifles. . . . Not an indelicate expression to us, or our country, or our ally, escaped him. His whole behaviour was that of an accomplished gentleman.

"The governor's motives for this trip to Paris," Adams adds, "I never knew." Neither does history. But John took the occasion of the trip to Passy to tell his old friend that "upon his Honour . . . he never wrote the Letters that were published in his name . . . and never had any Concern in Counterfeiting. . . ."* As for Paris, he was probably on a "special mission" which almost certainly had to do with Paul Wentworth, his "dear friend and close relation." They never knew the degree of it; Paul's public life is obscure, the secret part discoverable in some detail.

He is often thought to have been an American, but nothing is surely known of this Wentworth until, when Frances was about five, he appeared in Boston bearing letters to her father and John's. Well educated, no one knows where, he was wealthy—his own explanation being that he had married a rich widow in Surinam, Dutch Guinea, who had died childless and left him her estate. In 1757 he paid for a pew in Queen's Chapel, Portsmouth.

---

* Recent research suggests otherwise. He had urged his "warm friend" Stephen Holland to stay in New Hampshire and "use his arts" against the rebels. Holland organized a chain of friends to pass the British-made American bills, and was not discovered until a boy in a barn in Connecticut, looking in the hay for eggs, found a packet of letters implicating him in the highly effective operation—some of them written by the deposed Governor. One of Holland's accomplices, also exposed, fled to join Wentworth's Volunteers.

When Frances's first husband died, the Governor asked that Paul —of Portsmouth and "large property . . . now in London"—be appointed to the Council in his place; it was done, but he never attended any of the meetings. In 1770 he was still in London, where he dealt in New Hampshire lands; Milan, New Hampshire, was originally Paulsburgh. He paid for the survey of the province that John promoted; he was a substantial benefactor of Dartmouth, which gave him an honorary degree. For a time in London he was friendly with Franklin, who is said to have lived briefly at his house. His knowledge of the eventual Patriot leaders, north to south, was exhaustive and shrewd; no one knows how he acquired it.

By the time Frances lived with him in London he was wealthier. King George denigrated him as a stock-jobber: "a low wretch, buying and selling shares in the funds" (stock in the national debt), and "a dabbler in the Alley" (Change Alley). He was in fact a gentleman, an international speculator with agents in Amsterdam, Lisbon, and Hamburg and a reputation for uncommon financial integrity. Living in Paris at the time when he had instructed Frances to say he was in Holland, he was received by Louis XVI and dined by Vergennes, the French Foreign Minister. He was a close friend of the philosopher Abbé Raynal and of Beaumarchais, friend of America, and business genius who on the side wrote plays, such as *The Marriage of Figaro* which, set to music, are still performed. Beaumarchais warned Vergennes about Paul: he speaks French "as well as you do and better than I," and is "one of the cleverest men in England." It was easy to get carried away.

"No government"—thus a British historian—"was ever better served by its informers than that of George the Third, or possessed more accurate information of its enemies most hidden plans"; if the King had believed what he was told and made the concessions to the colonies that were urged on him, he "almost certainly would have preserved his Empire." Questionable, both claims. But there is no doubt at all—as Prime Minister North told his Majesty—that his "most important and truest informer," the same man who was urging the concessions that might have held the colonies, was Paul Wentworth super-spy. "He carried a private cipher on his person with receipts for various invisible inks. He went under twenty different names, kept as many addresses, and directed an intricate organization on the Continent." It was through Paul that the King got regular bulletins on the progress of America's highly secret and lengthy negotiations which brought about the Alliance with France that cost England the war, as well as the private correspondence of the Congress with its Commissioners at Passy—Franklin and Silas Deane—on the departure of ships carrying supplies from France to America, and other sensitive matters. Wentworth desperately believed that he could end a needless war on terms beneficial to both sides. His labors in trying to get the Commissioners to accept a conciliatory arrangement with Great Britain, then in trying to get the King to offer it, were Herculean. George admired his skill and his zeal, but thought his agent was circulating bad news to depress the funds and make a killing—further, since the Americans could offer nothing in return for France's support, that no Alliance would be made. The French feared him so much that Alliance was speeded lest his efforts to end the war might succeed.

Paul's instructions were "to take handsome lodgings, support them, take a mistress, induce intelligence, seduce it." He carried them out. The mistress, as Vergenne's agent reported, "is called Mdlle. Desmailles and lives in Rue Traversiere." Wentworth professed indifference to her, he observed, but "often goes to see her"; indeed he invited M. Favier, the "unsavoury" agent who was spying on him, to dine with him there. His seduction of intelligence was shrewder. He was the only man alive who knew that there was in London one prestigious Patriot in American pay, the close friend and confidant of Franklin, who was sufficiently cupiditous to be bought and clever enough to get away with it.

When a boy in Massachusetts Dr. Edward Bancroft had run off to sea and lived for a time in Surinam, where as a burgeoning scientist he had become interested in vegetable dyes and poisons. Later in England he studied medicine, then served his country as a spy for Dr. Franklin, subsequently for Silas Deane. There he remained until his connection with John the Painter, who proposed to lose the war for England by burning her shipyards, became known. Now more than ever the spotless rebel Bancroft took off for Paris, to the delight of Franklin and Deane, who housed him as their private secretary at Passy until he eventually established a place for his mistress. The British watched him to the point of assigning a spy to that nameless woman; the Americans trusted him absolutely. What everyone overlooked was the Surinam connection. Bancroft was on record as having served there as "Surgeon to a Gentleman of Fortune, Owner of two large Plantations"; the fortunate gentleman was Paul: "I engaged him Seven Years ago to live on my estates, and explore Nature to discover New Subjects of Commerce." Bancroft was reborn as "Dr. Edwards."

All sheets of Paul's private cipher survive—seven pages of proper names and common words to be designated in alphabetical order by digits (Washington was 206, Benedict Arnold 13), and signs (⊖ = not). So, written out in his own hand on December 5, 1776, exists the "Engagement of Dr. Edwards to correspond with Paul Wentworth . . . & the Means," which were extraordinary. Bancroft was to compose letters on Gallantry—his intelligence interlined in invisible ink which would turn "reddish and very legible" when brushed with the Brown Tincture. He was to deposit such matter for Wentworth "every Tuesday Evening after half past nine" in a "Hole at the root" of the "Tree pointed out on the S. Terrace of the Tuilleries." Letters to Bancroft were to be sealed in a bottle "tyed by the Neck with a common twyne," and placed under the "Box-Tree agreed on" at the W. side of the gardens, in front of the Louvre.

A scheme out of Hannibal, Missouri, a century later; but it worked, was never exposed, and never known to any but the King, a few top ministers, and almost surely John and Frances. Paul was a gentleman, so humiliated at the thought of being also a spy that he kept his secret as elaborately from the friends who would have applauded him as foes. He found the work utterly degrading but was tireless at it. Hounded by those who were spying on him, he lived in fear of assassination—or worse, perhaps, imprisonment as a common criminal. After his strongbox was broken into he burned all his papers but "the Cypher—which I carry very intimately about me." Everything he owned, he remarked, was in Surinam or his pocket. His salary came to no more, he cheerfully computed, than it cost him to support the American Wentworths, but to Lord North's consternation he refused any other "indemnification or emollument." What he wanted was what a gentleman could earn: a title and a seat in Parliament. On the news of Saratoga, the Prime Minister rushed him across the Channel to make an elaborately secret, last ditch effort to forestall the French Alliance. Empowered to satisfy all demands of the colonists except Independence, he also offered a loan of £30 million. Franklin told him that he had no power to make peace with Great Britain, and that America would never consent to it without Independence. As late as 1783 he was reported by John Adams to be still effectively in service—"making a party unfriendly to us" at The Hague. But by then he had begun to recede into the shadows he came out of. He never got the title; the seat in the House of Commons lasted only a few months. In 1790 he quit, sold Brandenburgh House,* and returned to Surinam where, according to the *Gentleman's Magazine,* he died "suddenly" in December of '93. So in England, reputedly a suicide, did Silas Deane.† Dr. Bancroft, rewarded for his trea-

---

*An anachronism everywhere encountered; the mansion was not so called until long after, or much known until Queen Caroline of Brunswick, consort of George IV, lived there while being tried in the House of Lords for sexual immorality. She died there, and the house was torn down for a factory.

†As Paul Wentworth learned, Deane and Bancroft were profiteering in purchasing supplies for Congress, and involved in various other forms of double-dealing. Deane, not Bancroft, was widely believed to be guilty of such practices, and after the war stayed abroad, took to drink and tawdry women, and in 1789 had so deteriorated as to be convinced, apparently, that he could vindicate himself in this country. He took his dose of laudanum, set sail, and died immediately; 170 years later a scholar, Julian Boyd, published an exhaustive investigation of his relations with Bancroft, and came to an unlikely but convincing conclusion. Bancroft had described the chemical characteristics of curare, a "preparation," he wrote, "capable of perpetrating the most secret and fatal villainy," and had brought a store of it to London from Paul's Surinam plantations. Knowing that Deane could never clear himself in America but could (especially when drunk or in introducing his papers in defense of his activities) incriminate them both, the kindly doctor spared him, put curare in his laudanum, started the rumor that

son with a handsome secret pension from the British government, lived out his life full of honor; a Fellow in the Royal Society, he made useful discoveries in the area of textile dyes. When he expired in 1820 his luster as a Patriot was in America untarnished, and he was seventy years in his grave before his connection with Paul Wentworth was discovered.

In 1792 Paul received from Nova Scotia (coals to Newcastle) nineteen able-bodied blacks guaranteed to multiply—a gift of Maroons from the deeply indebted John and Frances. Aside from that, almost nothing is known of his last years in the tropics. Perhaps he lived the life of the typical white planter of Surinam —an existence, according to eyewitness accounts, of savage, elegant decadence unparalleled: brutally whipped slaves, seraglios of sable sultanas, and white ladies who "indulge themselves just as much by giving way to their unbounded passions" (their "natural imperfections," it was believed, ripened in the steamy climate). In any event he lasted only three years at "Kleinhope," the distressed name of his chief plantation up the river from Paramaribo. He had, according to the only story, before leaving England sent to the West Indies—probably the Barbados—for a nephew, Nathaniel Wentworth, whom he adopted as a son. One night he heard a horse trampling his tropical garden, chased it off, caught a cold, and died of a fever. Nathaniel, his heir, deciding to return home, converted his rich properties to cash, took ship, and was lost at sea with his fortune. Rumors that the crew murdered him for his money were "never credited."

If details of the demise of Paul Wentworth seem no more plausible than that Silas Deane would commit suicide on setting out for his homeland, it is because they suggest more the Victorian imagination—adopted son and heir, fluky death, disappeared fortune—than eighteenth-century reality. They were furnished by Mrs. Gore herself, who at the time of those events was six years unborn. Thus Paul's end may be as obscure as his origin—and, finally, his identity. The genealogy of the Wentworth family has

---

he committed suicide, and, it is probable, wrote his obituary for the *Gentleman's Magazine.*

been traced with extraordinary thoroughness and skill, and a strenuous effort was made to locate him. Whatever Frances, John, the Rockinghams and Fitzwilliams believed, the conclusion is that he was not related to them. Conceivable, at least, that when he first showed up with a winning name, and letters to influential men so called, he had chosen it himself.

ᴄᴡIV

WILD STRAWBERRIES. It all began with the smell of them, in the summer of 1603, as the *Speedwell* plied its way up the Piscataqua River, in what is now New Hampshire, searching for sassafras—devoutly prized in London as "a plant of sovereign vertue for the French Poxe." The men landed, ate fruit, departed. Nine years later John Smith explored the region, and on his advice a small plantation was settled at Strawbery Banke, by two Hilton brothers from London, for the purpose of shipping fish to England. The coastal waters teemed with them; the forests were crowded with great white pines; and the streams had waterfalls for mills. Masts and inexpensive timber: geography is destiny.

History is destiny. By 1670 the Isles of Shoals, just off the coast, were dotted with huts of fishermen. One of the islands, "Smuttynose," was a beacon: it boasted a tavern, an Anglican church, and a problem with vice so severe that for a time all females were banned from it (which led to the lucky discovery that "as many men may share a woman as they do a boat"). The Puritans had of course arrived as well. The heretical John Wheelwright, who played football at Oxford with Oliver Cromwell, had been shipped to the little province, with followers, from the Massachusetts Bay Colony at the same time his antinomian sister-in-law Anne Hutchinson had been deported to Rhode Island. But early New Hampshire divines—at York, Dover, and Hampton—were known less for schism than scandal. The pastor at Dover excommunicated his rival for, among other things, Unchastity, only to be caught the next night in bed with his maid; the Reverend

Batchelor freely admitted at eighty to soliciting his neighbor's wife, and at ninety committed bigamy. New Hampshire was not Massachusetts. Even Cotton Mather understood that; in 1702 he himself told the story of the preacher from the region of Boston who addressed the settlers of Portsmouth. Reminding them of "the main end of Planting this Wilderness," the purer worship of Jehovah, he was interrupted in the middle of his sermon: "Sir, you are mistaken, you think you are preaching to the People at the Bay; our main End was to catch fish."

Exactly so, and in the same spirit a century later, beauty, rank, and reputation would render Frances Wentworth unique. She was, however, a Governor's lady in a very special place: an independent, materialistic colony competing with a long-stronger Puritan commonwealth, and growing into a rival province largely because of the emergence of a tiny affluent minority which established an oligarchy like nothing ever seen in Massachusetts. Viewed against that backdrop, the girl from Boston who would become the toast and talk of two capitals seems simply an end product of the history of Portsmouth.

With the early development of the Piscataqua trade, signs of gold rapidly began to appear at the mouth of the river. Merchant shipowners, who before long would build the ships themselves, set to exporting fish, fur, masts, and boards. In 1671 they could afford to import wine and brandy in the amount of three hundred tons; for polite manners and gracious hospitality the town would soon have a small fame. After the English example, the practice of concentrating wealth and the power that follows from it by arranging marriages to protect and promote the interests of property was established. Among leading families, as church records show, pregnancies occasionally preceded weddings.

The best way to enjoy and exhibit wealth was to build a big house. The golden age of construction began in 1716; Captain Macpheadris erected a stunning mansion and started the vogue for the "classic revival"—the Georgian or Palladian style, which in New England meant classic moldings, panelings and cornices, elegant mantelpieces, and graceful stairway balustrades—that distinguished Portsmouth architecture. In it he installed Frances's great-aunt, his bride Sarah Wentworth. Next came Sherburne's house, into which moved Dorothy Wentworth; then many others. These dwellings housed the finest silver, furniture, foods, wines, clothing, and portraits that a lot of money could purchase. The vaunted social life of the little capital existed primarily for their gratifying display. Nowhere north of Virginia was there such concern for the preservation and advancement of social status, family wealth, and power. Nowhere in North America, in proportion to the population, were there more carriages and servants. The town took its text from the pastor of Queen's Chapel: in the New World, announced Arthur Browne, "without nobility or orders of gentry," there must and ought to develop "some difference of rank, some inequality—how ridiculous the contrary. . . . !"

It took time, and very little. William, the first American Wentworth, had come to this country with Wheelwright, left with him on the expulsion from Massachusetts to settle first at Strawbery Banke and then at Exeter, where he modestly prospered. At Newcastle, just outside the Banke, his son Samuel had "libertie to entertain strangers . . . and brew beare—at the sign of Ye Dolphin." The way up was steep; Samuel moved to a combined tavern-dwelling hard by Puddle Dock in what was by then called Portsmouth. The Lieutenant-Governor lived in it; the Council met there; Samuel became active in civic affairs himself. Following a stint in the mast trade his son John, Frances's grandfather, bought the tavern, refurbished it according to the coming fashion, and fathered fourteen children. In 1717 Joseph Addison signed the commission that made him ruler of the province, and by mid-century no mercantile family in the capital was without its Wentworth.

Lieutenant-Governor John Wentworth sent three of his boys to Harvard—among them Benning, class of 1715, who dimly forecast his own reign by setting a record for breaking windows and paying fines, and Samuel, '28, warden of King's Chapel and father of Lady Frances. Son Mark, father of Sir John, skipped college to start getting rich at once; daughter Hannah married Theodore Atkinson, class of '18, also of Portsmouth and nearly as rich as

Mark. Theodore Atkinson, Jr., ranked first by social standing in the class of '57, was remembered chiefly for not being able to stand the food. Frances's second husband, '55, couldn't stand the conversation: "instead of Wit and Gay repartee . . . disputes of Original Sin . . . and such like." From religious exile to secular sophistication in three generations, from frontier brewery to moneyed mansions in two.

For the show of bounty, Frances was Portsmouth's handsomest vehicle and probably its most ambitious. No one who knew the place thought it odd that she had twice married first cousins: the number of families she could choose from without taking a step down had been reduced to two; protecting status with her first marriage, she promoted it with the second. That her husband was "the best of all royal governors" has not been demonstrated but is probable. The competition was scarcely serious,* he had the energy and desire, and in spite of mounting opposition to the Crown was the best liked. His achievement was nearly aborted, however, in an issue that proliferates.

Following Benning's death, John raised a question that infuriated Martha Wentworth and made a permanent enemy of his recent friend Michael: had not the titles to all those lands the widow Wentworth was bequeathed lapsed with the failure to develop them, and ought they not be regranted to people who would settle and cultivate them as planned? His Council, which was all the inheritance he had from his uncle, agreed they should, the single dissent coming from the only man on it not related to him by blood, marriage, or both. Ambitious Peter Livius, angry with the Wentworths for keeping him out of the extremely lucrative mast trade, took elaborate revenge. Accusing the Governor of trying to get the properties for himself through third parties,

---

*As Surveyor General with a hopeless assignment he had no competition. The pine-bearing wilderness of North America covered at least 100,000 square miles, his instructions being to mark and index every tree tall and straight enough to make a mast—orders from a government in which the Secretary of State immediately responsible for the colonies was convinced New England was an island. But John was a conspicuous success at the job. One of Benning's deputies in it never left Ireland.

he carried his case to London in person. There before the Board of Trade he charged "a connected and deep laid System of injustice" in New Hampshire, made possible by "Council, Judges—principal members of Assembly and all the wealthy merchants" being "linked together in an alliance or bond of blood." To the astonishment of nearly everyone, the Board found John guilty of "Mal-administration" and in effect recommended his removal. With Rockingham in the background, Paul Wentworth petitioned the King to reconsider the matter; it was referred to the Privy Council, which investigated and decided there was no foundation to the charges. His Majesty accepted the verdict; Livius explained his defeat by saying John had bribed Edmund Burke, who did him in, and left New Hampshire to become chief justice of Canada.

Opposition to the little aristocracy had followed quickly on its establishment and was in part moral. Blue noses sniffed at blue blood; there were people lying in wait for the like of Frances Wentworth. The same ones who deplored her tolerated her husband; but as the Revolution grew nearer their suspicions about his Loyalism approached the kind of paranoia which in Massachusetts had already accused Governor Hutchinson of authorship of a Stamp Act he had bitterly opposed, and burned down his house. Portsmouth had been quiet but socially tense for quite a while. John's first known civic action, taken long before he was in power, was to support the establishment of a theatre, as proposed by Benning, to replace the Wentworth Theatre Club that gathered at Stavers's. The Assembly, the only organized opposition and the source of Patriot leaders to come, howled at the thought of staged "Gallantries and Amours."

Connections between morality and class—as between church and class and church and state—are notorious. But there cannot be many demonstrations of how these relations work and what they ultimately mean as tidy as the one provided, in its divergence from Massachusetts, by the little history of Portsmouth. The Bay Colony had developed as a thoroughgoing theocracy; the Congregational Church was established, the Anglican Communion long prohibited. New Hampshire was never theocratic; its plain people were Congregational, but its patricians went to Queen's Chapel. The background in which Frances Wentworth, no more devout than her husband, attended the church of court every Sunday without fail—even, when a clergyman could be obtained, held services at Wolfeborough—is illuminating.

By 1730 the two colonies were not only in competition but dispute, the chief argument over boundaries. New Hampshire was at a disadvantage, there being only one full Governor, and Belcher partial to Massachusetts. In 1732 the Wentworths, Atkinsons, and others hit on the way to rectify this. They built an Anglican church, and named it after Caroline, consort of George II, who responded with gifts of silver communion and christening service. Arthur Browne arrived from England, via Providence, as a missionary for the Society for the Propagation of the Gospel, became a social as well as religious leader, and, until it broke, the administration's strong right arm. The Church of England became fashionable, the gentry converted, Portsmouth took on the look of an Anglican haven. The boundaries were decided in New Hampshire's favor, and Benning was its first Governor.

The animosity that overthrew John first formed against his uncle. In the course of his many trades and travels abroad, the Good Old Gentleman ("Don Granada" behind his back) had developed the air of a Spanish grandee. Middle-class citizens resented his imperial leadership, manners, second marriage, style of living, and religion. But the urbane cunning that had bested Massachusetts continued to dominate the vast majority—and in such ways as make clear that John's defense before Rockingham of his highly vulnerable and unpopular uncle was not the becoming act of family loyalty it appeared but an endorsement. An early attempt to build a college in the province had foundered on Benning's insistence that it be controlled by the Bishop of London, head of the Church in America. John was more diplomatic, and argued that lest Dartmouth appear hostile, as it was, to the Church of England, the Bishop should be appointed to its board. Wheelock replied that he'd move his school to some other colony first; he also believed that the Governor never gave up trying. He was quite right. And so was the hostile Peter Livius, except that he mistook his conspiracy for a more serious one. There was indeed a plan for "a connected and deep laid System," and John's Anglican zeal went to the heart of it.

Religion in the colony, he observed in a letter that did not surface until the present century, was as of 1769 "In very many places broke to pieces by sects": the time to "establish the Church in this province upon a permanent system . . . as wisely begun by my good uncle" was ripe. The first step would be the appointment of a chaplain, "whom I would find and recommend, for whose conduct I would be responsible"—and "if he should deviate from his duty I would suspend." Then lesser missionaries would be appointed, and lands granted in various townships to support them (Benning had also thought of that). Lest there be any doubt of the reason for such ecclesiastical fervor, he spelled it out: "very desirable effects in the administration of the civil government." He perfectly understood that "to embrace this opportunity requires caution, prudence and secrecy." But "by such a plan I think I could . . . in ten years establish at least forty good parishes . . . in the whole country."

Thus translates the charade that ended with the empty piety of Frances's graveyard inscription. He cherished the dream to the last: a divinely right little kingdom under total sway; Wolfeborough, to which all roads led, the seat and center of it; the Council *all* relatives; their meeting place, as wisely begun by his uncle, in Wentworth House. Dartmouth in the fold, Harvard become unnecessary. A church recognized by law, a churchman in his private command with a network of henchmen. A son to succeed him long after the stumps were gone. Glory to the brightest star in the firmament—and all, as they would come to see, for the greatest good of everyone.

SUMMONED UP by their colony's past, John and Frances Wentworth were called forth more faintly and yet perceptibly by ancestors on the other side of the water. The famous Lady Wentworth of English history, ambitious and the subject of scandal, was the Baroness Henrietta (1657?–86), mistress of the Duke of Monmouth—illegitimate son of Charles II and claimant to the throne —whose cause she backed with her money and who went to his execution proclaiming her "good name." (Her title descended to the wife, then the daughter, of Byron, the subject of greater scandal.) For John as ruler of New Hampshire the exemplar was plainer in the greatest of all the tribe: Sir Thomas Wentworth (1593–1641), First Earl of Strafford—whose end led the novelist to bestow on the Governor a dream in which he hears that his doom lies there.

As Lord Deputy of Ireland, a remarkably primitive colony at the time, Sir Thomas reigned like a King. He had set off for the place with a Wedding Scandal hanging over him (it was rumored he had murdered his wife to marry his whore), which evaporated as he ignored it—and an entourage of thirty coaches of six horses apiece. He was grandly welcomed at Dublin; moved into a castle and complained of his quarters; built a lodge in the woods, which all his life he loved. He labored mightily to populate the country, improve its agriculture, and was credited with its increasing prosperity. The Church of England in Ireland was weak, and though, as he said, he was "purely and simply indifferent" to its ceremonies he built it up, appointed Anglican bishops, planned for the day when Anglican worship would pervade the whole land, and meddled with Trinity College, Dublin, until its charter was recast to place it under the Crown. He wished to improve Dublin itself; there were private theatricals at his residence but he wanted a theatre, and opened one the Puritans had closed. Ireland exported among other things timber and great quantities of fish, importing such luxuries as wine and fine cloth. He fought duties imposed from England—especially on horses, whose stock he hoped to improve. He backed industries for the good of the people and his own pocket; he had a large income and large debts. He waited a long time for the King to make him an Earl, and put all hopes of an heir on an only son, who went to Oxford and then into exile, and never amounted to much.

The traits that biographers have pointed out in Strafford were, aside from his ruthlessness, John's: energy, ambition, grasp of detail, love of power, practical turn of mind, faith in law and order under the monarch, paternalism, sense of mission, self-confidence—there was even the identification of idealism and self-interest. But with all his success as ruler of Ireland, Wentworth failed utterly to comprehend the strength and bitterness of his subjects' feelings about him and England; when he left the country eight years of violence ensued. By then the Irish hated him, but he could say truly:

I wish extreme much prosperity to this people, and I should lay it up in my opinion as a mighty honour to become in some degree an instrument of it.

He rode voluntarily from Wentworth Woodhouse to be tried for high treason, of which he was found not guilty. But as the rigid agent of a King whose government faced its final catastrophe, he advised Charles I to appease the mobs by signing his death warrant. Thus he lost his head.

Sir Thomas reincarnate, Sir John was mindful of his prototype. He named a whole section of New Hampshire Strafford. When he himself lived at Wentworth Woodhouse and was made a colonial Governor there—where reposed all of Sir Thomas's papers, two volumes of which had been published—he would have visited the grave in the little churchyard and seen the sculpture over it. Four different portraits of the King's strongest defender hung inside. As boy or man he could not have visited Little Harbor without seeing the one, after Van Dyke, that Benning had on the wall. He owned such a portrait himself, and bequeathed it to his son. It is hard to believe that his plans, magnanimity, and lifelong resignation to misfortune had nothing to do with his most illustrious ancestor and the way he met his fate.

If John Wentworth's doom was not really in Strafford but his wife, as fiction has argued, it is hard to see how. Socially and politically, as it turned out, she was an asset; and if it is unsure what he knew or thought about her sexually it is certain that infidelity did not destroy him. Difficult to believe with Dyott that Madam was ostracized by the ladies of Halifax without her husband being aware of it, and discovering the reason. But by the time his career brought him to Nova Scotia it is hard to discover what he thought and felt, as opposed to what he said and wrote, about many things. Or how much he cared. As Surveyor General he performed feats of distance and endurance as great as ever; as Governor he ruled much as before, and won a second acclaim. But if the heroics came to seem self-imitative and redundant, that does not appear to have been Frances's fault. John seems never to have admitted it, but with New Hampshire no more governed in the name of Wentworth, stunned by expulsion from home and office, he was never again in the virile exuberance of his prime. Even before his flight into exile began, Frances was writing at Portsmouth: "He is so distress'd at the times . . . he has lost a great deal of flesh and all his Spirits I tell him but he don't own it."

The same ejection served only to activate her; when she spoke of exile she meant from England. And whatever her disgrace at Halifax she rose to become its grandest first lady—quite proper enough for Edward, in whom lay the seeds of Victoria. Lady or tart, it seems obvious that all depended on the situation. With the Rockinghams and Fitzwilliams, as with the respectable Prince, her conduct was for long periods (so far as can be learned) sexually irreproachable. Where there was less need for propriety—as with a different Prince, his companion, and evidently others in Halifax; with the bachelor John and possibly others in New Hampshire; perhaps with others still, particularly in London, we know nothing of—she appears to have done as she liked. Thus the answer to the question raised by Copley's portrait seems clear.

But the answer doesn't work: the question was never anything but a provincial one, as only the admirable Dyott is on record as having perceived. Even the worldly Prince William thought a lady who shed her decency a lady no more; Dyott put her down in his book as at once sexually available and the best bred woman in Nova Scotia. Many a British lady of the time was out to demonstrate that these qualities were compatible, and it was in that clear light that the lieutenant saw Frances—while almost surely misreading her husband: they were Americans both who had "lived a good deal in England and with people of the first fashion."

If John Wentworth profoundly suffered in New Hampshire an expense of spirit in a waste of name, it is at least possible that in

Nova Scotia, her health at last collapsed, his wife had received her own grievous wound—almost invisibly signaled, two centuries earlier, by the voyage of the *Speedwell*. Severe headaches, loss of sight and hearing, and convulsions are symptoms of syphilis in the secondary stage. In the third, *Table dorsalis* "is often confused with ulcerated stomach," and is "responsible for much invalidism and many deaths"; conceivably the Governor's "paralytic disease" was paresis. Diagnosis at this remove is itself disreputable; it would be more so if we knew less about William and the special form of condescension princes could sometimes bestow. Only a little while before Frances met him on his arrival from the West Indies, he cheerfully announced to the Prince of Wales "a sore I had contracted in a most extraordinary manner in my pursuit of the *Dames de Couleurs*," for which he was on mercury, the new cure.

Rank, suitable marriages, advancement—the lessons of Portsmouth could be learned too well. Very few so learned them; of all Wentworths only two, Frances's husband and her brother Benning, were deprived of their property and forbidden the territory; Michael Wentworth, an Englishman who owned a portrait of George III given him by the King, was welcome to stay. Colonel John Wentworth, also Frances's cousin, developed into a Patriot leader; his grandson John Wentworth became the giant, unsalaried Mayor of Chicago and author of the *Wentworth Genealogy* (3 vols., 1878, a prodigious feat; its index alone, small type and double columns, runs to 727 pages). But Frances's branch of the family—she was the third Wentworth woman to marry a Theodore Atkinson—grew thin and broke. There were little scandals involving her sisters Mary and Elizabeth; her niece and namesake Frances Apthorp conducted an infamous amour under her sister's roof with her sister's husband, bore him a child, resumed the affair, and then committed suicide. It was as if the weight of the past, and in-house alliance, destroyed the line on both sides of the water: the Rockinghams, Atkinsons Junior and Senior, and Benning, Paul (if he is to be included), and Charles-Mary Wentworth all died without descendants, only Benning and Atkinson having ever sired any.

A miniature of Frances's son shows him to have been as beautiful as his mother. Raddall's novelistic hunch that he was more Mary than Charles is plausible—as if his parents had doomed him with the name. By their fruits ye shall know them: Biblical wisdom, if lowered on Frances and John, is harsh. Folk wisdom points to inbreeding and the lack of peasant blood; it is much as if by marrying first cousins they paid the penalty for what in several states today constitutes incest. In any event Sir Charles, private secretary to Earl Fitzwilliam, died unmarried in 1844 and the title was extinct. At about the same time the pressure on Mrs. Gore to support her family with her pen was relaxed when "she succeeded to considerable property, through the death of a relative." Charles had left her his father's estate: Prince's Lodge and 23,000 acres in Nova Scotia, the family plate, papers, and portraits, plus his grandfather Mark's estate, willed him by John's mother. Charles's cousin Arabella Wentworth married Francis Gore, Governor of Upper Canada, and died without issue.

All over the map, descendant Wentworth bred with Wentworth till there were none. Martha Hilton (Wentworth) Wentworth set to work with Michael Wentworth at spending Benning Wentworth's fortune; in 1789 they entertained George Washington at Benning's mansion "in the grand style for which the house was celebrated." Six years later Michael died on a trip to New York—by rumor a suicide—with the observation: "I have had my cake and ate it." He and Martha Wentworth had one child, Martha Wentworth, who married a nephew of Sir John Wentworth —Sir John Wentworth, author of *Wentworth on Pleading* (10 vols., 1797–99); they were the last Wentworths to live at Benning's. Michael's wealthy older brother Peregrine died childless and left his niece Martha a fortune to replace the one her parents had gone through. She and Sir John returned to England, whence he had gone from Portsmouth as a boy, and died without issue.

Toward the end of his decline at Halifax—his spirits spent, his wife only a memory, his bride a remoter one—the twice deposed Governor received from the widow Raynard, in 1820 the occupant of what had been his estate at Wolfeborough, another memory: a key to the lock in his old front door, one pound, eight ounces heavy in his exhausted hand. In the spring of that year he died. Shortly after that the giant pine that crowned the Mount of Delight in the early summers of his marriage—totem of his power at its peak—was shattered by lightning. The gambrel covering of the mansion was replaced that season, and on the first chill morning of the fall—fifty years to the month from the time of Betsey Loring's coming there—Margaret Raynard built a pile of the old, dried shingles in the main fireplace and lit them. They gathered slowly to a roar, spurted up the great stack and out the top, dispersing in a myriad of tiny germinating fires. Descending shingle mated with shingle all over the roof, and before long there was nothing left of the House of Wentworth, County of Strafford, but a smoldering hole.

∾

Chapter Four

MISS MONCRIEFFE ON HER OWN

THEY GREW UP EARLY in those days. Margaret Moncrieffe in particular—a beautiful girl in a delicate situation. The daughter of a British officer living in the New York home of an American commanding General, she is reported to have been at thirteen "a woman in development and appetite." General Putnam's aide was also in residence, and anyone who knows about Aaron Burr could predict the outcome. In a recent version of the affair Major Burr confronts the inevitable charge and parries it: "I am told that she gives to me the honour of having been the first to take her virginity. But I do not think that would have been possible." It was not possible that he would have been the second. On such a sensitive point the young lady enters history.

The notion that Burr was the ruin of Margaret originates with his first biographer, who explains darkly that she was an "extraordinary young woman endowed with talents, natural as well as acquired, of a peculiar character." Licentious and dissolute at a tender age, he says, there is little room for doubt that she was a victim of seduction, the evidence being her own confession of a rhapsodic passion for the American officer, previously unnamed, who subdued her virgin heart. Matthew Davis names him: Burr, a piece of information he may have got from the Major himself.

The two men knew each other for forty years, and the biographer had his subject's trophies of victory, a treasury of letters from the countless other women Burr seduced. Which Davis burned.

He must have learned from Burr as well of Margaret's other talents, which arose from an apparent division in her commitments, sexuality at odds with politics. Living in Putnam's house at the foot of Manhattan, the British on Staten Island just across the bay, and given to diverting herself on top of the General's home with a telescope, she was, it suddenly dawned on Burr, a spy. Washington shipped her to a Patriot General less advantageously located. Left for a later biographer, who had got it from a man who got it from Burr, was the pretty tale of how the girl had managed to transmit her intelligence. It seems that Margaret was a great painter of flowers, sometimes for the pleasure of her father, who was on Staten Island with General Howe; Burr concluded that "the language of flowers" was a code. Later still another biographer claimed that the Major invented the whole business to get the girl's heart off his hands.

Especially where women were concerned, Burr's judgments were often as shrewd as they were breezy, and if he was the only one to spot Margaret Moncrieffe for a spy, so his hunch that Margaret Arnold was a traitor proved correct 150 years after he had it. The belief that he was right about Miss Moncrieffe, however, rests also on a quite different story, which centers on an account of a visit she once paid to some relatives named Wood, seven miles from Peekskill. "Surpassingly beautiful"—glossy dark hair, dazzling complexion, "eyes full of witchery"—she shocked the country people with the care she lavished on the "decoration of her person." But the Woods were full of young American officers from whom, pretending to be a Whig, she learned a good deal. One day, so the story goes, while riding as usual alone she had a fall from her horse, and was taken to a farmhouse, where some women on loosening her vest uncovered a letter, which a suspicious farmer confiscated. She hurried back to her room, and while packing for New York was arrested. The letter concerned troop movements; confession was got from a man who habitually transmitted such material to the enemy from the place where she deposited it during her solitary excursions. But her trial was repeatedly postponed until she was returned to her father without one.

The reader is assured in E. F. L. Ellet's *Women of the Revolution* (1849–50) that this tale is thoroughly reliable, having been furnished by a lady to whom the particulars were related by a relative who was an intimate of the Woods—the events by then over seventy years in the past. But Mrs. Ellet also cites a letter in a London magazine by an English officer stationed at New York, which was contemporaneous:

Without doubt it is generally known at home that Miss Moncrieffe . . . has been arrested by the rebels. She is still kept in durance at the house of one Elkins, near to a place called Peakeskill. . . . The ridiculous charge whereon she was arrested does not deserve a minute's investigation, though we hear that Newman, the rebel lieutenant who was implicated with her, has been broken and sent home.

The letter ends: "News comes that Miss Moncrieffe has been liberated and is now in this town, looking extremely well, in spite of her long imprisonment."

Female spies have traditionally been whores as well, in the line of duty, and it is curious that this one should be remembered more for clandestine activities involving the battlefield than the bedroom, for she had a more substantial story of that sort to tell. Mrs. Ellet alludes to it, remarking at the end of her account that Miss Moncrieffe eventually went to England, lived long, and died obscure—the details "only repulsive." Some years later a popular writer named Charles Burdett completed his version of *The Beautiful Spy* in the same way, noting that Margaret "lived many years after these events; but her career was one, the details of which would be unfit for publication." An odd remark, since he knew the details only because the lady had in 1794 apparently seen fit to publish them herself as the *Memoirs of Mrs. Coghlan, (Daughter of the late Major Moncrieffe,) Written by Herself, and Dedicated to the British Nation; being Interspersed with Anecdotes of the Late American and Present French War, with Remarks Moral and Political* (London: Printed for the Author, and Sold by C. and G. Kearsley, Fleet-street. MC. CC. XCIV). A document unique in the annals of the country, these are the only True Confessions to come out of the Revolution, composed by its only known courtesan, who recorded more personal indiscretion than all her provincial contemporaries combined. Few Americans are aware that their history contains any such woman; the handful of historians who know it have got more about her wrong than right; no one has ever looked far enough into her story to approach the mystery it eventually comes to.

ᠬᠥ I

This tale, as extracted from the digressive way she tells it in her *Memoirs,* starts with maternal ancestors in Nova Scotia: her grandparents, Captain Patrick Heron, who had come from Scotland and died Governor of Annapolis-Royal, and Margaret, daughter of Captain Jephson. It moves quickly into early years—which were less dissipated than unstable, to the point where she must have felt nearly an orphan. Her mother, the second Margaret, at fourteen had married Lieutenant Moncrieffe; two years later, apparently at New York in 1762, the third Margaret and future Mrs. Coghlan was born. Her mother, still not twenty, and her grandmother made a voyage to Ireland in which all hands were lost. Thus she and her brother Edward became heirs to their grandfather's properties in England and Scotland, and were taken into the house of General Gage in New York. Later they were shipped to Dublin to be educated, and during their absence Moncrieffe, by now a Major, married a New Yorker named Livingston (an "uncommonly forbidding person" and a rigid Presbyterian, says Margaret, "but her *purse* was irresistible"). He sent for his children; the girl was cared for by a governess for two years when the second Mrs. Moncrieffe died, leaving the purse to her husband. He eventually remarried again, this time a *"lovely"* woman who died in childbirth ten months later. Margaret had been taken in by Frederick Jay, her second stepmother's brother. Thus she found herself in the midst of republicans while her father was fighting for the King.

The war, in short, had begun to complicate her unsettled existence, and she was soon to become the object of the pointed attention of the three most important generals then in it. Her father was feeling pressure from both sides. Intensely loyal to George III, he was closely related by recent marriages to prominent members of the Continental Congress, and his long military experience in this country brought him repeated offers, she says, of commands under Washington. His daughter, meantime, lived with Patriots, and was finally invited back to New York in a letter from the good General Putnam, who explained that except in battle he was her father's friend.

Her account of the period does not square with Burr's. She did, she says, enjoy looking through a telescope from the gallery of Putnam's house on lower Broadway at the British fleet off Staten Island, but was mostly kept busy spinning flax for rebel shirts. It was only with Washington that she got into trouble:

One day after dinner, the Congress was the toast; General Washington viewed me very attentively, and sarcastically said, "Miss Moncrieffe, you don't drink your wine." Embarrassed . . . as if by a secret impulse I said, "General Howe is the toast." Vexed . . . Washington censured me. . . . My good friend, General Putnam, as usual, apologized. . . . "Besides," replied he, "such a child ought rather to amuse than affront you." —General Washington, piqued . . . then said, "Well, Miss, I will overlook your indiscretion, on condition that you will drink my health, or General Putnam's, the first time you dine at Sir William Howe's table. . . ."

From this Miss Moncrieffe got the idea that she might soon see her father, who regarded her as a prisoner and was demanding her release. Putnam as usual was agreeable, but Washington said she should be carefully watched, and ordered her to King's-Bridge, at the other end of the island.

Here General Mifflin commanded; here the girl was treated tenderly by his Quaker wife. And here, the future Mrs. Coghlan writes delicately, "my heart received its first impression,—an impression, that amidst the subsequent shocks which it has received, has never been effaced, and which rendered me very unfit to admit the embraces of an unfeeling, brutish *husband.*" Her lover is identified only as a Colonel in the American army with shining victories behind him. Marriage, it must have seemed to her, would solve all her problems, and she wrote Putnam that she was planning it. Most unexpectedly the guardian General said no: the man's political principles were "extremely obnoxious to my father," in whose blood the Colonel would not hesitate to drench his sword. Now Putnam did arrange her transfer to the British. She bid eternal farewell to her American friends, and turned her back on Liberty—a melancholy example, she writes, of the "horrors which ever attend the frustration of natural affection." (How much happier she would have been with her conqueror in "the wildest desert of our native country . . . than under the panoply of costly state, with . . . the royal warrior who fain would have proved the *conqueror* of France!") "We cannot," she remarks gently, "command our desires."

Thus they were commanded for her, and now in the midst of this courteous war her transfer to the British was accomplished. Regally. General Knox and his officers conveyed her by barge to Admiral Howe's flagship in the harbor; then she received an invitation to dinner from General Howe, and a predictable scene took place. "Being unfortunately asked for a *toast,* I gave General Putnam." A low voice said, "You must not give him here." But Howe was easy with such matters, and exclaimed: "O! by all means; if he be the lady's *sweetheart,* I can have no objection." This, Margaret observes, involved her in a new dilemma (she was young enough to be his granddaughter), from which she extricated herself by producing a letter from the man in question:

Ginrole Putnam's compliments to Major Moncrieffe, has made him a present of a fine daughter, if he dont lick her he must send her back again, and he will provide her with a fine good twig husband.

She does not remark that this is exactly what she had asked him for; rather that the missive furnished "a fund of amusement to the company." Then Howe sent her by carriage to her father, in whose arms she fainted. She was still thirteen years old.

It was a temporary calm. The British soon left Staten Island, took Long Island and then New York. There the unannounced Mr. Coghlan saw the girl at an assembly, and her desires were commanded again—forced, she says, "on a point where every thing most sacred is concerned." Without consulting her, Coghlan went to her father, demanded her hand, and was given it. (Clearly he had money, and in a mind that "only considered sensual enjoyments," she explains, "affection was not an object.") She refused to cooperate, was confined to her room and pressured by her brother until she yielded to an "honourable prostitution," and "took to my bed a viper, who has stung me even unto death." She was married by the Rector of New York; "dismal omen," he died three days later.

Several months after the wedding Mr. Coghlan was ordered with his regiment to Philadelphia, and left his wife on Long Island with her father for an extended period, an arrangement satisfactory to her, which ended with the bridegroom's abrupt return. He had sold out of the army and they were embarking for England. On the voyage to Cork he so abused her that the ship's captain threatened to lock him up as a madman; as soon as they reached anchor he took off for two weeks, leaving her the only woman in a fleet of men "not remiss in practicing their arts of seduction against me."

Perhaps the memory shook her up; at any rate what immediately follows is confused. On Coghlan's return he took her to Dublin and departed again. Nothing explains how they originated, but in London he picked up such a variety of calumnies against his wife that he determined to seclude her in Wales to break her spirit. On the way there she escaped. Ignoring the men who took her for an "amorous adventurer" run away from her parents, she reached Nantwich, where she got in touch with Sir Thomas Clinton, an intimate of her friends in America. An indiscretion, she calls it, without saying why. Perhaps because of the response, which was that and curious too. Clinton, whom she leads us to believe she had never met, sent her money and instructions, advising that since Mr. Coghlan had already charged that there was a carnal connection between them she should consider herself under his protection, the meaning of which was plain. Meanwhile Coghlan was on the trail. Having chased his wife to London, where she had not gone, he had visited her old benefactor Gage, who hinted that she might indeed be found living with Sir Thomas. Coghlan then went to Clinton's, and demanded to search the house, or have that satisfaction an injured husband was entitled to. Persuaded that she was not there, he left for London, swearing vengeance if he were deceived, which he was. The days of honorable prostitution were over.

It was while living with Sir Thomas that Margaret was first exposed to the ways of nobility, where "distinction keeps pace with vice"; Clinton did not propose that his protection be exclusive. She wrote a "penitent" letter to Mrs. Gage; the General arrived and fetched her off; a conference was held and the decision reached that she should get herself to a nunnery. Temporarily chastened, she acquiesced, and was shipped off for an extended stay at a Dominican establishment in Calais. An incongruous setting, and she was not long in it. After a celebration of All Saints' Day in which the bones and skulls of the long interred were displayed in the chapel, she determined to escape again. But before she had the chance her deliverer appeared—Clinton, now Lord Lincoln. His Golden Key worked on the mother superior; that night Mrs. Coghlan dined with his Lordship, and took passage to England, where she says almost nothing about her activities for a while, except to call them imprudent.

So they may have been, since at this point her father disowned her—for which she excuses him on the ground that her dishonor was not reputed but actual. It was his idea that she should learn the mantua-making business, and hers that she was entitled to a separate maintenance from her husband, who could afford it. He did not; embarrassed, she called on Lord Amherst, who remembered her in New York in her nurse's arms, but observed only that the negligée trade would be a curious way of restoring her to the paths of virtue. The situation was critical.

London, writes von Archenholz at about that time,

> is said to contain fifty thousand prostitutes, without reckoning kept mis-
> tresses. . . . Sometimes they escape from their prisons . . . and trade on
> their *own bottoms,* when, if they are unfortunate, or happen not to be
> economical, they are soon dragged to the gaol by their creditors.

As she may have known, but saw no other solution. Almost
frantic she called on Lord Lincoln, who welcomed her with a
satirical smile and the hope that she had learned how to improve her fortune herself. Now seventeen, she had, and after
a few false starts was off and running. Not for long with Lincoln, who was engaged in an election for the City of Westminster; by accident, she says, she became acquainted as well
with his opponent in the contest, the Right Honourable Mr.
Fox, whose affections were temporarily disengaged. For some
three years she engaged them, and makes clear that she would
have been happy had the arrangement lasted longer, her "soul
consecrated to sweet emotions" by this eloquent friend. But
he was too ambitious and illustrious for a frivolous woman,
and after he had commended her to Mr. Sheridan, who
agreed that she should make her debut at Drury Lane the next
winter, she left Fox as she left few others, with a tribute to a
tender, ardent lover.

Left him, that is, for another man, who had none of Fox's
shining qualities. But had one *"charm,* which . . . supported the
place of every other. Mr. Fazakerley was *rich."* Better yet, he was
generous. She told him that there was a probable "obstacle to our
connection," for she was pregnant. Fazakerley waived the objection, and for four years supported her without allowing her to
draw a farthing from Fox, by inference the father. They made the
Grand Tour, and so forth; but rich as he was Fazakerley had not
other qualities "formed to conciliate the affections of a delicate
woman," and she left him for Lord Hervey, by whom she had
another daughter. The child soon died, but the mother had already taken off for Ireland in pursuit of an amiable connection
with a lover so mighty as to obliterate even that first impression
that was never to be effaced. The roving habits of military life did

not, she explains, admit of any permanent attachment to Captain
B******. Perhaps not, but it produced two more children,
whereupon the Captain saw fit to marry Lady A—, who took them
both in. At this Mrs. C. is again a little shaken, first remarking that
she does not wish to "strew the thorns of jealousy" on the lady's
bridal pillow, then implanting them by reminding A— that she
is B******'s "former *friend,* the *mother* of his *children,"* and
concluding that prudence demands she draw the veil on what she
has just revealed.

She is no more prudent on the subject of her royal lover, who
is incoherently inserted next—a "certain Duke" who came somewhere along the line and of whom she is not fond. Princes, she
observes, "conceive that *women* are made merely for *them,* to be
the passive instruments of their voluptuousness," and are surprised if a Poor Indemnity is asked for the "dearest sacrifices that
have been made to sooth their passions." She says she ought to
know, having repeatedly applied for compensation from this one,
only to be met with "dead, monotonous, obstinate silence"; and
she retaliates with a sally that once had a small fame: "if this
princely Lothario shines not with *greater advantage* in the plains of
Mars than he excels in the groves of Venus, the combined forces
have little to expect from his martial exertions."

Transition from this General to quite another in another country was established by a Mr. Giffard, but terminated when—
harassed by her creditors and his finances "exceedingly de-
ranged"—it was decided that once again she should take off for
the Continent. It was the end of her English season, the box score
eight men, four children.

In Paris she took up with General D********, a hero in the
American war and a great lover in the French capital, who squired
her about town. But he had a young relative with him, and began
to suspect that his lady and the lad were also in contact; posting
himself in an "obscure corner" he was convinced and withdrew,
leaving behind the youthful Sir Robert Harland for consolation.
Urged however to change hotels she found Mr. Coghlan in residence, and so discovered yet a better place, where her arrangement was with Colonel McCarthy—who in turn introduced her

to the Marquis de Genlis, whose "temple of voluptuousness" was the center of gallantry and the scene of nocturnal orgies. Then a Mr. Beckett moved in; his table was crowded with royalty, and all the beauties were "emulous of each other for his affections." Mrs. Coghlan won them, but it was all a bit too splendid, and when Beckett's father refused to pick up the tab the young man ran off. She had no way of knowing it then, but that was the beginning of the end, down and out in Paris and London.

Since Beckett had eluded her, the proprietress seized on his mistress, appropriating her carriages, jewelry, and clothing. Worse, an officer of the police showed up with a *lettre de cachet* ordering her to close confinement. Once more *enceinte* she was so deposited, while her English friends worked for her release, pleading a French law against the imprisonment for debt of pregnant women. It was honored, and she was placed under royal protection at the Place du Temple. Money was then raised to spring her, and ten days before the fall of the Bastille she returned to London. (*L'addition:* four men, one infant.)

Her own great days were over, and word traveled fast. Surrounded by English creditors, arrested, she again got funds from Mr. Giffard, his finances now more ranged. But there was never enough, and she was cheated besides. Arrested once more she was taken off to a sponging-house, thence to the King's Bench, where she was imprisoned, chiefly because of a female milliner. Nothing worked; advised to sue John Coghlan for separate maintenance she did. And he—now living with a "woman of *notorious character*" despite the ties of Honour and Duty that should have bound him to her—was sentenced to provide it. But he did not, and no one else came to her aid. Such, she grieves, is the nature of friends: "While we can administer to their pleasures . . . they are our abject slaves," but when a woman is in jail, "incapable of making them any return," they are gone. Despite this incapacity, she was again pregnant; the English had no law to ease the condition, and she gave birth while incarcerated. There were moments of relief. An unexpected visitor, the amiable Captain B******, took this infant as well off her hands. At long last she got a legal separation from Coghlan and a small annuity, half of which she had to pay that milliner—and the clerk whom she "has lately taken to her *virtuous bed.*" Then, on a legal technicality, she was released. (No man, one child.)

But she was doomed. She had a dream that her father had died in New York, as indeed he had, and now her creditors pressed her with new vigor, believing her the heiress to his property. Imprisoned and released again, she and her brother Edward failed in an attempt to get some part of the estate left them by their grandfather. Next there was a reprise with "a certain wealthy Lord of Jewish extraction," quite unlike his namesake Sampson, whose Exquisite Sensibility prevents her from introducing scenes of his reputed prowess. Then she was jailed again, this time released by the bounty of a gentleman who would not give the pretty lady his name.

And so goes the tale to its inconclusion, which leaves her in the perilous limbo that is her reason for telling the story. Arrest after arrest pursues her; "my whole debts it is impossible for me to pay." Displaced from the station she was born to fill in the world, she offers her memoir as a plea for help. Its message is equally clear—born of the realization that her resources had been badly managed, and directed to the Dissipated Fair of her sex. The wages of sin is debt: "Make the false dissemblers, while they pay homage to your beauty, provide also for your interest." On the last page is a woodcut of a tilted gravestone.

⚭II

AND THAT IS THAT—a story that does not always make sense. Politically, for instance. Margaret loyally toasts Howe, regrets that her father is not a rebel, and that in joining him, as she wished to do, she turned her back on the land she loved and *Liberty,* an understandable infatuation. The French Revolution is at once "horrible" and "wholesome," a citizen's duty is to obey whatever laws he lives under, but her country is "the world!" Her chief appeal for help is to the Prince whose bedroom talent she has ridiculed; names of men she has already identified are occasionally protected with asterisks; in the middle of reciting the litany of her lovers she explodes at her husband for taking a mistress and her milliner a clerk.

But if the *Memoirs* are sometimes silly, they are also perfectly extraordinary. From the "lives," diaries, and correspondence of other Revolutionary Ladies, even sexual propriety is missing. For an American, as she counts herself, to monger your own scandal, or even to confess it, was to stand alone. Except that confession is an acknowledgment of guilt in an act of penance. Mrs. Coghlan's remorse is that in renting herself out she spent up the revenue. She admits to vanity and foolishness, dissipation, vice, and dishonor, but never even pretends, as she moves from man to man, to embarrassment, and repeatedly makes clear that she was not open to business for the money alone. The phenomenon of getting pregnant in jail is passed over; a pretty lady can always be serviced somehow.

It is remarkable how national sensibilities change. If the *Memoirs* are without precedent or parallel in eighteenth-century America, by the next they are unthinkable. Both the shocked Burdett and the repulsed Mrs. Ellet presumably read the New York edition of 1795, which had not at all disturbed "the society of grandees who compose the Female Jockey Club," whose introductory statement had endorsed the author and praised the sentiments of her spirit. By our own time responses have of course changed again. We are less likely to be struck with a world of men without end than, toward the start, by the early loss of a girlhood that was both bereft and privileged, in a war where embattled generals took pains with a child who would never today come to their attention. Toward the end the tale now seems sad, its heroine unaware that she herself is the embarrassment in a story that never looks back, where it is harder to care what man came next or if they stopped coming than to speculate when she might most appropriately have been named Mother of the Year.

It is also remarkable how sensibilities change nationally, for a testament unique in the American past was in eighteenth-century England imbedded in a tradition. A book forty years old when

Margaret was born is part of it—*Moll Flanders,* with her childhood in other people's homes, early seduction, transatlantic voyages, unabashed passage from man to man, financial vicissitudes, and imprisonments. But Moll was Twelve Year a *Whore,* five times a *Wife.* Margaret is closer to *Roxana, the Fortunate Mistress,* the well-born child whose father was the foundation of her ruin, and who leaves an unbearable husband to become a Moll of the upper classes for twenty-six years of unrepentant Wickedness. She goes from England to Paris, where she is taken on by a Prince, and bumps into the husband who doesn't see her; she takes the Grand Tour, and so forth, until she becomes exactly the prosperous business woman Margaret didn't. More thoughtful than Moll or Margaret, Roxana articulates some of their silences, sounding at points quite successfully liberated. Generous with her body she is jealous of her spirit; she stubbornly refuses marriage for the reason that where a wife takes insults, a mistress gratifies herself with another man. If at one point Moll looks back and appears to forget about no fewer than five of her children, so Roxana remarks when she loses a newborn baby in Venice that she is not sorry, the difficulties of travel being what they are. And it is Roxana who explains: if a whore has offspring, "her endeavour is to get rid of them," or she is "certain to see them all hate her and be ashamed of her."

Defoe had to imitate life before life was in a position to return the compliment; his novels had at least the precedent of the seventeenth-century memoirs of Mary Carlton, who is a vague forecast of Margaret Coghlan as well. The Crafty Whore of Canterbury committed bigamy twice, the second time posing as a highborn German lady; she was caught, tried, and acquitted, starred in a dramatization of her own story, then like Moll became a thief and unlike Moll was hanged. In seventeenth-century England as certainly not in America, the way to publicize the private lives of women had been paved as well by popular accounts of the likes of Barbara Villiers, the Duchess of Cleveland—great lady and stateswoman whose beauty and lewdness attracted such a parade of lovers as to make Margaret look like a flower on the wall. Thus in time Mrs. Manley was able to produce her *Secret*

Memoirs and Manners of Several Persons of Quality . . . (1714), which
border on the pornographic (in the "fire of the two meeting Sex"
the ravish'd maid received the amorous invader with "meltings-
full of delight . . . not at all behindhand in Extasies and guilty
Transports").

By 1785 the tradition in which Mrs. Coghlan would write was
completely established, as in George Anne Bellamy's *Life . . .
Written by Herself.* Here is the unstable childhood, the warning
against marriage for the wrong reason (passion alone), the horrible convent (where unchaste nuns were walled up), the succession of wealthy lovers (including, by rumor, another distinguished Mr. Fox), offspring, the extravagance that eventually
does her in, the trips to the sponging-house, then the King's
Bench, and finally her release. Though it verges on respectability,
this book was a *succès de scandale,* which may have prompted
another, *The Life of Mrs. Gooch Written by Herself* in 1792, where
tradition borders on formula: the early death of one parent, the
remoteness of the surviving one who, remarried and again be-
reaved, sends the child off to live at school, later forbids her to
marry the man with whom she could have lived happily forever,
and forces her into an ill-fated union with one who before long
rejects her for her rumored sexual misbehavior; the gothic interlude in the French convent, then the near-endless run of protec-
tors, including the Prince, in France and England; the debts and
jails in both Paris and London, where we leave Eliza, as we leave
all these women, suspended—with a pointed appeal for funds to
pay the creditors and get out.

It is odd that we know the end of almost all these people, no
matter how obscure, save Mrs. Coghlan's, vaguely reported to
have died forgot and brokenhearted in her dotage—as if, perhaps, she just continued from one gentleman to another, and in
and out of jail, until she could no longer trade, and went down
the dispose-all of history (in Paris, according to the most recent
empty claim, at the age of seventy-three). Mrs. Bellamy's *Life*
made money, but she was soon back in the King's Bench where
she died. Mrs. Gooch became a novelist of sorts, and passed on

in 1804. But nothing whatever is reliably recorded of Margaret after the *Memoirs* save only a 1795 letter—in a "neat strong hand" and signed M. Coghlan (it is her only relic)—to our Minister at London: a plea from an "American subject" for help in locating an English girl in France, displaced by the war between those countries. That is the last sign of her. She says she went to Paris in 1788, returned to Cavendish Street (a good address) in '89; she reports the death of her father in '91, and of the Colonel Moncrieffe with whom he is confused in '93; in prison at the end of that year she signs her manuscript, Written by Herself, and Printed for the Author the next. She begs help of the ambassador in '95, and then—well known, prominently connected, and already widely reprinted—she simply vanishes at the age of thirty-three. The search now resembles a colony of moles, until finally one of them, gone off half-blind like the others but in wholly the wrong direction, burrows his way to exactly the right place, which turns out to be the department of Obituary of Remarkable Persons in volume LVII of the *Gentleman's Magazine*—a journal replete, by modern standards, with errors of judgment and taste, but not in the area of vital statistics, which were a specialty of the house. There in type so small a hawk could have missed it is to be found a fragment noticing the demise, "In Cavendish-street, Portland-squ." of

> *Mrs. Margaret Coghlan, lady of John C. esq;*
> *and dau. of Colonel Moncrieffe.*

That's it, and nothing remarkable but the date: June 4, 1787. No dénouement, no Paris. No prison, no plea, no personal Printing, no Person. She was dead at twenty-five. ("After two days illness," according to the *Daily Universal Register,* "at three o'clock." England was celebrating the King's birthday.)

Rascals made mischief in those days as in ours, and in between was Charles Burdett, whose *Beautiful Spy* of 1865 carries the belated news that Margaret Moncrieffe's actual role in the New York underground of her time was heroine of a plot to assassinate George Washington. This discovery, the author announces, is founded entirely on facts newly gleaned by him from "the American Archives." There was, at least according to a rumor the General credited, such a scheme, and one of his own bodyguards was hanged in connection with it—the result, Washington explained, of trafficking with "lewd women." It is true that the place was crowded with whores—all of them, claimed Tom Paine, Tories—as well as with Tory agents, many of them women. But Burdett's claim to historicity is precisely as legitimate as his birth (he was a baby Burr); Peter Force's *American Archives* (1837–53) contains the record of the bodyguard affair but there is no mention of any woman in it; Hickey was hanged a week before Margaret was invited to town.

Yet modern historians are still on record with the flat statement that she really was a spy, and not one has been found to dispute it. The belief owes little to Burdett, more to Burr, most to Mrs. Ellet, and not much to evidence. But that letter from the British officer about the girl's arrest, outside Peekskill, where she had "relatives named Wood," sounds genuine. And near that town then lived one Mary Moncrief, at least once misidentified as Margaret's sister, the Tory wife of a man named Ward. Wood/Ward —an easy slip, especially since Mrs. Ellet seems to have got the story orally. It is hard to picture such wisps of smoke arising from no fire at all.

On the other hand the officer's letter has not been located, and it is easy to see how the simple fact of Margaret's transfer to the British, prominently staged before people who would not have known the innocent reason for it, could have sparked rumors that survive. But never reached her ears, perhaps, else it would be unaccountable that she doesn't mention them in her book, especially if she had a Loyalist story to tell. For her bootless Tory efforts Margaret (Mrs. Benedict) Arnold was handsomely rewarded by the King.

The whole matter remains a mystery to which history provides no answer. As for the *Memoirs,* they raise questions history has never addressed; authoritatively cited by many, they appear to have been doubted—even in part—by no one. Clearly there was no general outcry when they were issued. A review in the *British Critic* declared only that

This lady, who has long been known in the circles of gallantry, but who is now a prisoner for debt, imputes the cause of her misfortunes and her deviation from the paths of virtue to a marriage against her wishes. . . . The book seems to be written to procure a temporary supply to the author; and we shall not, by any unseasonable criticism, by any means counteract its effects.

Next year the editor of the New York edition pleaded, in view of her plight, that we *be to her faults a little blind;* the Female Jockey Club urged patience, wished her a speedy period to her afflictions and a new protector. The New York edition of 1864 has ponderous notes that credit the story, but for a trivial date, exactly as given. And in 1971 this edition was reprinted by the New York Times & Arno Press in a series called "Eyewitness Accounts of the American Revolution."

↬III

"MEMOIR," Richard Steele remarked long before Margaret, "is French for a novel." The temptation to discard Mrs. Coghlan's as just that—the fiction of some canny hack who had discovered the formula, worked it out, and never got caught—is powerful. But to be resisted: life in this case had imitated the formula to which it had been reduced. So long as she lived and can be checked against the record, her book is accurate far beyond the standard for the form and very close to history. This is not always true. Her mother, for instance, was not lost at sea but died—"a most exquisite Beauty . . . after a long and painful consumption," according to the *Mercury*—at the age of twenty-three in New York. But for the most part, where the facts can be uncovered they confirm the story as she gave it.

This is ultimately clear in what she has to say about people, though it is not always easy or even possible to identify them. As in the case of that first, anonymous lover. The idea that he was Aaron Burr, almost endlessly asserted, seems to rest chiefly on the assumption that any female exposed to Burr was lost; he was still fathering bastards at seventy-six. But it is very doubtful that he was the seducer of Margaret. For one thing, as he remarked, "seduction is a crime like no other. . . . I have never had an amour in my life in which I was not met half way." His second wife attested to this eloquently (and perhaps plaintively, since her appetite was said to be "unquenchable"), recalling how women by the hundreds "vied with each other in a continuous struggle to offer him some testimony of their adulation." But as Margaret's original lover—the Colonel with shining victories behind him and political principles odious to her father—Burr strikes out. The *Memoirs* are punctilious about rank; he was a Major. His single shining victory, the attempt to rescue the body of Montgomery, killed at his side in the attack on Quebec, was a failure. As for political principles, he didn't have any.

If her conqueror is lost to history, her ancestors are nearly so. Beyond the fact that both her grandfathers, Captains Heron and Jephson, managed to get arrested in Nova Scotia in 1737, about all that can be learned is that Patrick Heron did not, as his granddaughter claimed, die Governor of Annapolis-Royal but in 1751 was court-martialed, "broke for habitual drunkenness and conduct unbecoming," and died two years later.*

---

*Early in her book Mrs. Coghlan argues that on the death of her mother and grandmother she and her brother came into their grandfather Patrick Heron's estate through his will, as "proved in the *prerogative court* of Canterbury." If only because Heron had been living and would die in Nova Scotia, this seems doubtful. A search, however, reveals that since he left property in England his will dated 1748—leaving everything to his wife Margaret Jephson Heron and "my heirs on her body"—was indeed probated in the court of Canterbury. But by the time Heron's widow died, his daughter Margaret Heron Moncrieffe was gone too. As Margaret Moncrieffe Coghlan apparently did not know, Mrs. Heron's "goods, chattels and credits" were granted not to her grandchildren but to one Charles Gould, "for the use and benefit" of the widower Major Thomas Moncrieffe, "now residing at New-York." However, during the considerable period in London that began with Mrs. Coghlan's escape from the nunnery and ended with her dishonored and disinherited, she explains that all her expenses were paid by "Sir Charles Gould . . . at the *Major's desire.*" Thus she seems to

Individuals better known to history are still problems; memoirs had it in common with military dispatches that first names were rarely used. This helps explain the total confusion over the identity of Major Moncrieffe, for there were two of them here with the British. James, later Colonel, was an engineer credited with the English success at Charleston; in 1793, serving with the Duke of York, he died unmarried and childless at Dunkirk, exactly as reported in the *Memoirs*. Of Thomas Moncrieffe, the father who disinherited his daughter, they report several things: extensive service in this country, aide to various top generals, friendly with his enemy Putnam; captured in the Battle of Brooklyn; possessed of "rigid, austere principles"; married twice after the first Mrs. Moncrieffe died, both subsequent wives then dying; and died himself of a ruptured artery in New York.

All of which can be independently verified. Thomas was in this country a soldier of the King for nearly a quarter century before the Revolution. When old Fort Oswego was surrendered in 1756, it was he who went out with the White Flagg; when Fort Niagara was taken three years later he carried the news of victory to Amherst. He was with Captain Joshua Loring on Lake Erie, and deeply involved in Pontiac's War. He and Putnam had served long together, and during the Revolution there was at least one public "display of Affection" between them. In June of 1778 he was captured when "about 20 men with their faces blacked . . . came into Flatbush" and took him from his house; a month later he was back in New York. His second wife, who was indeed a rich Presbyterian Livingston (as General Mifflin and his wife were Quakers), died like the first one of consumption. His third —the unnamed lovely woman of the *Memoirs*—was Helena Bar-

---

have spent moneys that were not, as she believed, willed her. Another descendant of Patrick Heron and a genealogist, C. H. H. Evans of Bryn Cadwfra, Montgomery, Powys, Wales, has traced the line to Thomas, Earl of Moray, Regent of Scotland (d. 1332). As for the Moncrieffe line, Sir Iain Moncreiffe of that Ilk, incumbent laird of Clan Moncrieffe, writes from Easter Moncreiffe on St. Andrew's Morn, 1975, that it descends anciently from Thomas de Mouncref, and although an effort to place Margaret Moncrieffe Coghlan in it failed many years ago he is convinced that she belongs somewhere in the pedigree.

clay of Wall Street, who died in childbirth sixteen months, not ten, after the wedding. The promotions of his son Edward, who matriculated at King's College in a little class with Alexander Hamilton, show up in Howe's *Order Books*. Even the Major's moral severity can be recovered—as in a letter he wrote after his wedding to the heiress, where he says that "I have many arguments with some of my connections concerning the licentious spirit of this country. Tho' I am married, and probably to one of the best of the stock . . . I am not wedded to all the abuses of the country." ("Now," he goes on, "I come to Izard its a pity he should get poxed.") A New York newspaper reported his death there "from a rupture of an artery in the lungs." His will, filed in New York when Margaret was twenty-one, makes no mention of her.

It is because of his assignments in this country that Margaret can be located as an infant. In 1762, the apparent year of her birth, he was aide to Monckton, who was established at New York (where she was almost certainly born, the record of her baptism perishing in the great fire of '76 which destroyed Trinity Church). She would have been known in town as a baby by General Amherst, who left in '63 to be replaced by Gage, with whom she lived, as she did later with Putnam. Her revelation that this Patriot leader was approximately half-literate is hardly new. But a remarkable demonstration of the fact survives, the very letter Putnam wrote her inviting her to his home: "Yestorday Majir Leavenston was hear and said you had a mind to com to New york . . . be assured if you will com you shall be hartely welcom. . . ."* Even the letter she says she carried from him to her father when she was transferred, which diverted General Howe's dinner party, is verified—this because Ambrose Serle, secretary to Admiral Howe and an educated snob, was so bemused he copied the thing *verbatim & literatum* (and worse than she remem-

---

* How this letter got from her hands into those of Burr's biographers, who first printed it 150 years after she received it, passes comprehension; the supposition is that it did not. As Putnam's aide Burr, a Princeton man, habitually copied his letters. Presumably Margaret got the copy and the original was found in Burr's papers.

bered it) in his journal. And because William Howe's adjutant-general made the news of her arrival the only entry for the day in *his* journal, we know even the date of her transfer (August 7, 1776) and that second toast. Next winter a license to wed was issued by the Secretary of the New York Colony; on February 24 the *New York Gazette* announced that "Lieut. John Coghlan, of the 7th, or English Fuzilleers, was married by the Revd. Dr. Auchmuty, to Miss Margaret Moncrieffe. . . ." The Rector of Trinity Church, where her mother was buried, died eight days, not three, after performing the ceremony.

After that, in England, it is harder to verify Mrs. Coghlan, but scarcely impossible. The identity of her first protector is clear enough; Thomas Clinton, who became Lord Lincoln at the time reported, had the American friends mentioned from having served in this country as aide to his cousin and Howe's successor, Sir Henry Clinton. So the last lover—greatly unlike his namesake, the mighty "Jew of antiquity"—must have been Sir Sampson Gideon, Jr., the wealthy Lord Eardley. (Having been raised an Anglican he was at fifteen made a baronet to reward his ineligible father for the great sums he loaned the British government.) Mr. Fazakerley, in between, was almost surely S[amuel]. Hawarden Fazakerley, a permanent bachelor and as owner of the "family estates at Fazakerley," a township near Liverpool, definitely—as the *Memoirs* have it—*rich*. Of all the Mr. Giffards at the time only one—Thomas Giffard of Chillington, Staffordshire—appears to have been wealthy enough to afford her. And of all the lecherous Herveys only one, John Augustus Hervey (1757–96), could have terminated their affair by being made an "Envoy at a foreign court," as Mrs. Coghlan writes; he became ambassador to Florence in 1787. (His previous affair with one Mrs. Nesbitt was notorious, as was his uncle Augustus John Hervey's.) There was, of course, but a single Charles James Fox, the phenomenon of the age, who has been credited with having gone through a quarter of a million pounds, packed the House of Commons every time he spoke, become a scholar in five languages, and single-handedly "lowered the morals of the period"—by the time he was twenty-five. When Margaret is said to have lived with him, he was indeed a candidate for election (he won), and was pursuing his dissipated existence. But on joining the respectable Rockingham's administration he took a turn for the serious, which is in effect why she says they parted. Bad luck; he soon took another mistress, Mrs. Armistead, who already lived in splendor, "having known more men, and known them better, than any other woman of her day," and whom he eventually married.*

Even worse luck with her Certain Duke, the Warrior Prince. His Mrs. Armistead was Mary Anne Clarke, who had become rich through amorous connections, who wrote a far worse book than Mrs. Coghlan's, which was a great success, then blackmailed her ex-lover and got richer. But if the *Memoirs* record an unrewarding interlude with this man they are also prescient. As everyone knows, the Duke of York marched up the hill and then marched down again. But that was later, when (exactly as predicted) Frederick Augustus had turned out to be a commanding failure—first in France, where Colonel Moncrieffe was killed (having ill-rewarded him in life the Duke made it up by attending the funeral), later still in The Netherlands.

Then her luck ran out completely, for after leaving Fazakerley and Giffard (who, coming late in the story, are candidates for suspicion) the *Memoirs* say she went abroad when she was in fact deceased. Yet there is little to question in what was written over her name about Paris. By the time the *Memoirs* are signed at the end, the "late unfortunate" Duc d'Orléans had gone from libertine to guillotine, along with the deeply regretted Marquis de Genlis, whose "superb hotel" was in fact the Palais-Royale, with its *décorations lubriques* and the *luxe d'obscénité,* where the Duke competed in orgiastics against the record held by his grandfather. The Temple, where Margaret is said to have been put under royal

---

*The *Memoirs* have it that at the time Fox and Mrs. Coghlan separated she was pregnant but do not specifically say that the child, a daughter, was his. His only known offspring, illegitimate, was a son (whom Talleyrand for one remembered vividly: "how strange it was," he wrote, "to dine in company with the first orator of Europe, and only see him talk with his fingers"; the boy was deaf and mute). Either Mrs. Coghlan slipped on the gender of her first child, or Fox had a second one, or she was not pregnant by him.

protection, had been a castle, but was by this time a sanctuary for debtors. As for the great General D********, he can only be William Dalrymple (1736–1807), the single militarist with the proper American background and number of stars. Although he served in this country for thirteen years, he is recalled less for triumphs than as the hapless commander who was forced to withdraw the British troops from Boston at the time of the "Massacre." His record for gallantry, however, is more memorable; in postwar London, according to an anonymous contemporary, the whole object of his affection was a nameless young beauty "much celebrated for an admirable dexterity in certain manual operations," who died very young, grievously lamented by all "whose passions she was exquisitely delighted to raise, and which she had ever the generosity to gratify." Things in Paris are very *au courant,* and only once a little *de trop:* a tale of Margaret's miniature, a visit to the president of Parliament, and the intervention of Louis XVI on her behalf.

Back in London nothing seems askew. Though placed years after her actual demise, the drawn-out financial troubles and imprisonments appear authentic. Even the impregnation in jail makes easy sense with the realization that, there being little sexual segregation at the time, inmates were as available in as out; at the King's Bench, which was the principal clink for debtors, it was possible if one had any money at all to live "within the Rules" —in the immediate area, that is, outside the walls.

Completely genuine as well appears the silent villain of the drama, the undefended but ultimately recoverable and almost crucial Mr. John Coghlan. The name with that spelling was exceedingly rare in America, and except for his marriage the only clue to this man's activity in this country is the statement that shortly after the wedding he was ordered with his regiment to Philadelphia. Filed there is an old pension application which states that "John Coghlan was a Soldier in the Tenth Penna. Regt. In 1778 while in service he was seized with an inflammatory fever which particularly affected his head." It is tempting to attribute subsequent behavior to this affliction, but also impossible to believe that Major Moncrieffe married his daughter to a Patriot who soon took off for England—where the name was a bit more common. "Jn Coghlan, co. Glamorgan . . . and formerly a merchant of London," died in the same year as Margaret Moncrieffe Coghlan, and was probably father of a boy entered in the musterbooks of the ship *Resolution,* on which Captain Cook sailed round the world, as "Coghlan, John. Glamorgan, 15, A.B." Four years later, in May of 1776, William Howe's *Order Books* announce "John Coghlan, Gentleman, to be Second Lieutenant"—this at Halifax, where the Major was serving at the time. Save for his promotion the next year, nothing more of Lieutenant Coghlan is found in the records of the war—or of the rest of his life, until in March of 1807 his obituary gathers the loose ends, and recalls something about there always being two sides to the story of a broken marriage:

In St. Bartholomew's Hospital, in the most abject state of poverty and distress, and in the 54th year of his age, John Coghlan, esq. some time a Captain in his Majesty's 89th regiment of foot. . . . This unhappy man . . . had the brightest prospects. His father, a London merchant, though possessing great wealth, committed him to the care of his friend, the celebrated Captain Cooke, with whom he made a voyage round the world as a midshipman. Not liking the sea he at last entered into the Army. He served several campaigns in America . . . where he behaved very gallantly. At New-York, he married the beautiful and all-accomplished Miss Moncrieffe, so celebrated in the annals of gallantry as Mrs. Coghlan. From this unfortunate connexion . . . may be dated his misfortunes, and his misery. She was a rank Republican. . . . The lady soon chose another protector. . . . His domestic disappointment preyed on his mind, and he became dissipated and unstable . . . and entered with avidity into every fashionable vice and folly of the day. His extravagance and attachment to the fair sex gradually involved him in poverty and ruin; and rendered him, in the end . . . the broken down, pitiable object of a charitable institution. Highly favored by nature, he possessed great powers of body and mind; he was social and convivial; could at will "set the table in a roar"; and was accounted one of the handsomest men of his time. . . . He was very respectably connected both in England and Wales; yet, the humanity of the Officers of the Hospital retained the body a full fortnight in the *dead house,* in the vain hope that some relation might come forward. . . . The charity of a stranger furnished a covering for his remains, which were deposited in the burial-ground of the Hospital.

Two sides, but not necessarily of equal merit. According to his wife, Coghlan's temper was "naturally violent," and she portrays him as dissipated and uncontrollable some time before she left him to his fatal disappointment. Once more the record supports her. Captain Cook's *Journal* of the 1772–75 voyage mentions the midshipman only as one of the "wild & drinking" young gentlemen aboard, journals kept by other officers report nothing except that for his frenzied behavior Cook once discharged him from his station, and after another episode had him "Confin'd in irons."

ᴄᴏ IV

THIS IS THE WAY OF THE *Memoirs,* which are counterfeit as coined yet ring true wherever Mrs. Coghlan herself seems accountable. But how it is that this particular alloy has currency still, and who has passed it, is not easy to explain. Literary impostors walk the streets today undetected; the way to lay an ancient ghost which has not been known to exist is at first open to nothing but speculation. Perhaps shortly before her death (in childbirth? of smallpox?), Margaret simply supplied a lot of accurate information to some pale shade that wrote it up and filled in the blanks. Or had kept an off-and-on journal herself—or written a series of autobiographical letters (more common then than now) that fell into clever hands. More likely, and maybe prompted by the success of Mrs. Bellamy's memoirs (which were plagiarized and pirated while the lady yet lived), she was writing her own, two years later, when the story ended prematurely—and protracted insufficiently to meet the requirements of the form. Then someone saw an opportunity, and finished the job with an eye to the market that was served by six printers in three countries in a year.

Someone—a spirit which somehow had contact with the body that gave it rise. The possibilities are endless, but probability very limited. There was only one person of the time and place with recently published memoirs of a life that had roughly paralleled Mrs. Coghlan's, and who had known the places, prisons, and people—specifically, the Duc d'Orléans, the Marquis de Genlis and his magnificent establishment, the French and English jails— that Mrs. Coghlan is made to write about but did not live to endure or enjoy. And this is the same woman who remarks that in London in the mid-1780s she had so lost touch with her friends that "the only one with whom I was associated was the pretty Mrs. Coghlan, who then lived with Mr. Fazakerley, and went by his name." This autobiography was issued two years before Mrs. Coghlan's and by the same publisher, which in its elegant edition of the *Memoirs* advertised no book but *The Life of Mrs. Gooch.*

The guess that out of her own experience, and such facts as newspapers and magazines had printed, it was this lady who finished whatever she had got from Mrs. Coghlan passes every test save the crucial one of style. Eliza went on to become the writer; the all-accomplished Margaret was a livelier one. But neither woman composed with anything like the pen that sketched the Preface to the *Memoirs,* its conclusion, or the an- nounced *Remarks Moral and Political* obtrusively *Interspersed* throughout. Touching on matters alien to both ladies, most of them unheard of while Margaret lived, here is the heavy, mascu- line hand of some flunked Tom Paine (large on the London scene at the time), which sinks irony into sarcasm—with embellish- ments from Otway and Shakespeare—and shoves Mrs. Coghlan into opinions about the refugees of the French Revolution, the soundness of the Jacobin cause, and the plight of the Spitalfields weavers.

The odds at so late a date against identifying these smudged fingerprints would seem formidable. But style, if there be any, is a very individual thing, and there was only one political moralist of the time who wrote with exactly the sort of pen that inter- spersed those remarks about refugees, Jacobins, and weavers— that indeed had composed the same before, and decorated them with the same bits from *Venice Preserved* and *Lear.* He is the familiar Anonymous, in this case the author of *The Female Jockey*

Club, which turns out to be not an organization of ladies in the flesh but between the covers of a book, published in the same year and place as Mrs. Coghlan's. In the short chapter of this work that is devoted to her, and reprinted in the New York edition of her *Memoirs,* it is not the grandees of the group but the compiler of them who praises her sentiments, which are his own.

Mrs. Coghlan's famous Prince did not set out to conquer France until she was long gone. It is Anonymous in *his* book who had already written—of one who went to fight with "the *immortal* commander, the Duke of York, in Flanders"—"May he *prove* himself no less successful in the *plains of Mars,* than he has so often *proved* himself a conqueror in the *groves of Venus!"* The deceased Mrs. Coghlan is made to describe General D******** in Paris as the Second Agamemnon, "this favourite of the fair sex, that renowned warrior, equal to both and armed for either field." Two years earlier in another book the same nameless writer had devoted a whole chapter to "G-N-R-L D-R-MP-LE, Alias Agamemnon the Great," that soldier "Equally distinguished for gallantry in love, as for bravery in war . . . this son of Mars, this favourite of Venus . . . equal to both and armed for either field."*

All that remains is to put a signature to this strenuous spirit into whose hands, very likely, Mrs. Gooch delivered whatever Mrs. Coghlan herself supplied (for he seems as he says to have had not the least acquaintance with the woman whose life he mangled). He was generally nameless at the time; a reviewer for the *Gentleman's Magazine* pondered the question of authorship and, noting the Jacobin bias, concluded that it could not be either virtuous or English, apparent synonyms. But morality, political and personal, was the man's very banner, and the way he waved it utterly British. This the same journal was tacitly to acknowledge in its

---

*This was in *The Jockey Club* (1792), to which the Females were sequel. There was such a London club, and "to shew vice its own image" the author of these works began by portraying its members; he ended by including the likes of Tom Paine, whom he eulogized, and women—"for we are all jockeys, running our races," etc. (He was also up to more mischief than at first meets the eye, for he implies that the lady of felicitous dexterity who failed the General by dying so young, as reported by him in *The Jockey Club,* was Mrs. Coghlan.)

notice of the death, "At his apartments in Westminster," of "Charles Pigott, esq. author of 'The Jockey Club' . . . 'The Female Jockey Club' . . . and many other well-known publications." (As indeed he was, among them *The Rights of Man,* also *The Wrongs of Man,* and—despite his ceaseless castigation of gambling, "the abominable vice"—a work called *Pigott's New Hoyle.* He was anonymous for good reason; the publishers of *The Jockey Club* were committed to Newgate.) These books and others of a piece are all today as well forgot as the author of them—who might as well be remembered, if he is to be, as the character who ripped off the *Memoirs,* leaving Mrs. Coghlan to languish in a London jail at the edge of St. George's Fields, an easy walk over Blackfriar's Bridge to the publisher of them. At either place, such was the practice, donations could be made to the unfortunate prisoner, and picked up by whoever beside the publisher was in on the take. (Not Pigott, who died on June 27, 1794, deeply lamented by the *Times,* which noted that though his first name was Charles he was "commonly called Louse Pigott.")

Many at the time must have known what was amiss and afoot. Surely it was brought to Mr. Coghlan's attention that he was stuck with a quill out of the grave; surely the signs of Pigottry, which was popular, were read by some. But record of anything like that there is none, and we are left at the end of the road, where all that remains of Margaret Moncrieffe Coghlan is shrouded in what has been written for and about her. Her aim was simply survival; but come down to us in part by rumor and the rest by fraud she never as her own woman survived at all, never offered a word to the future that was not manhandled by one sex or the other. She kept her looks all the way, but her story lost its figure early and can be reshaped no further. History remembers more ladies than it can protect.

And if what it remembers is a distortion, what is needed to bring her finally into focus is not more information but some sense of a real woman, recovered from time. That is what is missing, but also what may never have been. The child of New York Island carried off forever from a warring land she never wished to leave, to get along as best she could in quite another, brave, candid, willing: *be to her virtues very kind.* 'Tis not so much pity she's a whore, and did not last long. Rather that this high-pitched little kid who only fainted once—who never having had a childhood could not provide any for the babies she gave away like dolls (Captain B****** understood), or keep their fathers either—was a case every bit as clinical as her husband's. She distributed her children as she had been distributed; in their fathers she looked for the one she never had. Checked as a child, she peaked on her appearance at Putnam's. The emptiness that pervades her record reflects the absence of the woman she never became. History protects more ladies than it can create.

Chapter Five

RETURN, MY DAUGHTERS, GO: FINALE

JOHN ADAMS had trouble saying it. "No Father, Brother, Son or Friend"—this was early in his autobiography—"ever had cause of Grief or Resentment for an Intercourse between me and any other Relation of the female Sex. My children may be assured that no illegitimate Brother or Sister exists or ever existed."

Nor any man pursued. What bothered Adams, as tales of President Jefferson's wickedness flew through the air, was the thought of being swept up with his peers. The War of Independence had not, as sons of the Puritans hoped, proved an end to scandal, its course in the new Republic having taken instead two sharp turns. Veering from sexual adventures of Revolutionary Ladies departed to those of Founding Fathers present, in exchange for English fashion, carried off at last by the Loyalists, it substituted French.

The new nation's moralist *par exemple* was Washington, but the moralist's voice belonged to Adams. Like practically everyone, he considered the first President blameless; unlike others he ignored the legendary affairs of Aaron Burr. Benjamin Franklin's "outrages to morality" were another matter. So too the report, which Adams accepted without question, of Jefferson's children by one of his slaves. As for the morals of Alexander Hamilton, they were "as debauched as old Franklin's." Worst of all, his "unblushing attempts upon ladies . . . of the purest virtue"—a clear reference to Mrs. Adams, who wrote of the Treasurer, "I have read his heart in his wicked eyes many a time. . . . They are lasciviousness itself."

Rumor nipped at the heels of the nation's leaders, occasionally taking a piece. Born of the British desire to discredit the Revolution itself, nurtured by an American irritability that one man alone should go untouched, mischiefs tried for nearly two hundred years to pin something on the father of his country. A few frauds, perpetrated early and in England, were ingenious, though easy to expose, and credited. Washington did warn a step-granddaughter of a "great deal of inflammable matter" in the human frame: "when the torch is put to it, *that* which is *within you* must burst into a blaze." But the nearest sign of that in his own life is the probability that for much of it he carried a torch for the wife of a friend, Sally Fairfax. Late in his career he wrote of the "moments, the happiest of my life," that he had spent with her. When the furnishings of the Fairfax mansion were put at auction, he bought the pillows from her bedroom.

Jefferson was "cold as a frog," according to Gouverneur Morris. According to Alexander Hamilton he was a "concealed voluptuary." At different times he may have been both. When scandal clouded his administration, he confronted the story that he had endlessly besieged the wife of a friend by admitting that once as a young man he "offered love to a handsome lady. I acknoledge its incorrectness." On the charge that he got children on a slave, by report the half sister of his deceased wife, he went silent to the grave. It's true that Sally Hemings had five children who strikingly resembled her owner, and it has been demonstrated that he was on the scene nine months before the birth of each. More than one authority disputes the tale, but Adams may well have been right in believing it. There are still blacks in America who claim descent from this union.

Legends of an old man's lecheries in France, which for Adams disqualified Franklin as a public servant, appear to have been little else. "When I was a young man," Franklin himself remarked, "and enjoyed more favours from the sex than at present, I never had the gout. . . . I . . . have the gout now." But the good doctor did, as Adams particularly deplored, have an illegitimate son who had an illegitimate son who had an illegitimate son who died short of puberty. He himself recalled how as a young man he got "frequently into intrigues with low women who fell in my way," and it was obvious that he was no great support to the institution of marriage.

As for the "fornications, adulteries, and the incests" of Alexander Hamilton—not, as persistent rumor had it, the son of George Washington and a wife said to have "gone whoring in the Barbados" but, as Adams called him, that "bastard Bratt of a Scotch pedlar"—the evidence was partly solid. Everybody knew about the Treasurer's protracted affair with a prostitute who had a husband who pimped for her and blackmailed him. Hamilton had admitted it in print. His "incests," if real, were never confessed. But "scandalized whispers" in fashionable circles had it that he was intimate with his wife's sister, Angelica Church. Mrs. Church wrote Mrs. Hamilton not to be jealous, but added that "if you were as generous as the old Romans you would lend him to me for a little while."

Adams recorded only his political disapproval of Aaron Burr; perhaps for once he was shocked into silence. It had become almost "a national habit to claim for nameless infants his illustrious fatherhood"; Burr in turn explained that when a lady so honored him he was too gallant ever to show himself ungrateful by denying it. He fathered a bastard daughter at seventy-six; was caught "pantaloons down" a few weeks after his second marriage; and the day he died was divorced by Madame Jumel, the wealthiest ex-whore of the age—who, according to one of Hamilton's biographers, had been the cause of the duel in which he was killed.

∾ I

OF A PIECE WITH FAITH in the moral superiority of republican government was the notion that the expulsion of Englishmen and Loyalists meant the end of Fashion in America. What happened instead was that the French Alliance, the publicized presence in the French capital of American leaders and in America of French army officers—soon of aristocrats exiled by their own Revolution—brought a new vogue. The war was still being fought when a French General noticed that the wives of prosperous men were "clad to the top of French fashions." At a dinner in 1788, the last President of the Continental Congress in attendance, "the women had their bosoms very naked," reported Brissot de Warville. "I was scandalized by the indecency in a republic."*

Brissot was looking in the right direction, for the influence of his country on this one was most apparent in formal attire for women. Abigail Adams reported from France that "to be out of fashion is more criminal than to be seen in a state of nature, to which the Parisians are not averse." To be in fashion meant in the style called Classical Empire: the gown modeled after togas of republics long gone, made of diaphanous muslin, worn over a filmy chemise and designed to cling as in ancient statues. Reference to "transparent depravity" was inevitable; inevitable as well that in the new capital at Washington would appear "what I

---

* The naked bosom has an unremarked history in this country—the earliest symbol of which was a noble young woman bare either to the waist or the feet and known as the Indian Princess. Entitled simply "America," she turns up in many seventeenth-century paintings. She derived from the Indian Queen, equally exposed and long a cartographer's symbol for the western hemisphere. Unaccountably, unless intended to indicate descent from the Princess, British cartoonists at the time of the war often depicted the colonies as a scantily dressed and frequently topless young white woman. When post-Revolutionary America went neoclassical in spirit, the symbol of the country as the Goddess of Liberty—more circumspectly clothed than fashionable women of the time—emerged. She evolved into the buxom, heavily robed Columbia, but Uncle Sam canceled all that.

hope," wrote a lady at the party, "will not often be seen in this country, an almost naked woman." ("No one dar'd look at her but by stealth.") This, a gentleman explained to his wife, was in imitation of Paris ladies: "half the body naked & the rest perfectly visible." (People could look all they liked; the woman was "not at all abashed.") French fashion in America, he predicted, was an end to female chastity. The reasoning was that a nation importing its styles from the French would soon bring over as well their notorious infidelities. Jefferson in Paris was as shocked as Mrs. Adams. "Domestic bonds here," he wrote, "are absolutely done away. . . . Conjugal love has no existence." The "French mania" was to run through both his administrations.

But without doing the harm anticipated. To the bewilderment of the French themselves—over seventy of whom left memoirs, journals, or diaries of their stay here—ladies provocative at court did not carry through. Conversation with them, Chastellux was dismayed to announce, "leads no further." The frequent observation was that where in Europe unmarried girls had no freedom at all and married women enjoyed considerable latitude, the situation here was reversed. Thus two expectations proved false. The moral progress realized in a new form of government was not accompanied by any striking improvement in moral tone, and the public display of private charms did not destroy marriages.

Such post-Revolutionary wickedness as Europeans did notice was largely in the public sector. We are indebted to a foreigner for knowledge that in 1794 New York still featured streetwalkers "flaunting their licentiousness in the most shameless manner" and "many houses of debauchery in a locality which for some reason unknown to me is called 'Holy Ground.'" But he was more attracted to private scandal, and rejoiced in the tale of another Frenchman who, promised a tender beauty at one of the houses, greeted on her arrival the "daughter of the home to which he had brought a letter of introduction, the celestial Venus with whom he had dined!" ("What to do? . . . Happiness put a seal upon his lips.") He was even more pleased for a Frenchman who made his way through a household: rich widow, daughter, Negro servant.

A very public scandal, the "general topic of conversation in all circles," was the appearance of that almost naked woman at the Washington party. Born Betsy Patterson of Baltimore, she later remarked of her costume, "to tell the truth there was as little as possible of any gown at all. . . ."* The year before she had at eighteen "seduced into wedlock," according to Adams's son John Quincy, a nineteen-year-old Frenchman. ("All clothes worn by the bride," noted an observer, "could have been put in my pocket.") The groom was Jérôme Bonaparte, who was entirely dependent on his brother. Napoleon disapproved the match and asked the Pope to issue a bull that would annul it, which the Holy Father was "troubled not to find any reason" for doing. Meanwhile Betsy, who continued to dress with "the daring of the Directoire," and her husband dined just outside New York with the lord of the manor at Morrisania.

Their host was Gouverneur Morris, "the great lover with the wooden leg," which replaced one he was said to have lost in escaping a betrayed husband. He had lived six years in Paris, several of them as our minister, and no American had a better knowledge of fashionable France. What things might have been like if his country had adopted a Parisian way of living is suggested by his diary, which shows as well how his experience abroad may have prepared him for a large scandal at home.

A lesser known Founding Father, Morris was a leader in holding the balance between radical and conservative extremes. He drafted important documents, including the instructions for Franklin and the peace Commissioners, and first worked out the decimal system of coinage. He was also known for his "daily oblations to Venus." In Paris they were offered chiefly to Adèle, twenty-eight and wife to the Comte de Flahaut, sixty-three. At the start she rejected him, saying that she could not be unfaithful— to the Bishop, diplomat, and statesman Talleyrand, that is. "By degrees, however," he noted, "we come very near it."

---

*The standard historian of American costume remarked in 1903 that she had seen robes of the early Republic "brought out of old trunks in staid New England homes . . . so low necked that they were indeed incroyable . . . and slit up the side nearly to the waist. One was a wedding gown of a parson's wife. . . . Desperately immodest."

Paris made a deep impression. "Every Body agrees," he wrote Washington, "that there is an utter Prostration of Morals" but that "general Position can never convey to an American Mind the degree of depravity." He learned a good deal from Adèle. It seemed that not to be, in France, a natural child of Louis XV gave a certain distinction. Her son was Talleyrand's. Her sister had left her husband for another important cleric, and traveled with him dressed as an acolyte. She had a friend who received all her lovers dressed as a boy. She knew a count who was the reputed lover of a marquise, his sister. (They occupied the same room, it was observed, at hotels in this country; James Madison protested in the name of "American manners.") Morris asked if another count was really the child of the late King by his daughter; Adèle explained that so it was thought and so she believed. She pointed out that the mistress of a count whom he esteemed was his daughter.

"Je brûlais de vous combattre corps à corps," Adèle told him. When she was ill and her prescription unavailing, "I exhibit another Medicine which works wonders. The Roses blush on her Cheek . . . she is very well." But the arrangement was complex. One night she could get rid of her husband for but half an hour; on another occasion she did not get rid of him at all, and Morris had her "in the passage . . . Mlle. is at the harpsichord . . . [Monsieur] downstairs . . . the doors are all open." This was in the Louvre, where the de Flahauts resided. When the Revolution convulsed Paris, Morris stuck to his post, wisely but vainly advised the King, and plotted his royal escape. He also planned Adèle's, who made it to England.

On leaving Paris himself, Morris had other amours. Back in this country he called on the beautiful Mrs. Morton of Boston, poet and niece of Frances Wentworth. Pestered by a jealous husband, she proved alternately receptive and indisposed. She told him a "curious history"—presumably of the tragic affair her husband had conducted with her sister. Chances are he remembered it. Later he dined at the Morton's: "Monsieur was cordial all things considered."

Adèle had escaped to England on the last day of September,

1792. During that night in the State of Virginia, Anne Cary Randolph of the Virginia Randolphs, whom Morris had met as a girl of fourteen, bore a child out of wedlock and disposed of it. The father, also a Randolph, was thought to be her sister's husband. He was jailed to await trial, and Anne, who was called Nancy, was placed in the custody of their attorneys, Patrick Henry and John Marshall. Thomas Jefferson, whose daughter was married to Nancy's brother, was in the courtroom. The Negroes who had the evidence which would probably have convicted the accused could not by law testify, and they were acquitted.

Jefferson asked his daughter to support her afflicted friend; she replied that it would be easier "could I suppose her penitent." In any frame of mind Nancy was ruined, at eighteen unmarriageable. She lived on with her sister and her sister's husband in the role of spinster: "I was permitted to sit at table where I did not presume to enter into any conversation or taste of wine. . . ." But then the husband, ill, was given an emetic and died. His younger brother, the great John Randolph of Roanoke, accused Nancy of having killed him, and of long intimacy with one of the family slaves. He told her to leave; according to him, she was next evicted from the house she went to for having made immodest advances to a doctor. She moved on to Richmond, where by rumor she survived as a prostitute. By now thirty-one and destitute, she remained there while her brother's father-in-law was inaugurated for his second term as President.

NANCY WAS TRAPPED, but as Betsy Patterson Bonaparte at last discovered, post-Revolutionary Ladies who escaped abroad could always go home again. Napoleon was crowned in the year of Jefferson's re-inauguration; he never had approved her marriage to his brother. When she and Jérôme sailed for Europe, she was forbidden to land in France. She went to England instead, and gave birth to Jérôme Napoléon Bonaparte, whose father gave in to his brother. A Paris court annulled the marriage; Jérôme Senior wed a Princess and was crowned King of Westphalia. Betsy went back to Baltimore and moved in with her father, known as the richest man in Maryland. She hated the place, and when Napoleon settled a generous allowance on her she returned to Europe. Renowned on the Continent for beauty and wit, she lived high. When her father remonstrated, she replied that she was no different from other women who had left America. "I never heard of one who wanted to return. . . . Besides I think it is quite as rational to go to balls and dinners as to get children which people must do in Baltimore to kill time." It was impossible for her "ever to be contented in a country where there exists no nobility." Business disgusted her, and the men of Baltimore "are all merchants. . . . Commerce clogs the brain."

But the system she loved betrayed her, and the one she abhorred rewarded. Though endlessly plotting her son's future as a legitimate Bonaparte in France, she sent him to Harvard, and when he married an American there was no hope left. She returned for the last time to Baltimore, where for her lifelong disobedience her father had willed her only "a few small houses and lots." Leaving her son $1.5 million she died at ninety-four, a business woman in a Baltimore boardinghouse.

A Greenwich Village boardinghouse was sheltering Nancy Randolph when Gouverneur Morris learned of her situation. Morrisania needed a housekeeper, and she took the job. His friends informed him that they were "hurt" by this domestic arrangement; it is doubtful that he cared, but on Christmas, 1809, he wrote in his diary: "I marry this day Anne Cary Randolph. No small surprise to my guests." The Morrises flourished. Gouverneur was revered as the eulogist for both Washington and Hamilton, and when he was sixty-one Nancy gave him an heir. But then John Randolph resurfaced. After spending a day and a night at Morrisania, he concluded that to free herself for "lewd amours" Nancy had made her husband a prisoner in his own estate. He wrote her a letter, which for his protection he sent to Morris, repeating all the old charges. Nancy responded with forty pages, noting that for the birth of her deceased child he had the wrong date. Morris said that since she had told him the whole story it gave him no concern. And wrote, heavily underscoring the words, *"She never deceived me."*

And she long outlived him. He left her Morrisania and a large income—with the proviso that if she remarried it would be increased. She never did, but she did read his diaries, and lived until 1837, when she was buried beside him. Four years later St. Ann's Church was consecrated at the spot—given and named by Gouverneur Morris, Jr., "for the Glory of God and in Memory of His Mother." Red brick and still Episcopalian, it sits a little shabbily in the midst of the rubble, rubbish, and gutted buildings of the South Bronx; a sign outside reads "Iglesia de Santa Anna."

TWO YEARS BEFORE Nancy Morris died, the last of the Revolutionary Ladies—Hannah Van Horne and Elizabeth Lloyd Loring, who were also born in the same year—had died across the water. An age had passed since a Loyalist girl from South Carolina had exulted, on debarking in England, "When I first set my foot on British soil I could have kissed the gravel on the salt beach! It was my home. . . ." So, on landing, thought many Americans. They looked forward to their reception, to recognition of what Loyalty had cost them, and to providing informed advice on the conduct of the continuing war.

These people remain for many Americans a strange group who for some foolish reason were on the wrong side: educated, wealthy, snobbish, and Anglophile. That is a rough picture of the richest of them, perhaps seven thousand in number, who managed to get to England. In many cases they were simply the most successful of the colonists—sometimes victims of their victories, targets of those who had not shared their good fortune. Among other things they were loyal to what they had won through ambition, ability, and effort. Few if any of them had approved British policy as a whole, and some had opposed it with energy and skill. Their general view was that war had been brought by a small body of malcontents who had misled the colonists into thinking themselves oppressed. (A distinguished historian recently called them "the freest people in the world.") What the Loyalists really opposed was Independence—as, at the start, had virtually all Patriots, including some of their leaders even after its Declaration was signed. In declaring war in 1775 the Continental Congress specifically disavowed any "design of . . . establishing independent states."

The Loyalist diaspora was larger than is generally recognized, involving perhaps 100,000 people—proportionally equivalent to the total population today of North and South Dakota, Kansas, Nebraska, and Minnesota. It still comes as a surprise that as many colonists fought for George III as for George Washington. The Continental Army never came to more than 35,000 men, of whom the General had at most only a third under his personal command; at one time or other some 50,000 provincials fought for England. The Loyalists too were a mix, many of those who went to Canada and Nova Scotia having been tradesmen and farmers. There were Hessian, Huguenot, and Dutch Loyalists, black Loyalists (whose descendants in Sierra Leone are still English-speaking Anglicans), and Indian Loyalists. (Mohawks on a reservation in Ontario, descended from those who accompanied Sir John Johnson when he fled to Canada, still celebrate Holy Communion with the silver service donated by Queen Anne.) The Loyalists as people were, finally, valuable. Even though the most successful of them went to England, lesser ones became "the makers of Canada," according to one of its historians—"an army of leaders"; from Maine to Georgia the "choicest spirits" went forth "to people our northern wilds." Given their quality and numbers, it appears that the colonies in giving birth to the Republic simply hemorrhaged.

The refugees in England soon discovered that the country was not home at all, but alien and expensive. The North administration was not interested in their views on the war, and they were not welcomed into the mainstream. They huddled, waiting for the victory that would allow them to return to real homes. The news of Saratoga "confounded & staggered"; by the French Alliance they were "struck dumb." Some wished, though it would have meant risking their lives, they had never left. Assuming as they did that they would be returning, the Crown had done little to ease their plight; when Yorktown at last removed the sustaining fiction they realized that nothing could help but compensation.

England was under no legal obligation but recognized a debt of honor, paid partially their claims on lost property, issued pensions, and put former officers on half pay. The notion that where Patriots made great sacrifices for Independence the Loyalists "lost everything" would have bemused the King's government, which bestowed on them some £6 million sterling.

One American in England became a great success, Dr. John Jeffries, Harvard class of '63. First apprenticed in Boston to Dr. James Lloyd—leading physician and Betsey Loring's uncle—Jeffries had refused a general's commission to serve with the rebels, and in London was made Surgeon General of the King's Forces in America. In 1780 he was serving in Savannah when his wife died in England; the stricken doctor sold his commission to Joshua Loring and returned to London. An extremely successful specialist, he also maintained a general practice for Americans, who were "very frequently disordered . . . and at the same time unable to pay." He was lonely, as his diary shows, and despite "a descendant with a pair of scissors" it is clear that he was well acquainted with a number of "charming alluring Women of the Town"; eventually he settled on a mistress. But it was for neither venery nor medicine that Jeffries was famed. Rather for having on January 7, 1785, made a trip from England to France—Dover to Calais—by air. Scientifically as curious as Franklin, he had been attracted by the balloon ascensions of Jean-Pierre Blanchard, and proposed the journey to him. It was a difficult one. To stay aloft the men had to jettison Jeffries's equipment, then despite the cold their clothing. (Whereupon it occurred to the doctor that they'd had a good deal to drink at breakfast, and they reduced their weight by "five or six pounds more.") In France they were re-clothed by a crowd and escorted to Paris, where Lindbergh's would one day rival their reception. Jeffries was greeted at Versailles by the King, caught the Queen's "lovely eyes" on him, delivered to Franklin the first recorded piece of airmail, was cheered at the Opéra and the Comédie. Best were the "lovely lovely women," one of whom moved into his hotel and flooded his bed with tears when he left. "The celebrated physician and scientific aerialist" addressed the Royal Society, and remarried.

Visiting Boston he found himself so welcome that he stayed, practicing until his death. When the centenary of his flight was observed in 1885, speakers noted that nothing had come of it. (Of what use was it? "Of what use," Franklin had long before responded, "is a baby?")

The fate in England of Nathaniel Hatch told more. Also born in Boston and educated at Harvard, he had married "a famous heiress Elizabeth . . . the widow of Nathaniel Lloyd, a wealthy Boston merchant"—which is to name the mother and father of Elizabeth Lloyd Loring. Hatch inherited Strawberry Hill, his father's estate in Dorchester, where a decade later Betsey married Joshua. He also had a house in town. When the Sons of Liberty tried to intimidate the consignees of the tea in '73, and did so, he alone dared face them. On the night of the great influx, April 19, 1775, he too sought refuge in Boston, then went on to England. Little is known of him until nine years later when he got up from a dinner with Loyalist friends and, overwhelmed with loss, cut his throat.

In their bewilderment, the likes of "poor Mr Hatch" were heedless of precedents for their disaster. During their own civil war, English Royalists had fled across the Channel, their properties appropriated. When the Edict of Nantes was revoked so many Huguenots left France—some for America, whence, for instance, the name Gouverneur—that whole provinces were nearly depopulated. It had been but a generation since the English themselves seized the lands of the Acadians and drove them from Nova Scotia. But history found the Loyalists unprepared. And where it is claimed that France never did recover from the loss of the Huguenots, America was bursting so rapidly into the future that its distinguished exiles—save for families and friendships sundered—were never really missed.

Nor, once the shock of colonies lost was absorbed, did England grieve. How easily it could dismiss the land that had dismissed it is suggested by a later, British equivalent of a Revolutionary Lady.

When Adèle, the Comtesse de Flahaut, dined in England at Holland House, her hostess pronounced her "an agreeable adventuress" whom "a volume would not suffice" to describe. As volumes attest, Lady Holland knew a bit about older husbands and adventures herself. Born Elizabeth Vassall in 1770, she was a great beauty who at fifteen had married Sir Godfrey Webster, thirty-eight—apparently for his title, since she was an only child and her father rich. Webster was a sullen, violent man who owned Battle Abbey—built by William the Conqueror but to Elizabeth a "detested spot" where she bore him five children, three of whom lived. But Lady Webster, now twenty-three and traveling in Italy, succumbed to Lord Holland, nineteen. They went off together, returning to England for the birth of a son. For an enormous sum and custody of their three children, Sir Godfrey consented to a divorce; when he shot himself Elizabeth got her inheritance and the children back.

Holland was Henry Richard Fox, nephew of Charles James Fox, the nation's foremost Whig. The newlyweds quieted the sensation the divorce proceedings created by gathering round them in the magnificence of Holland House "a coterie of social, literary, and political talent, which in the annals of the country has never been equalled." To his wife, Holland was "the most agreeable man in England," and it was agreeable to him that his brilliant self-educated lady should rule. So she did, bossing about the greatest men of her day as they sought her favor. To one powerful lord she said, "I am sorry to hear that you are going to publish a poem. Can't you suppress it?" When Monk Lewis complained that he was made to write burlesque, which he never did, she told him, "You don't know your own talent." She traveled like a Queen, with a huge retinue and a fabled silver chamberpot. Once, having faced the "imminent perils" of riding a public train, she commanded its speed reduced to a crawl. She treated her servants well, her guests like servants, and her children scarce at all. She despised George Washington but adored Napoleon, sending him books and fruit in exile. It was shortly after eating *les pruneaux de Madame Holland* that he died, willing her a gold snuffbox given him by the Pope. A quarter century later, Holland having perished, his lady was observed for the first time to lean back in a chair, and a few days later she died too. Her will virtually excluded her children.

A tyrant, she is remembered as having met her match only once. She grandly informed an American scholar, George Ticknor, that New England had been settled by convicts. It had been settled by Ticknors, among others—including Vassalls. He mentioned to her the Vassall (now Longfellow) House in Cambridge and the monument to a Vassall which is the first thing visible on entering the gloom of King's Chapel in Boston. He could have gone on. Two of her Vassal ancestors are named in the Massachusetts Charter of 1629, and John Vassall—her great-great-grandfather, part of whose estate she inherited—came to that province in 1635. Until they were driven out by Patriots, there had long been, as there would not be again, prominent Vassalls about Cambridge and Boston. Elizabeth herself was not, not by birth, really English at all. Her grandfather had moved from America to Jamaica, where her father had lived; her mother was a New Yorker. By denying her ancestry and ignoring her progeny, she gathered everything to the bosom of her marvelous self, and all collapsed when she did.

ONE OF THE ODDITIES of the American Revolution was that when Loyalists and English departed their church remained. Disestablished, it thrived, despite the fact that at the time of the war Anglican ministers here had but the status of missionaries. In 1789—the centenary of the opening of both Trinity Church and King's Chapel—the Protestant Episcopal Church declared that, independent of foreign authority, it would continue the liturgy of the Anglican Communion in America. Anti-British feeling was one problem; another was that there were no bishops in this country, and no way of creating bishops, hence no confirmation. To remedy this, Samuel Seabury, Jr., was sent to England to be consecrated. Since he could not swear allegiance to the Crown he was denied, but in Aberdeen the deed was done. The church went on to flourish, the only large Protestant denomination that did not split, north from south, in our Civil War. Thoroughly converted to this country, the Episcopal Church is about all that remains of American Loyalism.

The relationship between Loyalists and the Anglican clergy had been close. The Boston Wentworths were pillars in the support of the Reverend Henry Caner, who was carried off to Halifax by John Wentworth. The Reverend Arthur Browne was a powerful presence throughout two Wentworth administrations at Portsmouth. As a young man, Seabury Junior was assistant to his father during the period when Seabury Senior baptized Betsey Loring on Long Island. Hannah Van Horne was married at Christ Church, New Brunswick, New Jersey, where, when she was a girl, the future first Bishop also served. Margaret Moncrieffe in all likelihood was baptized at Trinity Church, where both her parents are buried, and she was married there by its pastor, the Reverend Samuel Auchmuty, who soon died—his end hastened, it was believed, not by her inauspicious wedding (though he took to his bed the day after it) but by the burning of his church. Following his death, his house—which stood in the vicinity of "Holy Ground"—was "immediately taken over" as a brothel.

The world of Revolutionary Ladies was small, and its upper crust was thin. Mrs. John Montresor, wife of the presumed model for the villain of *Charlotte Temple,* the country's first popular novel, was herself the subject of one of Copley's most stunning portraits. When her father lost his head to a cannonball, her mother married Samuel Auchmuty. John Montresor engineered the fireworks for William Howe's Mischianza and took his wife's half sister to the party Peggy Shippen was not allowed to attend. When Margaret Moncrieffe proposed a toast to a rebel General at Howe's dinner table, she was seated "next to the wife of Major Montresor, who had known me from my infancy."

It is as if everybody was connected with everyone else. The Montresors with the Lorings—they sailed from Halifax to New York on the same little ship. Having lived in New York for many years, Frances Montresor would have known Hannah Van Horne, perhaps as Mrs. Foy. As Mrs. Carleton, wife of the Governor of New Brunswick, Hannah clearly knew Frances Wentworth, wife of a neighboring Governor; John Wentworth once wrote Thomas Carleton that his wife "longs to shake her shoes" with them in New Brunswick. Hannah could not have avoided

Peggy Shippen Arnold had she wished to; they were close neighbors at little St. John and then in littler Fredericton. It may have been that Aaron Burr kept secret all his life his knowledge of Peggy's role in Arnold's treason because as an orphan he had been taken in by Philadelphia Shippens. Frances Wentworth and Betsey Loring were friends and, although they may not have known it, related by marriage; Frances did not know that she was similarly related to General Howe. Long after the war, her "large & celebrated estate"—Wentworth House at Wolfeborough—was advertised for sale by John Jeffries.

Still visible after nearly two centuries are the faintest of this good doctor's tracks. Shortly after selling his medical commission to Joshua Loring, who was unqualified for it—and while Jeffries was between marriages, making do with Women of the Town of London—Elizabeth Loring was not far off, awaiting the arrival of her husband. He did not join her in England until the end of 1782. A year and a half before that, Dr. Jeffries noted in his diary that

Mrs. D requested I would call on her frequently—this Eve reced a Letter from Mrs Loring (Betsy Lloyd) dated Reading, March 1—'81 (secret).

A few days later is another entry:

Eve, wrote *Mrs Loring,* Reading, Berkshire, *secret.*

⌒∾ II

BETSEY LORING'S FOREBEARS owned Lloyd's Neck in 1670, the ancestors of Hannah Van Horne were in New Amsterdam by 1645, and the great-great-grandfather of Frances Wentworth was banished to New Hampshire in 1637. By the time of the Revolution, the biological roots of its Ladies were already deep in America: there ought to be a plot of native soil where the roots of their spirit could be uncovered.

There are two or three such places, the first of them got at by summoning a few forgotten victims of seventeenth-century scandal. A nameless woman who "suffered an Indian to have carnal knowledge of her" and was made to have "an Indian cut out exactly in red cloth, and sewed to her right Arm." A wife sentenced to wear the letters AD on her sleeve; another with an elderly husband found guilty of committing the same with "divers young men." And especially a young woman who confessed to fornication: "The judgement of her being whipped was respitted for a month or six weeks after the birth of her child, and it was left for the Worshipful Major Hathorne to see it executed." Her name was Hester Craford.

But the prototypal Revolutionary Lady was not Hester with the scarlet A on her breast; Hawthorne admired her, but was enough the son of his ancestor to execute judgment. She is instead the fruit of Hester's misadventure, her daughter Pearl (1642–?), not herself a scandal but the product of one that has never left the national consciousness since first it was published. Chillingworth —the husband who failed Hester in the romance—made the sign of his inadequacy the beneficiary of his will, so that Pearl became "the richest heiress of her day, in the New World." At the end of his book Hawthorne fades her into myth: where was she? "None knew—nor ever learned. . . ." But Hester received "letters with armorial seals upon them," and gifts which "only wealth could have purchased. . . ."

She was once observed embroidering a baby's garment. The pearl of great price was fertile, a "seed pearl." Issuing from her were not only the provincial ladies of Henry James who, also made rich, depart for European adventure, but forgotten Ladies as well, who blossomed in the flesh after long dormance. As seed sewn in a cranny on the roof of the House of the Seven Gables in Puritan Salem bloomed over a century later to gladden a little a gloomy mansion, so a few women in the time of the Revolution burst belatedly into flower to lend a grim scene a little color.

In another line from Hawthorne, these women descend to us as well from the spirit of a tiny settlement in earliest Massachusetts that was like a crack in the rock of Plymouth Colony nearby. There in 1625 Thomas Morton built a house on a hill overlooking the water and named it Mare-Mount. A vigorous anti-Puritan, he and his men erected in the spring a great pine pole, garlanded and ribboned, with antlers at the top. About it they drank and were merry with their women, singing Morton's "Let all your delight be in Hymen's joys." Governor Bradford deplored such "dancing and frisking"; they had "anew revived and celebrated the feast of ye Roman goddes Flora"—held a carnival of the sexes around a blatant symbol in memory of a courtesan.

A clear and present danger to the Pilgrims, Morton traded firearms and firewater to the Indians for fur, and erected a new pole each May. Captured by Miles Standish and shipped to England, he was back in 1629. This time his Maypole was chopped down, Merry Mount renamed, and his house razed. He kept returning from England until he died.

Morton claimed the Separatists, as he called the Pilgrims, were out to get him because of his trading profits and because he was an Anglican. They were certainly right in fearing his Maypole— a pointed reminder of a force that also caused them trouble. Right as well in tracing it back to pagan celebrations of Flora, though Morton was pleased to note that Bradford didn't know the pole was "a trophy erected at first in honour of Maia," the Greek goddess from whom we presumably get "May." His story has often been told, but it was Hawthorne's "Maypole of Merry Mount" that made it stick. Here is introduced the sweet Lady of the May, who is told she should wear more decent clothing, and the Lord of it whom she married. But if, as Hawthorne has it, Merry Mount and Plymouth represented "jollity and gloom contending for an empire," it was an unequal contest. "Loose characters" joined Morton, but there were never more than ten men in residence and there were no ladies at all. "Their consorts," wrote Bradford, in drinking the rum and beer, and in the other "beasly practises of the madd Bacchinalians," were Indian girls: the men were "traytors to their neigbors and *cuntrie.*" Morton confirmed it:

Lasses in beaver coats come away,
Yee shall be welcome to us night and day.*

---

* A few contemporary observers judged the Indian women lascivious and wanton, a few others chaste and modest. The contradiction is probably explained by

"Since the SUMMER POLES *were overthrown,*" an Englishman would soon observe, "How times and men are chang'd." It was so in both countries. The Maypole had already lost to the whipping post in America, and Morton's colony been obliterated. Yet in the struggle for cheer his celebrations were not just a throwback to ancient sexual rites but a forecast as well of a time in the same part of the world when Anglican ladies would come away —with fine wines and merry mountings new. The pole the Separatists chopped down, festooned in the spirit of women to come, was precisely a century and a half later erected again. Was crowned again with horns—by Hannah, Frances, Margaret, Betsey, and Betsy. And was again cut down, its devotees—Daughters of Merry Mount—once more driven from the land.

NO AMERICAN ROOTS but there are older ones—here Hebrew, to be got at once more through Morton, by way of exiled Loyalists like the deposed colonial Governor of Massachusetts, who said his later life in England seemed "a dream or other delusion." The longer he was from it, the fairer looked his homeland. So with others, who began thinking of the colonies as a lost idyll or Golden Age—prosperous, loving, beautiful. With naked nostalgia they dreamed of Eden, from which they had been expelled.

The dream was not new, but roughly a repeat of John Smith's "bountiful fantasy" in which he described what he named New-England as a land of abundance and promise extraordinary. Even after his troubles Morton could call it, in his account of them, *New English Canaan* (Amsterdam, 1637). He saw "a kind of paralell"; here was another "land that flowes with Milke and Hony." (It "to mee seeme Paradice . . . Natures Masterpeece.") He also saw it

---

Roger Williams, who noted that "single fornications they count no sin, but after marriage . . . then they count it hainous. . . ." Parkman among the Hurons saw it the same way. This is a little like what Europeans would remark of American women in the new Republic.

in sexual terms. Three hundred years before Hart Crane would picture the territory that lay before Columbus as "a woman, ripe, ready to be taken," he portrayed Massachusetts as a "faire virgin" awaiting a lover in her "Nuptiall Bed." He viewed it additionally as a land which bestowed fertility, pointing out for the well-being of English women that the beaver is "of such masculine vertue that if some of our Ladies knew the benefit thereof they would desire to have ships sent of purpose to trade for the tayle alone."

Emblem of a virtue to match the fecundity of earth and female, Morton's Maypole was central to the vision of his book. It is much as if he saw its destruction as an act of animal and vegetable doom. Embodiments of civilization and its discontents, the Separatists were cutting off not only their church from England's but man from nature. "New Canaan" could never realize its promise with Pilgrims; when he considered what they had already done in the place, Morton's use of the name became ironic. Neither was New England "Canaan" according to Puritan doctrine; Jesus had abrogated the assignment of special promise to any particular place. But the Pilgrim Fathers, markedly Old Testament in character, did think of the country as providentially provided. They too saw the analogy between their migration and Abraham's: "Get thee out of thy country," said the Lord, "and from thy kindred . . . unto a land that I will show thee: And I will make of thee a great nation. . . ."

Long before Patriots had begun to realize that promise, Puritan patriarchs had died. One of them, a voice crying in the Massachusetts wilderness, had obliquely warned a prosperous handful of his parishioners, with their "proud fashions," of what awaited them as "haughty daughters of Zion in this place." Increase Mather accurately predicted in 1676 what would happen to Revolutionary Ladies in 1776—and tipped as well the fate of their husbands. For in crying out he clearly invoked the time Jehovah foretold to Isaiah how, "Because the daughters of Zion are haughty, and walk with . . . wanton eyes . . . the Lord will discover their secret parts . . . take away the bravery of their tinkling ornaments . . . bracelets . . . bonnets. . . ." And how, finally, their "men shall fall by the sword," and their "mighty in the war."

It was in the War of Independence that America's true Daughters of Zion were found out, stripped, and felled. But in the struggle for a different Liberation they were harbingers of triumph. The rights of eighteenth-century women were few. If, like Betsey Loring, they held property it became their husband's as long as he lived. A man could divorce his wife for adultery with ease, as Hamilton's mother discovered; it took a state legislature to free Betsy Browne of the Ranger. When Peggy Shippen came into the world her father gave thanks, but noted that she was of the "worst sex." What no prophet foretold was how with her frank eyes, extravagant gown, brave baubles, bangles, and beads, no Revolutionary Lady would ever need feel inferior to her Lord. She inhabited a man's world; only men were formally educated —though to judge from their letters it would be hard to say whether it was John Wentworth or Frances who attended Harvard. By adequately valuing themselves, body and soul, and by asserting a freedom American wives were known not to possess, a small group of women achieved two hundred years ago something very like equality. Simone de Beauvoir caught the paradox: ". . . those women who exploit their femininity to the limit create for themselves a situation almost equivalent to that of a man."

But their men did fall in a war. The women won individual victories in a general defeat—which was not entirely inappropriate, since Loyalism meant, among other things, the perpetuation of the class structure of England in a nation that did not want it and was well on the way to arranging things differently. As even Frances Wentworth could see, while writing to her titled sponsor about the provincials in 1775, the English have "too mean an opinion of them . . . think them Fools & Cowards . . . my Lady they are neither."

DAUGHTERS OF ZION, of Merry Mount, Pearl—for precedent of failure and a disappearance from history there remains at last one of the daughters-in-law of Naomi: at the very farthest reach the obscure, mute, but presently archetypal figure of

Orpah. If Revolutionary Ladies, flung back across the sea to the motherland, are finally seen as from some tremendous distance, where all particulars fade from sight, the germ of their collective narrative can be found in the Old Testament once more. It rests in the story and book of Ruth, where the role of destiny is played by Naomi, not to be found in their story save as the hand of fate, which is invisible.

Now between Abraham and David were fourteen generations, and between Abraham and Boaz were eleven generations. After Abraham had come into Canaan there was famine in the land of milk and honey and he went into Egypt. It was in the time of a later famine that Naomi quit Bethlehem to journey into Moab, where she dwelt ten years. Both her sons took wives of the women of Moab; the name of one was Orpah, and the name of the other was Ruth. When the husband of Naomi died, and both her sons as well, bitterly she made ready to return to the land of Judah, her daughters-in-law with her. But piercing the heart of this whole matter Naomi cried out to them, "Am I likely to bear any more sons to be husbands for you?" "Return, my daughters, go." Orpah, "she who turns away," departed for Moab her home. But Ruth cleaved to Naomi, entreating her to be allowed to follow after, go where she went, lodge where she lodged, take up her people and her god.

When they were come to Bethlehem, Naomi told Ruth to wash and anoint herself, pose as a maidservant, and lie down for the night at the feet of the exalted Boaz. Ruth did as she was bidden, Boaz took her to wife, and the first time he went to her she conceived Obed. Obed begat Jesse, and of his rod was David the King, father of Solomon, and so it was that Ruth continued the line that reached Joseph, husband of Mary, of her was born Jesus and a New Covenant. The god Ruth had chosen was Jahweh. Her triumph was of a woman converted to a different land who remained in it. So the women who stayed in New English Canaan had chosen the country that would prosper above all others of the earth.

Orpah also did as she was told—returned to her ancestral home straight across the sea from Judah. Unlike Ruth and her sons she was never heard of more. But in time it came to pass that there were those in the new land who recalled her from ancient days when suddenly they recognized her daughters.

RESOURCES
INDEX

Resources

MUCH THE GREATEST PART of the research for this book was conducted in the library of a somewhat isolated land-grant university—a fact that those who (like me, once) never put such an operation to the test are slow to credit. For the rest, I am grateful to the public libraries of New York, Boston, and Portsmouth, New Hampshire; the Widener and Houghton libraries of Harvard; the Library of Congress and the University of Pennsylvania library; and the historical societies of New York, Pennsylvania, and Massachusetts. Special debts to other repositories are acknowledged below.

After the Pattee Library of the Pennsylvania State University, my principal research obligation is to Professor Richard E. Winslow III, a friend and former student stationed at another base, who learned of my project in midstream, stowed himself aboard, and completely without orders served mightily. He not only corrected errors, several of them time-honored; he also dug up and shipped in materials I had not begun looking for, and others I might never have thought to seek. The research for these chapters is as much my own as the writing of them, but Winslow made things easier. I note some specific debts to him in what follows.

Here I want to express my appreciation of his selfless devotion to another man's book and his talent for burrowing. (In addition to some of those institutions already mentioned, Professor Winslow would like to thank the public libraries of Erie, Buffalo, and Toronto; the libraries of SUNY at Buffalo, the University of Toronto, and Gannon College; and the historical societies of New Hampshire and of Western Reserve, Cleveland.)

One. PRELUDE

The specifics in my sketch of Early American Scandal are taken from nearly as many sources as there are instances of it. Of uncounted works examined, the most useful was *Women in Stuart England and America* (London, 1974) by Roger Thompson of the University of East Anglia. Two books by William Hart Blumenthal, *Women Camp Followers of the American Revolution* (1952) and *Brides from Bridewell* (1962), though in the long run disappointing, offered help. John C. Storms's *Origin of the Jackson-Whites* gathered in 1936 the pieces of their legend, presenting them as facts—a book not really discredited until 1971 in David S. Cohen's doctoral dissertation, "They Walk These Hills: A Study of Social Solidarity Among Racially Mixed People of the Ramapo Mountains" (University of Pennsylvania).

A great deal has been written on the early American novel, but attempts to link its fictions with history have been for the most part amateurish. The identification of John Montraville of *Charlotte Temple* with John Montresor in life is commonplace; the only solid evidence for it, so far as I know—the duplication of Montresor's post-Revolutionary life in England by Montraville in *Charlotte's Daughter*—has not been presented before. For standard heroines of the period, the most recent collection is Paul Engle's *Women in the American Revolution* (1976). Little more than I have given is known of Dorcas Griffiths, but much has been claimed for Agnes Surriage, Lady Frankland. The most intelligent account of her is Stella Palmer's "Dame Agnes Frankland, 1726–1783, and Some Chichester Contemporaries" (*Chichester Papers,* no. 45, 1964).

Hannah Van Horne is to be encountered, if at all, in the journal of the Baroness von Riedesel, which is best read in the edition of Marvin L. Brown, Jr., called *The Baroness von Riedesel and the American Revolution . . . 1776–1783* (1965); her only other notable appearance has been in *The Baroness and the General* (1962), a biography of the Riedesels by Louise Hall Tharp. In both instances the account of her is limited to the brief period she spent in the company of the Baroness.

There are several genealogies of the Van Horne family, the best of them to be found in the *Somerset* [N.J.] *County Historical Quarterly* (VII, 1918). For Hannah's life in New Jersey and New York, files of the *New-York Gazette & the Weekly Mercury* and of the *Proceedings of the New Jersey Historical Society and Documents Relating to the Colonial History of the State of New Jersey* provide a few facts. For Foy, her husband, and Dunmore, his superior in New York, I relied mainly on W. H. W. Sabine's edition (1956) of the *Historical Memoirs . . . of William Smith* (Dunmore's chief justice), and L. F. S. Upton's *The Loyal Whig: William Smith of New York and Quebec* (1969). For the Dunmore-Foy administration in Virginia one good book among several is Ivor Noël Hume's *1775: Another Part of the Field* (1966); files of the *Virginia Gazette* of Williamsburg are also useful. Dick Winslow was searching several of these and other sources while I was in pursuit of a lady in another part of the forest, but we separately turned up Thomas Moncrieffe's letter about the Van Horne and other belles of Revolutionary New York in the *Papers of Sir William Johnson* (VIII, 1144).

When Hannah's trail vanished on her parting with the Baroness—leaving me convinced that she did not then become, as alleged, Burgoyne's mistress—I went looking for the identity of that nameless woman. In Lieutenant James M. Hadden's *Journal Kept in Canada and upon Burgoyne's Campaign in 1776 and 1777,* as edited by Horatio Rogers (1884), I failed to discover the mistress but picked up Hannah again. For her sketchy life as Mrs. Carleton, the best sources prove to be W. O. Raymond's little biography of Thomas Carleton, published by the New Brunswick Historical Society (I, 1894) and another by W. F. Ganong in the *New Brunswick Magazine* (II, 1899). *The Winslow Papers, A.D. 1776–1826,* W. O. Raymond, ed. (1901), and volume III of Beamish Murdoch's *History of Nova-Scotia, or Acadie* (1867), offer a few details.

The only extended treatments of Betsy Browne Rogers are in John R. Cuneo's *Robert Rogers of the Rangers* (1959), which supersedes other biographical attempts on the Major and his wife, and in Kenneth Roberts's *Northwest Passage* (1937), a novel in which the research on Betsy is not as thorough as on other aspects of the book. (Mr. Cuneo and I are in disagreement but I am thankful to him for deciphering Rogers's hand where I was unable to.) In Mary Cochrane Rogers's *Glimpses of an Old Social Capital . . . Reverend Arthur Browne and His Circle* (1923), a last descendant fills in some background.

Part of the story of John Roche, Betsy's second husband, can be found in Samuel Eliot Morison's *John Paul Jones: A Sailor's Biography* (1959) and in Lawrence Shaw Mayo's *John Langdon of New Hampshire* (1937). A few facts rest in volumes III, V, and VI of *Naval Documents of the American Revolution;* Nathaniel Bouton's *History of Concord* (1856) gives a brief but standard portrait of "Roach." Death certificates for both Betsy and her sailor husband are on file at Concord.

The manuscript of the journal Daniel Morison kept at Michilimackinac, incriminating the violent Ensign Johnston, is in the Burton Collection of the Detroit Public Library; it was published in 1960 by the Mackinac Island State Park Commission, as in 1967 were the proceedings of Rogers's court-martial at Montreal. The original of Betsy's divorce petition and the letters she received from Rogers are in the William L. Clements Library of the University of Michigan, which supplied me with them. The library also furnished the letter of Captain (later Colonel) George Turnbull telling General Gage that Rogers for marital reasons was jealous of Ensign Johnston.

Peggy Shippen Arnold is the only woman in this collection whose story has been fully told. I was unable to discover anything genuinely new and significant about her, else I would have given her more space. She is effectively portrayed, along with Arnold and André, in a scholarly thriller by James T. Flexner called *The Traitor and the Spy* (1953), as well as in Willard M. Wallace's *Traitorous Hero* (1954) and Milton Lomask's "Benedict Arnold: The Aftermath of Treason" (in *American Heritage*, October, 1967). The painting of Peggy that probably does her justice is by Thomas Lawrence, executed when he was "about fifteen" and on his way to becoming the most fashionable portrait artist of his day. This picture, in which she appears intensely feminine, is now displayed in Philadelphia at the Historical Society of Pennsylvania, which also has some of her letters, composed in a no-nonsense, masculine hand.

Two. MRS. LORING

This, as related, is where the book began—some time before the author was aware that a book had begun. At first intending simply to discover a family relationship to Mrs. Loring, if one should exist, I developed a yen to learn everything I could about the lady—somewhat troublesome for an instant historian working in an era about which he knew extraordinarily little. (Gates, Howe, Clinton—famous generals: on which side? A pleasure to discover one of each on both.) How to proceed? I knew no better than to pull one volume after another off the shelves in such sections of the library as stack books on the war, the period, and the histories of places. I searched indices for mention of "Howe's mistress," cursed volumes unindexed, collected titles from countless bibliographies, chased what seldom turned out to be real leads, and once in a long while noted mention of ladies who could conceivably have been Betsey's sisters under the skin. All this in an explosion of inefficient energy.

But after reading over and over the same lines devoted to Mrs. Loring I reached a lucky conclusion, which was that only one historian consulted had given the lady independent thought, John R. Alden of Duke University. His classic *History of the American*

Revolution (1969) did not give much space to her, but I sensed that he knew more than he wrote. This turned out to be true, and after a brief correspondence Professor Alden sent me many Loring notes on scraps of paper—material he had assembled, he explained, for a book on General Howe which he had abandoned. By that time I already had many of his references but by no means all; in particular I had not yet come across the *Papers of the Lloyd Family of the Manor of Queen's Village, 1654–1826* (2 vols., 1927), which were vital. (Other major sources not mentioned in the text of this chapter were C. H. Pope and K. P. Loring's *Loring Genealogy* [1917] and E. Alfred Jones's *The Loyalists of Massachusetts* [1930].)

Mr. Alden was generous with other things as well, including the inscriptions on the graves of Elizabeth and Joshua, and black and white photographs of their portraits, which are in England. The fact that these likenesses exist was much the biggest news: if as in legend Betsey was in life a handsome blue-eyed blonde then it was possible that there was truth in the stereotype that has kept her alive. But from these prints one could not be sure. I wrote the descendant who owns them—he would, I think, choose anonymity—and after many long delays (no fault of his) I received from him color reproductions which were conclusive. A bit of a cliffhanger: by the time I got the pictures the research was done, and I had a suspicion of how things would turn out.

Along the way, I made a somewhat tedious study of General Howe, from which I concluded that most scholars feel as much in the dark regarding his motives in this country as his enemies had been. Even as I make these notes I read an acknowledged authority who announces that Howe's strategy in the war "still defies rational explanation," and that the position taken at the end of my account of the matter is "controversial." It is the position Howe himself took, in defending his action or inaction before Parliament, when he explained that he had "endeavoured to conciliate His Majesty's rebellious subjects . . . instead of irritating them by a contrary mode of proceeding. . . ." How or why this is disputed is not stated. (Regarding his mistress or mistresses, it might be noted that Howe left in England an exceptionally attractive and loving wife who would, according to one of his biographers, have liked to accompany him here.)

The situation with Joshua Loring turned out to be much like that of his wife: one writer after another draws the quick sketch of complaisant husband, cruel and corrupt jailer, and troubles not to fill it in. The primary source of such worn material on both Lorings is Judge Thomas Jones's *History of New York during the Revolutionary War* (2 vols., 1879, but written nearly a hundred years earlier). This is a lively book, composed by one who was much on the scene, but he does not appear to have been acquainted with anything more than gossip about the Lorings. So far as is known, the guarded defense of the Commissary of Prisoners given in these pages has not been risked before.

How to find the time and place of the heroine's birth? It was awkward to give a lady's life its first airing without these facts; for a long time the task appeared doomed. From the *Lloyd Papers* I inferred that Betsey was probably born at Lloyd's Neck sometime in 1752. But until she is reported as an infant in Boston, following the drowning there of her father, there is no mention of her in these volumes. Failing a family Bible, what one looks for is record of baptism; I knew the Lloyds were Anglicans, and that Betsey's grandfather, the lord of the Manor, maintained an Anglican pew in the Presbyterian church at Huntington, Long Island, the nearest town. Its records, however, make no mention of her. Thus it seemed that she might have been born in Boston, where her father had been employed and where her parents were married in the New South Church. But there is no sign of her there either, nor in the records of King's Chapel, which I made a special trip to consult. Where else to look?

Right next door in the library, as it turned out, but it was the tenacious Winslow who discovered the fact. Betsey Lloyd was indeed born on Long Island and baptized at Huntington. But since it was an Anglican affair in a Presbyterian building, the deed was registered in the records of the more suitable St. George's Church of Hempstead, L.I. As published in the *New York Genealogical and Biographical Record*, X, 134:

> *1752, Oct. 15. At Huntington, Elizabeth,*
> *d. of Nathaniel and Elizabeth Lloyd.*

The fifteenth was a Sunday that year.

Three. LADY WENTWORTH

Compared with husbands of other Revolutionary Ladies, John Wentworth has fared well. Lawrence Shaw Mayo's *John Wentworth* (1921) is a tasteful biography, and a later John Wentworth's *Wentworth Genealogy* (3 vols., 1878) notices him extensively. An excellent short account of him is in John Langdon, *Sibley's Harvard Graduates,* class of 1755, as continued by Clifford K. Shipton. (For the many Harvard men in this book I have mined these carefully researched and stylishly presented little biographies.) All these treatments of the Governor are sympathetic. But save for mention of her quick remarriage, her social brilliance, her reported appointment as Lady-in-Waiting to the Queen, and her incomparable beauty, none of them has much to say about his wife, or anything at all about the gossip that surrounded her. (Her Copley portrait hangs in the Berg Collection of the New York Public Library, where it dominates a room full of more famous paintings.)

The only extensive and candid account of the historical Frances Wentworth turns out to be fiction: Thomas Raddall's *The Governor's Lady* (1961) gives a novelistic dramatization of her wayward life in both Portsmouth and Halifax. The author writes me that the main source for these tales was in both places "tradition." (He lives in Nova Scotia; for New Hampshire we are both indebted to Dr. Dorothy Vaughan of the Portsmouth Public Library.) But what is most remarkable about Mr. Raddall's fiction is the thoroughness of his research—right down to the correct names of bizarre refreshments served at such and such a social event.

I have read as well his history of *Halifax, Warden of the North* (1948), which for a time features Frances's role and reputation in that place. In both books Prince William and the good-natured Lieutenant Dyott find their easy way to her bed: how Mr. Raddall delineated these affairs with such assurance was a mystery—until he called my attention to the existence of *Dyott's Diary* (R. W. Jeffrey, ed., 1907), which had inadvertently been omitted from his *Halifax* bibliography. Much of what Dyott reported was corroborated in a fine biography of *King William IV* by Philip Ziegler (1971), who describes his subject's liaison with Mrs. Wentworth as revealed in the Prince's correspondence. (I obtained the letter in which William washes his hands of his promiscuous mistress from the Maritime Museum at London; not all that her ex-lover wrote about her is legible, and many's the squinting that has failed to decipher the rest.)

Though not all of Mr. Raddall's inferences agree with mine, he has been of great assistance. He put me in touch with the Dalhousie University Library, which furnished materials he had sent there—such as the inscription on Frances's grave—and had not used in his books. He directed me to the story of John Wentworth's mulatto child at Preston, Nova Scotia, and to the repository of a considerable correspondence between the Wentworths and the Rockinghams, little of which has been published. I thank P. I. King of the Northamptonshire Record Office, Delapre Abbey, Northampton, for excavating and microfilming many of these letters for me; where Mr. Raddall made little use of them, I relied on them heavily. The same is true of the Wentworth correspondence with the Fitzwilliams, now in the Archives of the Sheffield City Libraries, and supplied by their director, R. F. Atkins. I have quoted from these, and otherwise used them tacitly, with permission of the present Earl Fitzwilliam and his Trustees.

Traditions concerning Frances's life in New Hampshire are to be found, among other places, in Charles W. Brewster's *Rambles about Portsmouth* (two series, 1859 and 1869); largely taken from Brewster is Thomas Bailey Aldrich's *Old Town by the Sea* (1893). I also used other histories of Portsmouth, one of New Castle (by John Albee, 1884), and the files of two journals, *The Granite Monthly* and *Historical New Hampshire;* of occasional help was the *New England Historical and Genealogical Register.* Mr. Winslow, whose parents conveniently live in Portsmouth, turned up several

of these materials for me. He also procured for me information
on Wentworth House at Wolfeborough (now Wolfeboro)—in
particular B. F. Parker's *History of Wolfeborough* (1901) but also
W. P. Bowman's *Lake Wentworth* (1956) and *The Saga of a Palace*
(1962) by Robert F. W. Meader. For the Wentworths in Halifax,
sources not mentioned in the text include the *Winslow Papers* and
Murdoch's *History of Nova-Scotia* (vol. III), both cited above. The
story of Prince Edward, his mistress Julie, and their long friendship with Frances and John is admirably told by Mollie Gillen in
The Prince and His Lady (1970).

Where there are few tangible remains of other Revolutionary
Ladies, Portsmouth today is redolent of the world of Frances
Wentworth. Her house and the houses of friends and relatives are
handsome yet; when the tavern refurbished by her grandfather
was torn down, a portion of it went to the Metropolitan Museum
of Art in New York. But the story of Paul Wentworth in that area
—and in this country generally—is not to be dredged up. On the
other hand it is easy to glean a first-hand account of his activities
as a spy in Paris from Benjamin Franklin Stevens's *Facsimiles of
Manuscripts in European Archives Relating to America, 1773–1783*
(1898), twenty-five huge volumes "distributed to 200 libraries by
Andrew Carnegie." A part of my account of Paul's espionage is
anticipated in Lewis D. Einstein's *Divided Loyalties* (1933). Julian
Boyd's suspicions about the death of Silas Deane (exhaustively
aired in the *William and Mary Quarterly,* XVI, 1959) have been
disputed, but I concluded that the case had been strengthened by
the challenge to it.

The *Wentworth Genealogy* by John Wentworth (1815–88),
grandson of the New Hampshire Patriot John Wentworth, another of Frances's cousins, was accomplished despite the loss of
many of his papers in the Chicago fire of 1871. Himself among
the most colorful of the tribe, he arrived in Chicago with $30. Six
foot six and three hundred pounds, he once told a cheering
crowd: "You damn fools . . . you can either vote for me . . . or
you can go to hell." Elected Mayor of the city, he refused to draw
a salary. Even after he published his family tree, the identity of
Paul Wentworth continued to concern him, and he learned that

there had indeed been Wentworths in the Barbados—whence, via Surinam, Paul may have come to this country. But how he acquired his comprehensive knowledge of American leaders (not to mention French as good as a Frenchman's) remains mysterious. He did not, John Wentworth concluded, belong to the family of American Wentworths, and his relationship to English Wentworths, if any, could not be discovered.

There have been several histories of New Hampshire since the first one, written with Governor Wentworth's help by Jeremy Belknap. The best, to which I am remarkably indebted, is Charles E. Clark's *The Eastern Frontier: The Settlement of Northern New England, 1610–1763* (1970). I have also taken into account Jere Daniell's *Experiment in Republicanism* (1972). Evidence for my notion of a family precedent for John Wentworth as Governor of New Hampshire is taken chiefly from C. V. Wedgwood's *Thomas Wentworth, First Earl of Strafford . . .* (1962).

For living signs of the past it is a pleasure to examine a map: the Geodetic Survey of New Hampshire's "Wolfeboro Quadrangle" (in what since 1840 has been Carroll—no longer Strafford—County). The old Governor's Road is now Governor John Wentworth Highway; it runs across the foot of "Moose Mountains" along a course that used to frighten Frances Wentworth. Smith's Pond, which her mansion overlooked, is now Lake Wentworth; in it are to be found Stamp Tax Island and—no bigger than a barn—Turtle Island, where she dined outdoors. At water's edge is a steep little hill labeled "Mount Delight." Her house was never in any manner rebuilt, but a third of an inch off the lake's northeast shore is an almost invisible white dot in the green background, indicating a clearing in the woods where remains a large cellarhole.

Four. MISS MONCRIEFFE

Unfinished business. If, as I repeatedly assume, the place and time of Margaret Moncrieffe's birth remain uncertain because of the burning of the records of Trinity Church in the great New York fire of 1776, the place of her burial is a mystery for reason unknown. In her day Cavendish Street, London, where she died, belonged to the parish of St. Marylebone, but its church has no record of her. Foreigners of the period were often put to rest at St. Pancras, but it has none either. Private cemeteries had not yet been established in London; my only thought is that if she perished without funds or protection, and no one came to the aid of her remains (as somebody did her husband's), she went to a potter's field. Cause of death is also unknown, although Charles Pigott insinuated that she was the extraordinary young lady, lamented by General D********, who expired of sexual excess—dying early of "constant and exquisite fruition."

As for her disappearance in life, not literature—apparently after publication of her *Memoirs*—I once toyed with the notion that history has black holes in time analogous to those astronomers posit in space: regions of such gravitational pull that no light can escape. The actual trouble, however, was mundane; I had often seen mention of the *Gentleman's Magazine,* but was unaware of its department of vital statistics which, when I finally came upon them, provided many things beside the date of Mrs. Coghlan's death—among them the obituary of her husband. (For finding in old newspapers a good deal about the Moncrieffes in New York I thank Dr. Kenneth Scott of Douglaston, New York.)

As already related, what cracked the case of the purloined memoirs lay sleeping in *The Female Jockey Club,* which supplied the praise of Mrs. Coghlan that I had read as a preface to the New York edition of her book. After the Jockey Club of England, perhaps, I took it for a club, though I could find no hint of its existence. It was while combing English periodicals for notice of the *Memoirs* that I came across what appeared to be bare mention of a book by that name. A young scholar who at the time needed a little research project quickly discovered that it was indeed a book, written by the posthumously identified "Louse" Pigott. I read it, locating at once the lines that would serve as a preface. Then I read *The Jockey Club,* to which the Females were sequel, and found the passages that would be put in Mrs. Coghlan's sealed mouth two years later.

As also remarked, the peculiar thing about the *Memoirs,* given the element of fraud, is their overall reliability. My conclusion is that Margaret was responsible for most of what is stated during the period in which she lived, although on stylistic grounds I suspect that the rhapsodic description of her first lover, still thought to be Burr, was inserted by Pigott—as, on the same grounds, the incoherent abuse of the Duke of York. What was invented for her after she died, such as the sojourn in Paris, was easily dreamed up, or taken from other memoirs. Actual events which occurred after her death, such as the death of her father, are to be found in the periodicals from which they were taken.

Despite the resemblances of Mrs. Coghlan's book to the reminiscences of other women of the time, and the evidence that suggests Mrs. Gooch as the person who finished it, I stuck with the hunch that the ghost was male; from style and sentiment, further, I figured him to be an imitator of Tom Paine. My guesses are rarely so accurate: Paine and Pigott were in London a pair, except in talent—both authors of *The Rights of Man,* both specialists in the exposé, both hostile to England's whole political system, Opposition as well as Government. When in her book Pigott has Margaret go out of her way to extoll the virtues of Thomas Erskine, famous lawyer, it is because Erskine was defending the publishers of both Paine and Pigott, who were in jail for selling their works.*

In terminating my own affair with Mrs. Coghlan, I am glad to acknowledge help from an unexpected quarter. Unknown to me, Winslow sent a version of this chapter to the incumbent laird of Easter Moncreiffe, Perthshire—Sir Iain Moncreiffe of that Ilk, Albany Herald of Arms, and himself a writer and genealogist. He responded by remarking that his great-uncle William, co-author

---

*The Pigotts were another pair, descendants of John Dryden. Robert, Charles's brother, decided in 1776 that England, because of America, was going out of business; he took to the Continent, where he became acquainted with Franklin and Voltaire. A dedicated but unlucky gambler, he once bet a fortune that his father, who had died a few hours previously, would outlive another man's. He was a fanatical vegetarian who despised bread and hats, and started a vogue in Paris for caps. Charles was jailed not for writing but, while drunk, for talking treason.

of *The Moncreiffs and the Moncreiffes* (1929), had been unable to place Margaret in the clan. (Sir Iain's scholarly uncle Willie became a pioneer rancher in Wyoming, friend of Buffalo Bill and Teddy Roosevelt; his daughter Alexandra was in 1975 reported the object of the affections of Prince Charles.) Sir Iain also described my work to C. H. H. Evans of Wales, honorary editor of *The Harleian Society,* a genealogical organization and publication. Mr. Evans is a descendant of Mary Ann Evans, called George Eliot, and also of Patrick Heron, Margaret Moncrieffe's grandfather. He had long been confused about the American Moncrieffes, on whom he was working professionally. I was able to help him, and he me: irrationally I had set out to identify all the alleged lovers of Mrs. Coghlan and by this time had pinned down the proper Clinton, Fox, "Sampson," and General D********. (This last much the toughest; I went through the entire "D" section of the *Dictionary of National Biography*—Daborne to Dyve, 1,284 pages, double columns—looking for an officer with the right number of stars to his name; there are hundreds of lesser warriors entered in this monumental work, but it missed Dalrymple, whom I found in *The Jockey Club*—and might in a matter of seconds have found, had I looked there, in Mark M. Boatner III's really excellent *Encyclopedia of the American Revolution,* 1974.) For the others, Mr. Evans steered me to genealogical sources I knew not of, so that for no very good reason save to establish the general validity of the *Memoirs* I am at last able to finger as lovers beyond reasonable doubt the correct Hervey (they were a randy crew), Fazakerley, and Giffard. Mr. Evans also supplied me with a copy of the Canterbury copy of Patrick Heron's will.

It is odd to think that at this distance we are in a position to know more about matters that concerned Margaret than she did —such as that Heron did not leave her assets she thought were hers on the death of her mother, and that for a time she was supported by them anyway. It is probable that she was told and believed that this grandfather, who perished in obscure disrepute, had died Governor of Annapolis-Royal. I occasionally try to imagine how she would feel if she knew she was long remembered in her native land, when at all, as a conquest of Aaron Burr and a Tory spy—especially if she was neither.

Five. FINALE

A good deal of documented gossip concerning the Founding Fathers was recently gathered in Fawn M. Brodie's *Thomas Jefferson: An Intimate History* (1974). Some of her conclusions are disputed and some of her arguments weak, but the research is exhaustive and one can draw his own conclusions. For other material I have used the standard biographies of Washington, Franklin, Hamilton, and the rest—in particular Howard Swiggett's *The Extraordinary Mr. Morris* (1952).

The best account of Betsy Patterson is probably S. A. Mitchell's *A Family Lawsuit, The Story of Elizabeth Patterson and Jérôme Bonaparte* (1958). For Nancy Morris, Swiggett is again reliable; John Randolph's written denunciation of her, and her reply, are given in full by William C. Bruce in his *John Randolph of Roanoke, 1773–1833* (1922). (Randolph's spleen is sometimes attributed to physiological impotence.) When I gave the address of St. Ann's Church to a cabdriver, he said: "You got a machine gun?" The day I was there no one present had heard of Anne Morris.

There ought to be a full-scale biography—materials for it exist —of Dr. John Jeffries; the best short account is in *Sibley's Harvard Graduates*. His own *Narrative* of his famous flight, as presented to the Royal Society with *Meteorological Observations,* was published in London and has been reprinted. His diary, 1777–1819, is at Harvard, and a copy of it is in the Jeffries Family Papers at the Massachusetts Historical Society, where the entries regarding Mrs. Loring (XXX, 190) were photocopied for me by Mr. Winslow.

A very satisfactory account of Elizabeth Vassall, Lady Holland, is to be found in the *DNB*. Concerning American Loyalists in England there are several books, the best of them Mary Beth Norton's *The British-Americans* (1972); a recent study by the same author (in the *William and Mary Quarterly* for July, 1976) shows how Loyalist women in exile felt even more "abandoned and adrift" than the men. Kent Britt's "The Loyalists," in the *National Geographic* (April, 1975), also furnished some fresh material.

The New England Canaan of Thomas Morton (1883), with introduction by Charles Francis Adams, Jr., is still serviceable, but I was helped in understanding the whole business by the work of a friend and former student, Robert D. Arner (in particular his "Pastoral Celebration and Satire in Thomas Morton's 'New English Canaan,'" *Criticism,* XVI, 3 [Summer, 1974]). In this connection I also took account of but am partly at odds with Larzer Ziff's *Puritanism in America* (1973).

Daughters of Merry Mount, of Zion and Pearl—what, finally, of Orpah? "There is no good cause to disparage her," advises *The Interpreter's Bible* (II, 836). "But she lacked the imagination of Ruth."

Index

in Halifax, 100–6 *passim,* 109,
110, 113, 115, 117, 118,
119, 133, 137, 138, 139,
187, 206, 207, 208
in Portsmouth, 88, 91–7
passim, 109, 113, 115, 120,
130, 132, 134, 137, 138,
206, 207–8, 209
and son, Charles-Mary, 96, 97,
98, 103, 106, 114–15, 117,
122, 140
John Wentworth, marriage to,
92, 113, 115, 116, 206
and Paul Wentworth, 99, 109,
126, 128, 129
and Prince William, Duke of
Clarence, 101, 102, 103,
110, 113, 115, 118, 119,
120, 138, 139, 206, 207
Wentworth, Lady Henrietta,
135–6
Wentworth, Henry, 115
Wentworth, Sir John, 69,
87–124 *passim,* 126, 128,
129, 131–41 *passim,* 187,
193, 206, 207, 208, 209
Wentworth, Sir John: *Wentworth
on Pleading,* 140
Wentworth, Col. John, 139,
208
Wentworth, John, 131
Wentworth, John, 139, 208
Wentworth Genealogy, 139, 206,
208–9
Wentworth, John, Jr., 116–17,
117 *n.*
Wentworth, Mark, 92, 93,
131–2, 140
Wentworth, Lady Martha
(Wentworth), 140
Wentworth, Mary, 139
Wentworth, Michael, 90–1, 92,
93, 111 and *n.,* 132, 139,
140
Wentworth, Mrs. Michael
(Martha Hilton; Mrs.
Benning Wentworth), 91,
92–3, 111 and *n.,* 132, 140
Wentworth, Nathaniel, 128

Wentworth, Paul, 98, 99–100,
109, 123–9 *passim,* 127 *n.,*
133, 139, 208–9
Wentworth, Peregrine, 140
Wentworth, Samuel (Frances'
great-grandfather), 131
Wentworth, Samuel (Frances'
father), 86, 115, 131
Wentworth, Samuel (Frances'
brother), 115
Wentworth, Mrs. Samuel
(Frances' mother), 99
Wentworth, Sarah, *see*
Macpheadris, Mrs.
Wentworth, Sir Thomas, *see*
Strafford, 1st Earl of
Wentworth, Thomas, 115
Wentworth, William, 122, 131
Wentworth family, 88, 122,
128–9, 131, 134, 139, 140,
187, 188, 206, 208–9
Wheatley, Phillis, 75
Wheelock, Eleazer, 95, 134
Wheelwright, John, 129, 131
Whitman, Elizabeth, 21, 24, 25
Whitman, Walt, 75
Whittier, John Greenleaf, 39
William IV, King (Prince
William Henry, Duke of
Clarence), 101–2, 102–3,
110, 113, 115, 117–21
passim, 138, 139, 206, 207
Williams, Roger, 190–1 *n.*
Wimble, Capt., 77
Winslow, Penelope, 101
Winslow, Richard E., III,
199–200, 201, 205, 207–8
Wolfe, Gen. James, 65
Wright, Patience, 19–20

"Yankee Doodle," 64–5
York, Prince Frederick
Augustus, Duke of, 151,
164, 169
Young, John Philip, 57

Ziegler, Philip, 102, 207

A NOTE ABOUT THE AUTHOR

Philip Young is Research Professor of English at Pennsylvania
State University. A noted critic, he is author of *Ernest Hemingway:
A Reconsideration* and *Three Bags Full: Essays in American Fiction.*

A NOTE ON THE TYPE

This book was set, via computer-driven cathode ray tube, in
Garamond, a modern rendering of the type first cut by Claude
Garamond (1510–1561). Garamond was a pupil of Geoffroy Tory
and is believed to have based his letters on the Venetian models,
although he introduced a number of important differences, and it
is to him we owe the letter which we know as old-style. He gave to
his letters a certain elegance and a feeling of movement that won for
their creator an immediate reputation and the patronage of Francis I
of France.

This book was composed, printed, and bound by The Haddon
Craftsmen, Inc., Scranton, Pennsylvania. Typography and binding
design by Camilla Filancia.